T0305211

Rethinking Work, Ageing and Retirement

Series Editors: **David Lain**, Newcastle University, **Sarah Vickerstaff**, University of Kent and **Mariska van der Horst**, Vrije Universiteit Amsterdam

---

This is a new multidisciplinary series that brings together researchers from a range of fields including management and organizational studies, gerontology, sociology, psychology and social policy, to explore the impact of extended working lives on older people, organizations and society.

Forthcoming in the series:

Menopause and the Workplace:
Theorising Transitions, Responsibilities and Interventions
Edited by **Vanessa Beck** and **Jo Brewis**

Rethinking Financial Behaviour:
Rationality and Resistance in the Financialization
of Everyday Life
Ariane Agunsoye

Find out more at

bristoluniversitypress.co.uk/
rethinking-work-ageing-and-retirement

Rethinking Work, Ageing and Retirement

Series Editors: **David Lain**, Newcastle University,
Sarah Vickerstaff, University of Kent and
Mariska van der Horst, Vrije Universiteit
Amsterdam

Find out more at
bristoluniversitypress.co.uk/
rethinking-work-ageing-and-retirement

OLDER WORKERS IN TRANSITION

European Experiences in a Neoliberal Era

Edited by
David Lain, Sarah Vickerstaff and
Mariska van der Horst

BRISTOL
UNIVERSITY
PRESS

First published in Great Britain in 2022 by

Bristol University Press
University of Bristol
1–9 Old Park Hill
Bristol
BS2 8BB
UK
t: +44 (0)117 374 6645
e: bup-info@bristol.ac.uk

Details of international sales and distribution partners are available at bristoluniversitypress.co.uk

British Library Cataloguing in Publication Data
A catalogue record for this book is available from the British Library

ISBN 978-1-5292-1500-7 hardcover
ISBN 978-1-5292-1501-4 ePub
ISBN 978-1-5292-1502-1 ePdf

Cover design: Andrew Corbett
Front cover image: Alamy/Andrew Corbett/RR190M
Bristol University Press use environmentally responsible print partners.
Printed in Great Britain by CPI Group (UK) Ltd, Croydon, CR0 4YY

Contents

List of Figures and Tables

Figures

Tables

Notes on Contributors

Nathalie Burnay is Full Professor of Sociology at University of Namur (Transitions Institute) and at UCLouvain (IACCHOS Institute), Belgium.

Emma Garavaglia is Lecturer in Economic and Labour Sociology and member of the WWELL Research Centre at the Università Cattolica of Milan, Italy.

Anna Hokema is Researcher at the German Institute for Interdisciplinary Social Policy Research, University of Duisburg-Essen/University of Bremen, Germany.

Clary Krekula is Professor of Social Work at Linnaeus University, Sweden.

David Lain is Senior Lecturer in Employment Studies at Newcastle University Business School, UK.

Áine Ní Léime is Senior Researcher and Deputy Director at the Irish Centre for Social Gerontology at the National University of Ireland Galway, Ireland.

Chris Phillipson is Professor of Sociology and Social Gerontology at the University of Manchester, UK.

Mariska van der Horst is Assistant Professor and Lecturer in Sociology at Vrije Universiteit Amsterdam, the Netherlands, as well as Honorary Researcher in the School of Social Policy, Sociology and Social Research, University of Kent, UK.

Sarah Vickerstaff is Professor of Work and Employment in the Division for the Study of Law, Society and Social Justice, University of Kent, UK.

Acknowledgements

The editors would like to acknowledge funding from the Norwegian Research Council for the project 'Challenges and possibilities for mobility for the 50+ population' (2016–18). This edited collection emerged as a result of working on this project; we would like to thank the Principal Investigator, Anne Inga Hilsen, for her important work in helping set the groundwork for this volume.

The editors also acknowledge that Chapter 4 by Clary Krekula was previously published in the journal *Ageing and Society*. The full citation is Krekula, C. (2019) 'Time, precarisation and age normality: on internal job mobility among men in manual work', *Ageing and Society*, 39(10): 2290–307. The original article is located here: www.cambridge.org/core/journals/ageing-and-society/article/time-precarisation-and-age-normality-on-internal-job-mobility-among-men-in-manual-work/6C1B86C78F1BDDC036A88B32A43137B6. The copyright holder of the article is Cambridge University Press (Cambridge, UK) and it was published with a Creative Commons (CC-BY) open access licence. Professor Krekula kindly gave us her approval to use this work in the current volume. We have made a small number of minor edits to the article in preparing it for publication.

Series Preface

David Lain
Sarah Vickerstaff
Mariska van der Horst

Work and retirement in older age are undergoing radical change, which in itself is nothing new. Retirement as a fairly predictable life stage involving full exit from employment at a set pension age only emerged in most industrialized countries in the second half of the 20th century, and it tended to be less common for certain groups, such as women. From the 1970s onwards there was a marked increase in early exit from paid work as employers, trade unions and governments sought to deal with the economic problems associated with globalization and industrial restructuring by using early retirement as a means of shedding labour. In the last 20 years this trend towards early exit has been reversed, and governments now want people to extend their working lives. In this context, state pension ages are rising, occupational pensions are changing and/or are in decline, and private saving is becoming more important. The boundary between employment and retirement is also becoming more blurred as individuals increasingly do paid work while drawing a pension.

These policy changes extend the theoretical option of continuing in employment, which may create new opportunities for those who want – and are able – to work. At the same time, it arguably makes retirement timing a hypothetical choice for which people can be held more accountable. Individuals must now assume greater financial responsibility for remaining in work as long as they need to. For a significant number of older people this may be difficult to achieve, however, given evidence of widespread age discrimination in the labour market and reduced employment opportunities for this group. This is in addition to difficulties individuals experience in the labour market at any age – for example, due to racism or ableism, or constraints on time and energy stemming from outside paid work, such as care responsibilities. Work itself also appears to be getting more precarious, albeit to various degrees across countries, and the management of older workers is becoming less straightforward given uncertainties around retirement.

It is in the context of these changes that the book series Rethinking Work, Ageing and Retirement emerges. It will bring together researchers from a range of fields including, but not limited to, management and organizational studies, gerontology, sociology, economics, psychology and social policy. It will explore the impact of extended working lives and changes to welfare states and labour markets on people, organizations and society. Areas we expect the series to cover include the management of older workers and their experiences in employment; the changing financial context of work and retirement; and the impact of health, technology, training, caring and volunteering on employment and retirement in older age. The series also the offers the opportunity to examine paid work and/or retirement planning at earlier ages and to take a full (working) life course perspective. This is particularly important as the earlier stages of individuals' working careers may impact on their later retirement opportunities, and policies to extend working lives have implications for younger workers who need to prepare for more years in employment.

Different volumes may focus on specific groups and resulting inequalities; they may likewise be focused on a specific country or be comparative in approach. The reference to 'rethinking' in the title denotes the fact that we want critical perspectives on these topics, which may challenge 'mainstream' thinking and assumptions. We therefore welcome manuscripts that develop new theories and/or increase our empirical understanding while also being theoretically informed and innovative. Please get in contact with us with your book ideas should you be interested in writing for this exciting new multidisciplinary series.

This first book in the series is edited by us, the Series Editors, and explores a topic of great importance in the context of pressures to extend working lives: job transitions in older age. In an area of research that is dominated by quantitative analysis, it brings together leading scholars examining job transitions through qualitative approaches. In doing so, it seeks to make a critical theoretical contribution by situating these transitions in the context of a wider neoliberal trend that is occurring across the European countries covered.

PART I

Introducing Older Worker Job Transitions in a Neoliberal Era

1

Job Transitions in Older Age in an Era of Neoliberal Responsibilisation

David Lain, Sarah Vickerstaff and Mariska van der Horst

Introduction

In 2011 the European Commission made the following announcement:

> The European Commission today issued a White Paper on pensions. It puts forward policy initiatives to support Member States in the reform of their pension systems. The measures proposed by the White Paper aim to help people who are able to work longer and save more for their retirement. They aim to raise the average age at which people retire, reflecting the rising life expectancy, to encourage complementary private retirement savings. (European Commission, 2011)

This White Paper reflected a trend that was already evident in Member States, a trend that would only intensify in the following decade. The language in such policy documents is of helping people to continue working. However, a recent policy review has concluded that in Organisation for Economic Co-operation and Development (OECD) countries the emphasis is on making older people take personal financial responsibility for themselves, rather than being supported to work longer should they wish to do so (Street and Ní Léime, 2020). The financial need to do paid work is increasing, due to rising state pension ages and reduced/restricted access to early retirement options and disability and unemployment benefits in many countries. Likewise, the role of the state in delivering retirement incomes is declining, with the private sector taking a more significant pensions role and inequalities likely to rise as a result.

The progressive shift from defined benefit to defined contribution occupational pensions in the UK and other countries has been a profound change (Lain, 2016). In such schemes the individual, not an employer, now bears the risk that the money invested on their behalf results in a sizable pension pot when they retire. Predicting what this means in reality is difficult given that individuals cannot know how far this money will stretch. The experience of COVID-19 in the UK illustrates how exposed people are to risk and the inequalities that emerge as a result. Survey evidence from the relatively early stages of the pandemic suggested that 13 per cent of older workers expected to change their retirement plans, with those experiencing a reduction in their pension wealth being more likely to work longer, and those in richer households being more likely to retire earlier (Institute for Fiscal Studies, 2020).

Despite financial pressures to extend working lives, policies to actively *support* older people to work longer are meagre (Ní Léime et al 2020). As we shall argue in this chapter, this reflects a wider trend of increasing 'neoliberal responsibilisation', whereby it becomes the responsibility of individuals to become 'active', entrepreneurial individuals and take whatever opportunities are available to them to work until they are in a financial position to retire. Jobs held by older individuals are not always sustainable in the long term, due to unemployment, work intensification or changing levels of health, and the need to change jobs in order to continue working arguably therefore becomes even more important (Lain, 2016).

In this context we have seen a rise in employment of older people across OECD countries, partially reversing a trend towards earlier exit occurring since the 1970s (for a discussion on the historical and policy context see Chapter 2). Researchers following a rational choice perspective have sought to explain rising employment as relating to changing financial incentives made available in the institutional environment (Ebbinghaus and Hofäcker, 2013). The argument is that people have to work for longer because they cannot afford to retire. Nevertheless, it remains the case that significant numbers of both men and women are out of the labour market before state pension age. In this context, there has been a burgeoning academic literature on the factors that encourage or inhibit longer working lives and the conditions required to retain older workers. Much of this literature is quantitative and explores the factors influencing employment (or anticipated employment) in older age including: health, wealth, motivations, domestic circumstances, caring responsibilities, line manager attitudes and behaviours, and work-related/human resource management factors (see Hasselhorn and Apt, 2015 for a review). However, relatively little attention is placed on the role of job changes as a means of extending working lives in European countries (Hasselhorn and Apt, 2015; Hilsen and Midtsundstad, 2015; Lain, 2016).

There is a literature on so-called 'bridge jobs', and this seems to suggest that people change their working arrangements in the build-up to retirement.

This literature is predominantly related to the US context, although the term 'bridge jobs' is growing in usage in the European context and is often used to identify a wide range of different changes in employment in older age. An exception is Brunello and Langella (2013) which examined individuals moving from a full-time job with ten plus years of tenure to a new job after age 50 in a range of EU countries. They concluded that such moves were less common in the EU countries covered than in the United States. However, the analysis is not presented at a country level, and it only covers the period up to 2008, prior to some of the country-level policy changes to extend working lives. Furthermore, given the nature of the research design, it does not capture the experiences of individuals making such transitions.

More fundamentally, as we argue in the final chapter in more depth, the concept of bridge jobs is not very helpful for understanding job transitions in older age. By variously labelling a diverse range of transitions that occur in later life as 'bridge jobs/employment' – including transitions between and within firms and fluctuations in working time – it tends to obscure more than it reveals (for a sympathetic review of this literature see Wang et al 2014; for a more critical assessment see Earl and Taylor, 2017; Lassen and Vrangbæk, 2021). The bridge employment literature also arguably fails to address *why* people make transitions, or how they are experienced, because it is under-theorized and lacks qualitative inquiry (see Chapter 9).

In order to partially remedy this gap in the literature, this book draws on the lived, and thus far often overlooked, experiences of older individuals attempting to make job-related transitions in Ireland, the UK, Belgium, Italy, Germany and Sweden. In doing so, it focuses on an oft repeated but rarely amplified point that older workers are not a homogeneous group and that the individualization of retirement has led to an increasingly diverse range of later life working trajectories (Vickerstaff and Cox, 2005). In this chapter we set the context. We first outline our arguments about extended working lives policies in an era of neoliberal responsibilisation, and why this increases the potential importance of job transitions as a means of continuing in employment. We then add some empirical substance to this by presenting statistics on changes in job transitions between 2000 and 2019 across a range of countries. This helps set the context for the later chapters in this book that draw on qualitative research.

Extending working lives in an era of neoliberal responsibilisation

Rising pension ages, a reduction in state support for older people and the promotion of private sector alternatives is often presented uncritically in the literature, as if the way in which these changes have been enacted are almost inevitable. The proportion of older people in OECD countries will increase over the coming years, as a result of the large baby boomer generation reaching retirement age, declining birth rates and increased life expectancy. There are a number of alternative approaches to dealing with these demographic changes, but as Macnicol (2015) argues, these more progressive options are usually sidelined as countries seek to implement the neoliberal proposals advocated by international organizations such as the World Bank and OECD. Macnicol (2015), writing from the UK context, has argued that much of the demographic change is a consequence of large birth cohorts reaching retirement age, rather than large increases in longevity. As a result, there are a range of ways in which the UK could seek to address these, partly temporary, peaks in the number of older people. These do not all involve large state pension age increases or a further withdrawal of financial support for older people. The fact that these options have been dismissed without much consideration reflects a wider political trend towards neoliberalism. Street and Ní Léime (2020, p 87) make a similar point:

> the neoliberalist political agenda in many countries has foreclosed progressive action [with regards to extended working lives]. The transcendence of neoliberalist tendencies in most countries' political economies has instead seen governments committed to reining in public sector spending, even if it means dismantling traditional social insurance and safety net programmes. This is consistent with beliefs about the limits on state intervention typical of the neoliberal turn and has contributed to tax cuts and deregulation, stagnant wages, struggling national labour markets, austerity and a departure from universalist social policies, all culminating in increased income inequality and insecurity for individuals. It is no surprise that the main idea gaining the most traction and dominating international policy circles is the 'live longer, work longer' solution.

In response to this, according to these authors, 'in most places, governments have ... shifted more responsibility for ensuring retirement income away from governments onto individuals' (Street and Ní Léime, 2020, p 96). According to Krekula and Vickerstaff (2020), the 'neoliberal discourse [is one] of helping individuals to help themselves', which inevitably means working longer in most cases. However, as Street and Ní Léime (2020: 94) point out, there is little 'evidence that governments have enacted effective policies that enhance older individuals' employability'.

In order to make sense of what this might mean for job transitions in older age, it is useful to place these trends in a wider context of 'neoliberal responsibilisation', which draws on Foucault's (1991; 2008) governmentality perspective (Pyysiäinen et al 2017; Laliberte Rudman and Aldrich, 2021). According to Lemke (2001, p 203) 'neo-liberalism is a political rationality that tries to render the social domain economic and to link a reduction in (welfare) state services and security systems to the increasing call for "personal responsibility" and "self-care"'. Rose (1999) plots the rise of neoliberalism to ideas circulating in reaction to the 'social state' in the post-war period in countries such as the UK and the US, and the subsequent election of the Thatcher government in the UK in 1979. Rose (1999) argues that neoliberalism is not simply a form of laissez-faire politics in which the state withdraws from governing. Instead, the role of government is to provide a framework under which the market can succeed. This required 'governing at a distance' – rather than ruling by diktat. The important point was to get individuals to govern themselves by taking responsibility for themselves: 'To govern better, the state must govern less; to optimize the economy, one must govern through the entrepreneurship of autonomous actors – individuals and families, firms and corporations. Once responsibilized and entrepreneurialized, they would govern themselves within a state secured framework of law and order' (Rose, 1999, p 139). Within this literature, it is often proposed that attempts to persuade individuals to take personal responsibility for themselves are based on an 'appeal of increased personal freedom' (Pyysiäinen et al 2017, p 217). In the field of extended working lives, for example, state pension ages might be increasing. However, with the expansion of age discrimination legislation across Europe, extended working lives are presented as an opportunity for people to take advantage of, as self-actualizing, autonomous individuals.

At an EU policy level, this trend is perhaps best manifested by the shift towards promoting 'active ageing'. Moulaert and Biggs (2013, p 28) argue that 'active ageing' has become a central concept in EU policy making since the late 1990s; this is based on the assumption that people should 'be able to be able to lead a productive life and to be free to make personal choices'. The concept therefore rests on the idea of promoting autonomy and self-reliance as self-evident virtues, as this European Commission statement from 1999 cited by Moulaert and Biggs (2013, p 30) demonstrates: 'Preparing for longer, more active and better lives, working longer, retiring more gradually and seizing opportunities for active contributions after retirement are the best ways to secure the maximum degree of self-reliance and self-determination throughout old age.' Active ageing takes a broad definition of activity in people's lives, but Moulaert and Biggs (2013) argue that it did not take long for an 'economic version' of active ageing to dominate at a policy level, as reflected in this European Commission statement from 2011:

> We need to enable older people to make their contribution to society, to rely more on themselves and to depend less on others and for this we need to create conditions that allow people to stay active as they grow older. 'Active Ageing' promises to be such an approach because

it seeks to help older people to: remain longer in the labour market; contribute to society as volunteers and carers; remain as autonomous as possible for longer. (Cited in Moulaert and Biggs, 2013, p 31)

There is very little in the European Commission active ageing initiative to ensure older workers are supported in working longer, beyond the publication of very general recommendations – for example, access to good working conditions, training and so on (see European Commission, 2012). Perhaps the most relevant wider development at an EU policy level, however, has been the EU Directive on Equal Treatment in Employment and Occupation (Council Directive 2000/78/EC). This included age as a protected characteristic for the first time, and mandated members to introduce legislation to protect people from discrimination in relation to recruitment, training and working conditions. It did not, however, preclude countries from permitting the use of mandatory retirement ages by employers, and only the UK, Denmark and Poland have abolished them (OECD, 2017, p 66). In a range of other countries, allowable mandatory retirement ages have been significantly increased, however, to 67 in Finland, 68 in Sweden, 70 in Iceland, France and Portugal, and 72 in Norway.

Arguably the greatest impact of age discrimination legislation has been giving individuals the theoretical right to continue working up to, and often beyond, state pension age. In countries such as the UK and the US, where mandatory retirement ages have been abolished entirely, retiring at any age therefore becomes a theoretical choice that people can be held accountable for. In the UK and US there is little concrete evidence that it has increased recruitment of older people (Lain, 2016). Furthermore, recent survey research on employers in nine European countries suggests that despite age discrimination legislation employers remained less likely to favour employing an individual once they were in their 50s (Lössbroek et al 2021). Wider evidence from a range of countries suggests that older people are still assumed by employers to be 'less productive, more resistant to change, less open to training and development opportunities, less competent, more costly and more prone to illness' (Conway and Monks 2017, p 587). In this context, older people are known to find it more difficult than younger people to find a job if they become unemployed (Lain, 2016). Age discrimination legislation is therefore arguably more significant as a means of promoting the idea that employment is an individual choice available to older people, than a form of support for those seeking work. Correspondingly, the Women and Equalities Committee inquiry into older people and employment reported that while 'the Government told us that the Equality Act 2010 provided "strong protection" against [age] discrimination and was working as intended. ... Our [expert] witnesses disagreed' (Women and Equalities Committee, 2018, para 23).

In a context where there is little actual active support for people to continue working, policy approaches to extending working lives have focused on restricting access to pensions and other forms of benefit (see later). The question, therefore, is how do individuals respond to neoliberal responsibilisation in the form of pressures to work longer when there are relatively few support structures in place to do so? The assumption in the governmentality literature is that the intention of policy is to get individuals 'to see themselves as responsible for their own fate, to actively assume responsibility for outcomes in relevant areas of their lives' (Pyysiäinen et al 2017, p 216). As 'appeals to freedom' are often part of this, it might imply that individuals come to see themselves as enterprising, autonomous individuals and embrace ideas associated with active ageing and working longer. From a job transitions perspective, it might mean that they enthusiastically seek out and exploit new employment opportunities. Some individuals, perhaps those in more privileged positions, might embrace the appeals to freedom and this notion of themselves as autonomous individuals choosing to work longer. However, Pyysiäinen et al (2017) argue that another possible response is 'psychological reactance', whereby in this case the individual attributes pressures to work longer as being beyond their control. However, at the same time they nevertheless seek to exert and retain some control over the situation by assuming responsibility by becoming more 'realistic' about the options (Laliberte Rudman and Aldrich, 2021). This could mean, for example, continuing to seek out employment opportunities despite the challenges but scaling back aspirations and expectations. As Pyysiäinen et al (2017, p 230) argue, 'even if autonomy and controllability in one's action situation would appear very limited ... one could still persistently continue to use one's actions as means to "fight back" and to prevent losing even the last remains of one's personal control over the situation'.

This does not imply that individuals in this situation are not anxious about their prospects for extended working lives; indeed we might expect what Lain et al (2019) refer to as 'ontological precarity' anxieties about the future among older workers to be fairly widespread. This could mean that those in employment may be reluctant to try to move into new work, for example, because they worry about their prospects in the wider labour market in the context of pressures to work longer. On the other hand, for those in particularly challenging employment situations (for example, where their paid work has ended or is ending) we should not assume that they necessarily respond with complete passivity; anxiety may prompt people to act. It is suggested that this process of 'psychological reactance' is key to understanding how people will increasingly react to financial pressures to work longer in the context of 'neoliberal responsibilisation'. They will progressively assume responsibility for their own job transitions as a means of extending their working lives in order to try to regain control in an uncertain context.

It should also be noted that we are not arguing that countries have all arrived at identical states or degrees of 'neoliberal responsibilisation'. Countries inevitably 'started' from different positions with regard to welfare provision and labour market institutions in the early 2000s, and differences between countries are unlikely to completely disappear over such a period. We might more fruitfully think of there being a neoliberal trajectory, to use the terminology of Baccaro and Howell (2017), a common path along which countries are headed from various starting points. This ties in with wider arguments that welfare states and labour market institutions are being gradually transformed as a result of incremental change (Streeck and Thelen, 2005), which does not presuppose that they have all arrived at exactly the same destination.

Rising employment under neoliberal responsibilisation

In this changing context employment rates of older people have been rising significantly across a range of OECD countries that are characterized as belonging to very different types of 'welfare capitalism' in the past. These welfare state regime country groupings, influenced by the work of Esping-Andersen (1990) and Hall and Soskice (2001) are commonly used in comparative research (see, for example, Amable, 2003; Ebbinghaus, 2006; Buchholz et al 2011). Before looking at the rising rates of employment, it is therefore useful to set the context by looking at the earlier predictions of Buchholz et al (2011) and Ebbinghaus (2006):

- **Liberal** forms of welfare capitalism are said to be found in developed English-speaking countries, including the **United Kingdom** and **Ireland** and the United States and Australia. These countries are said to have ungenerous welfare states, comparatively flexible labour markets, weak trade unions and relatively insecure employment. Early retirement was said to be relatively low in the past compared with 'conservative' countries (Ebbinghaus, 2006). Buchholz et al (2011, p 25) predicted a tendency towards late employment in these countries, albeit of an increasingly insecure nature (presumably with significant job transitions).
- **Conservative** welfare regimes are said to be found in continental European countries, represented here by **Belgium, Germany**, the Netherlands and France. These countries are said to have relatively rigid regulated labour markets, where trade unions play a significant role and movement between occupations is constrained by the importance of occupational certificates and age discrimination in education. These countries are said to have comparatively generous social insurance benefits, including pensions, based on the principle of status maintenance (replacing earnings at relatively high levels, but with little redistribution). In these

countries Buchholz et al (2011, p 25) predicted a 'strong trend towards early exit', and Ebbinghaus (2006) predicted that early retirement would be hard to reverse.

- **Fragmented** welfare regimes were said to be found in Mediterranean countries, represented here by **Italy**, Spain, Portugal and Greece. Labour markets within these countries were seen as relatively rigid and regulated for those employed permanently in large firms, with a significant number also on the periphery in more temporary work. Welfare states are fragmented, generous in relation to pensions but less developed with regard to other areas of protection and disproportionately of benefit to those working in permanent jobs in large firms. Female employment is said to be relatively low because caring responsibilities fall on women in the context of weak state support. Buchholz et al (2011, p 25) predicted early retirement among those in protected employment, and longer working lives for the self-employed and those in informal forms of employment.

- **Social democratic** welfare regimes include **Sweden**, Denmark, Norway and Finland. Labour markets are seen as less regulated than in conservative welfare regimes, but there is a high level of coordination between trade unions and employers' federations. Welfare provision is said to be universal, generous and redistributive, with a focus on gender equality, lifelong learning and full employment. Buchholz et al (2011, p 25) anticipated that there would be trends towards late employment in older age, but this employment would be relatively long and stable compared with liberal countries such as the UK and Ireland.

Table 1.1 shows that while countries have different starting points in 2000, partly in line with the arguments of Buchholz et al (2011) and Ebbinghaus (2006), there have been significant increases in the employment rates of countries in all types of welfare regimes in contrast to some of the aforementioned predictions.

Overall, in 2000 the average employment rate for those aged 55 to 64 across the countries examined was below half, at around 45 per cent. There was, however, quite a variety between countries, ranging from 26.3 per cent in Belgium and 27.7 per cent in Italy, to around 50 per cent in Ireland and the United Kingdom, and 65 per cent in Sweden. Nevertheless, it is clear that in all of the countries a significant number of people in this age range were not in paid employment. Some patterns emerged with regard to employment rates based on country clusters, as might be expected following the arguments of Ebbinghaus (2006) discussed earlier. Employment rates were typically lowest in conservative and fragmented countries and highest in social democratic countries (and, to a lesser degree, liberal countries). However, there was significant variation within country clusters. Of the countries examined in this volume, Ireland and the UK had relatively

Table 1.1: Employment rates at age 55–64 by sex, 2000–19

		All			Men			Women		
		2000	2010	2019	2000	2010	2019	2000	2010	2019
Liberal	Australia	46.1	60.6	64.5	57.6	68.6	70.3	34.2	52.7	59.0
	Ireland	45.9	50.4	62.9	64.4	57.8	70.9	27.4	43.0	55.0
	United Kingdom	50.8	56.9	66.2	60.0	64.8	71.0	41.8	49.2	61.5
	United States	57.8	60.3	63.7	65.7	64.4	69.8	50.6	56.4	58.0
Conservative	**Belgium**	26.3	37.3	52.1	36.4	45.6	57.3	16.6	29.2	47.0
	France	29.9	39.8	53.0	34.1	42.4	55.4	26.0	37.3	50.9
	Germany	37.6	57.7	72.7	46.4	65.0	77.1	29.0	50.5	68.4
	Netherlands	37.6	53.2	69.7	49.7	63.5	78.3	25.5	42.8	61.2
Fragmented	Greece	39.0	42.4	43.2	55.2	56.5	56.1	24.3	29.1	31.6
	Italy	27.7	36.5	54.3	40.9	47.6	64.6	15.3	26.1	44.6
	Portugal	50.8	49.5	60.4	62.2	55.8	66.5	40.9	43.8	55.1
	Spain	37.0	43.5	53.8	55.2	54.5	61.1	20.1	33.1	46.9
Social democratic	Denmark	55.9	55.8	71.8	64.4	61.0	76.2	46.7	50.7	67.5
	Finland	42.3	56.3	66.8	43.7	55.6	64.8	40.9	56.9	68.6
	Norway	65.2	68.6	72.8	71.4	72.2	76.8	58.9	65.0	68.7
	Sweden	65.1	70.6	77.9	67.7	74.2	80.0	62.4	67.0	75.7
Country average		44.7	52.5	62.9	54.7	59.3	68.5	35.0	45.8	57.5

Note: Countries in bold are those covered in the later country-specific chapters.

Source: data extracted from www.oecd.org/employment/database

low non-employment rates compared with their liberal counterpart, the US. Likewise, employment in Belgium and Italy was comparatively low compared with other countries in their respective clusters (at 26/27 per cent). In Germany employment was below the country average (at around 38 per cent), but nevertheless higher than in Belgium, another conservative country. Employment in Sweden was comparatively high (at 65 per cent) compared with social democratic Finland.

While there was some variation in employment rates in 2000, all the countries saw an increase in employment in the period up to 2019, partially reversing the long-term trend towards early exit since the 1970s. Overall, the country average employment rates rose from 45 per cent to 63 per cent over this period. In all but one country more than half the population was working in 2019, the exception being Greece which of course experienced significant financial difficulties in this period. In the UK, a country experiencing particularly strong neoliberal responsibilisation, employment rates had increased to such an extent that they surpassed that of the US (rising to 66 per cent). Likewise, employment in Ireland rose from only 46 per cent in 2000 to 63 per cent over that period, roughly equivalent to that of the US.

In conservative countries there was likewise a consistent increase, but lower overall rates in 2019 in Belgium and France compared with Germany and the Netherlands. This, in part, reflects lower initial employment in Belgium and France in 2000, but it is noteworthy that employment nevertheless rose particularly significantly in Germany, rising to 73 per cent in 2019 – higher than any of the liberal countries, contrary to the expectations of Buchholz et al (2011) and Ebbinghaus (2006). The explanation given by Ebbinghaus and Hofäcker (2013) for the rise in employment in Germany focuses on the reversal of benefit/pension pathways to earlier exit which necessitates employment, rather than active labour market policies supporting employment of older people.

In the fragmented Mediterranean there were increases in all countries, but considerable variation in employment rates nevertheless remain. In Italy, one of the countries explored in this volume, we see a particularly pronounced rise in employment, from only 28 per cent in 2002 to 54 per cent in 2019. Employment in Portugal stands out as being relatively high in 2019, at 60 per cent, with Greece showing relatively little increase (and this being concentrated among women). As noted earlier, we see some of the highest employment rates in social democratic countries. Interestingly, in Sweden we see a rise from 65 per cent to 78 per cent.

Overall, therefore, we see a rise in employment for those aged 50 plus across the countries examined, albeit from different initial positions in 2000. In each country, this was true for both men and women. In a number of the countries employment rates for women in this age group in 2000 were particularly low, and rose markedly – this includes five of the six countries examined in this volume, that is, Ireland, Belgium, Italy, Germany, and to a lesser degree the UK. In the other country, Sweden, female employment likewise rose markedly over the period, but from a much higher initial level in 2000.

Policy changes and neoliberal responsibilisation

Considering the increase in overall employment across countries, we now explore wider policies to encourage these trends. The primary means by which neoliberal responsibilisation has occurred from a policy perspective is increases in the financial need to work because of a retrenchment in support available for older people. As Ogg and Rašticová (2020, p 1) point out, 'Perhaps the most visible measure of these policies has been the increase in age of eligibility for pensions.' Table 1.2 presents a number of changes to state pensions in the period from 2000 to 2018 in each of the countries examined in this book: Ireland, the UK, Belgium, Italy, Germany and Sweden. Results

Table 1.2: Changes to state pensions

		Normal pension age c. 2009	Normal pension age 2018	Scheduled increases in normal pension age post-2018	Reduced early pension possible in 2018?	Gross pension earnings replacement rate based on 2018 rules for someone on average earnings	Change in gross replacement rate – 1956 cohort vs 1940 cohort	Change in future gross replacement rate – 1996 cohort vs 1940 cohort
Liberal	Australia	65 for men; 63.5 for women	65.5	66 in 2019; 67 in 2023	No	30.9	-3.1	-10.8
	Ireland	65	66	Originally scheduled to rise to 67 in 2021; 68 in 2028 (rises paused in 2020)	No	27.0	6.1	6.1
	United Kingdom	65 for men; 60 for women	65.3	66 in 2020; 67 in 2028; 68 by 2046	No	21.7	-4.8	-11.3
	United States	66	66.4	67 in 2022	Yes	39.4	-1.7	-2.0
Conservative	Belgium	65	65	66 in 2025; 66 in 2030; ultimate projection: 67	Yes	46.8	5.4	-1.9
	France	60	63.3 (earlier if long contributions)	Ultimate projection: 66	Yes	72.3	-2.1	-5.4
	Germany	65	65.5	67 by 2031	Yes	38.7	-4.3	-8.1
	Netherlands	65	66	67 in 2021; ultimately: 71.3	No	70.9	-5.3	-9.9

Table 1.2: Changes to state pensions (continued)

	Normal pension age c. 2009	Normal pension age 2018	Scheduled increases in normal pension age post-2018	Reduced early pension possible in 2018?	Gross pension earnings replacement rate based on 2018 rules for someone on average earnings	Change in gross replacement rate – 1956 cohort vs 1940 cohort	Change in future gross replacement rate – 1996 cohort vs 1940 cohort
Fragmented Greece	65 (earlier if long contributions)	67 (earlier if long contributions)	None scheduled as yet	Yes	49.9	-7.9	-16.7
Italy	65 for men; 60 for women	66.6	67 in 2019; ultimately 71.3	Yes	79.5	15.2	4.2
Portugal	65	66.4	Life-expectancy rises; projection: 67.8	Yes	74.4	-0.1	-0.7
Spain	65	65.5 (earlier if long contributions)	67 in 2027	Yes	72.3	-6.3	-23.4
Social democratic Denmark	65	65	67 in 2022; 68 in 2030	No	74.4	-5.5	-6.3
Finland	65	65	Life-expectancy increases; ultimate projection: 67.9	Yes	56.5	0.6	-4.3
Norway	67	67	None scheduled as yet	Yes	45.4	-28.3	-31.6
Sweden	65	65	None scheduled as yet	Yes	54.1	-0.4	-5.7

Source: authors' compilation based on OECD Pensions at a Glance, various years for each country are presented alongside those other countries historically said to belong to the same kind of 'welfare-state regime' or version of 'welfare capitalism'.

From Table 1.2 we can see that irrespective of the type of welfare state regime, in the majority of countries 'normal' state pension ages have already risen during this period, and are set to rise to around 67 in the next few years in most countries. This change has been particularly pronounced in the 'liberal' UK, where state pension ages will reach 67 in 2028 with no possibility of accessing a state pension before this age. In Ireland state pension age reached 66 as early as 2014 with no possibility of obtaining an earlier, reduced pension. However, plans to increase state pension age to 67 by 2021 were put on hold in 2020 and made the subject of a pensions commission, due to the political unpopularity of the move (see Chapter 8).

In a number of countries individuals can obtain a reduced pension earlier (see Table 1.2), but as 'normal' state pension ages rise countries are increasing the early age of receipt or reducing the generosity of early pensions accordingly. The trend towards later pension ages therefore affects countries in all of the four different welfare state regimes. Sweden's adherence to the 'normal' pension age of 65 does not imply a lack of pressures to work longer. The earliest age at which a reduced, early pension can be claimed will rise from 61 to 64 in 2026. Furthermore, the concept of a 'target age' of retirement has been introduced as a policy lever, argued to be 'the necessary average retirement age to make it possible to uphold the economic levels in the pension system' (Liff and Wikström, 2020, p 6). With a target retirement age projected to reach 69 in 2023, it seems inevitable that the 'normal' pension age will be revisited.

In addition to the general trend of having to wait longer to reach normal pension age, the generosity of state pensions is also declining in most countries. Table 1.2 shows the gross future pension 'earnings replacement rate' for individuals entering employment in 2018 at age 22; this assumes that these individuals will have average earnings throughout their career and will make all the required pension contributions. This shows that there was considerable variation, not only between countries but within welfare regime types. As we might expect, the lowest replacement rates are typically found in liberal countries, but they range from lows of 21.7 per cent of previous earnings in the UK and 27 per cent in Ireland, to 39.4 per cent in the US. Interestingly, according to these figures, the generosity of the German pension is below that of the US. This might be seen as particularly surprising as Germany was considered one of the countries where in the past early retirement was most entrenched (Ebbinghaus, 2006). Indeed, pensions in Belgium and Germany are significantly less generous than in their conservative counterparts, France and the Netherlands.

Gross replacement rates are typically highest in the Mediterranean fragmented welfare states, ranging from 72.3 per cent of previous earnings in Spain to 79.5 per cent in Italy. The exception to this was Greece which saw significant retrenchment in pensions following the country's financial crisis. It is important to note that these pensions are not quite as generous as they might appear, however, as they are measured against wages that have a lower buying power than is the average for OECD countries (measured in 'purchasing power parity') (OECD, 2019, p 193). Furthermore, due to comparatively low female employment rates across the life course, couples may be heavily reliant upon the man's pension. For these reasons, high replacement rates in pensions are particularly necessary. In the social democratic countries of Scandinavia we see some variation in pension earnings replacement rates, ranging from a high of 74.4 per cent in Denmark to 45.4 per cent in Norway.

The final two columns of Table 1.2 show the extent to which pensions are becoming less generous (if at all). The penultimate column shows how the replacement rate has changed for individuals born in 1956 (retiring in about 2018) compared with those born around 15 years earlier (born in 1940). In 12 out of the 16 countries pension levels were lower for those retiring in 2018 than they were in the past. These changes ranged from a 0.1 per cent decrease in Portugal to a 28.3 per cent decrease in Norway. Most of the countries experiencing an increase in pension replacement rate had nevertheless also experienced an increase in pension age. Furthermore, projected gross replacement rates for those born in 1996, entering the labour market in about 2018, fell in 14 of the 16 countries (relative to the cohort born in 1940). The dominant trend across this diverse range of countries is the rising state pension ages and declining pension levels.

Of course, pension levels are not the only policy changes of relevance to extended working lives, so it is worth briefly reviewing some of the broader changes. According to Street and Ní Léime's (2020, p 97) review it has also been the case that 'recourse to disability and unemployment benefits has been severely restricted in many countries'. Policies to support older workers and their employability have been marginal and access to early retirement pathways has been restricted.

In **Ireland**, in addition to an increased state pension age noted earlier, a government provided 'Pre-retirement Allowance' was discontinued in 2007, which removes the possibility of workers in physically demanding occupations retiring early (Ní Léime et al 2020). In addition, sickness benefits have become more restricted, with a two-year time limit on income replacement benefits for insured individuals (OECD, 2018a). In terms of supporting older workers to work longer, training and lifelong learning programmes provided by the government have been accessible to older workers since 2015, but the focus has been on younger participants with low numbers of older workers participating. In line with other EU countries, age discrimination legislation has been introduced, and since 2015 employers have to justify compulsory retirement age if they have one (Ní Léime et al 2020). However, there are a range of 'objective justifications' that employers may use to compel older workers to retire at their contractual retirement age.

The **United Kingdom** has gone the furthest, compared to the other countries covered in this book, in terms of how far they have gone down the path of neoliberal responsibilisation. State pensions have historically been provided to women before men, at 60 rather than 65; however, pension ages have now been equalized between the genders and are rising rapidly as we saw earlier. Without the possibility of an early reduced state pension, economically inactive older people are dependent upon unemployment and disability benefit provision, which have been reducing in real terms since the early 2010s and subject to a series of punitive sanctions for non-compliance with increasingly strict rules (Taylor, 2017). The main measure introduced to facilitate extended working lives has been the abolition of mandatory retirement ages in 2011. This changing situation has arguably created a sense of anxiety among older people, who worry about their prospects of being able to stay in work long enough to be in a financial position to retire (Lain et al 2019).

In **Italy**, rising state pension ages have been accompanied by reforms to unemployment and disability benefits which seek to transfer people from the schemes into paid work. For example, Lista di Mobilità was provided for employed people dismissed from their employment. It was, according to OECD (2018b, p 5), 'the most generous social protection exit scheme in Italy', albeit one restricted to those working for small employers (Mopact, 2017). In 2012 this allowance was abolished, and a new benefit introduced (Assicurazione Sociale per l'Impiego, or ASPI). This new benefit was time-limited and depended on participation in any active labour market activities offered and could be withdrawn for refusing a job with a salary 20 per cent more generous than the benefit (OECD, 2018b, p 5). In relation to disability benefits, these have been subject to stricter controls since 2009, to reduce access to so-called 'fake invalid people' (OECD, 2018b, p 5). While the financial need to work has increased, as Mopact (2017, p 6) state, 'employment policies and active labour market policies in favour of older workers (in view of an extension of their active life) are still rare'.

Germany has moved from what Ebbinghaus and Hofäcker (2013) describe as an 'early exit regime' to being one of 'early exit reversal'. Older workers can still draw their state pension from the age of 63, but are subject to significant pension deductions. Alongside the changes to pension ages, from a policy perspective increases in employment among older people have been importantly influenced by restricting access to cash benefits. For example, workers aged 57 and older could draw until 2008 on comparatively generous unemployment insurance benefits (sometimes topped up by former employers) for three years with no means test or obligation to search for work or enter activation schemes. The Hartz reforms cut this period for unemployment benefit recipients aged 58 and older to 24 months (Hess, 2016). Subsidies have been introduced to hire older workers, but in terms of policies to support older workers, 'comparably few improvements were made in the field of education and lifelong learning' (Hess, 2016, p 157). Interestingly, one form of early retirement was introduced in 2014: 'Rente mit 63' (pension at 63 without deductions) with 45 qualifying years, but this option favours especially men with long and uninterrupted work careers.

In **Belgium** early retirement since the early 1970s had been common following the introduction of the 'pre-pension system', the aim of which was to make room for young unemployed people to enter the employment market (Burnay and Vendramin, 2020). The system enabled people who had worked for 40 years to draw a pension from age 58. Access to this system has been increasingly restricted since 2012, and the name changed to 'unemployment with company supplement', with older people now required to remain available for work. In addition, a time credit system in place since the mid-2000s, which enabled older people to reduce their working time as a means of extending their working lives, has also been restricted. Burnay and Vendramin (2020, p 157) argue that the time reduction system was merely a transitionary stage 'between a period of early exit from labour market and a period of extended full-time careers'. In addition, access to disability insurance has been tightened (Burnay and Vendramin, 2020, p 160). In terms of support for working lives, this has arguably been limited to a requirement in 2015 for companies to have a plan to retain older workers, something that is deemed to have negligible impact in real terms (Burnay and Vendramin, 2020, p 158).

In **Sweden** eligibility conditions for Disability Insurance have tightened considerably since the late 1990s (Palme and Laun, 2018). In 1997 lower medical eligibility requirements were removed for older people and they then had the same job-seeking and mobility requirements as younger people. From 2003 the benefit was no longer automatically provided on a permanent basis, and eligibility would be reassessed every five years. More fundamentally, from 2008 new eligibility rules were introduced which required the individuals to prove that their ability to work had been permanently lost. These changes resulted in a sharp reduction in the number of older people on this programme (Palme and Laun, 2018). Alongside these changes, in 2001 the maximum period for receiving unemployment benefits was cut to 300 days in 2001, and the income replacement rates for these benefits were cut after the first 200 days. After 300 days if individuals are still unemployed they are moved onto what are described as 'workfare' programmes by the OECD (2018c).

Job transitions in comparative context

Having outlined the nature of neoliberal responsibilisation, we now set the context for the later chapters that explore the lived experience of older people navigating job transitions. Each of these chapters draws on qualitative research conducted by the authors which has received the appropriate ethical approval. To set this context we conclude this chapter by exploring how job transitions of older people have changed since 2000. The individualization of retirement has meant that people face the possibility or risk of more varied later working life trajectories. Chapter 2 provides a brief history of the influences that shape the transition from work to retirement and the growing precarity that characterizes work-endings. The impact of COVID-19 on older workers' employment prospects, which is only now beginning to be researched, will have further strengthened the 'zone of insecurity' which is later working life.

In order to give an initial impression of the prevalence of job transitions, Table 1.3 shows job tenure for dependent workers aged 55 to 64 in 2000 and 2015. Given the age band used, we can assume that those with less than five years' job tenure were recruited in their 50s or 60s. Overall, we can see that across the countries covered, the average proportion of workers recruited in older age (50 plus) was similar in both 2000 and 2015 at around 17 to 18 per cent. The rise in employment shown in Table 1.1 was not, therefore, solely about people continuing in long held jobs, and transitions into new jobs must have been part of the equation. Looking at Table 1.3 we can see that in 2015 there were significant variations in the proportions of older recruits between countries, including within country clusters. In conservative and fragmented countries older workers had a relatively low likelihood of having been recruited in older age (with the exception of Greece), with around 70 plus per cent of workers in these countries being in relatively long-term jobs lasting ten plus years. Recruitment into new jobs in older age was relatively high in liberal Australia and the UK, but lower than the country average in Ireland. It is also relatively high in social democratic Denmark and Sweden, but lower than the country average in Finland and Norway, where 15 per cent were recent recruits. Overall, job retention remained the most important route by which older people remained in work in all countries, albeit to varying degrees, which in part reflects the difficulties of changing jobs that individuals face in older age.

Job redeployment

Given the importance of job retention to working longer, in Chapter 3 we examine the use of redeployment to a new job and its impact on older

Table 1.3: Job tenure for dependent workers aged 55–64 (percentage breakdown)

		2000				2015			
		Under 5 years	5–10 years	10+ years	Total	Under 5 years	5–10 years	10+ years	Total
Liberal	Australia	..	..	..	100%	29.7	20.1	50.3	100%
	Ireland	23.3	11.7	65.0	100%	16.5	15.0	68.5	100%
	United Kingdom	28.9	17.3	53.9	100%	24.9	18.1	57.0	100%
Conservative	**Belgium**	11.0	9.2	79.8	100%	10.2	11.7	78.1	100%
	France	12.7	12.8	74.4	100%	12.8	11.5	75.7	100%
	Germany	15.9	14.5	69.6	100%	17.3	12.1	70.6	100%
	Netherlands	..	..	..	100%	13.3	13.5	73.2	100%
Fragmented	Greece	15.1	8.4	76.4	100%	19.3	9.3	71.4	100%
	Italy	12.8	7.7	79.5	100%	12.4	10.2	77.4	100%
	Spain	20.5	9.0	70.5	100%	15.8	10.6	73.7	100%
Social democratic	Denmark	22.8	12.9	64.3	100%	26.4	19.3	54.3	100%
	Finland	14.6	9.9	75.6	100%	17.1	13.0	69.9	100%
	Sweden	12.0	10.4	77.6	100%	21.1	13.4	65.5	100%
	Norway	..	..	..	100%	15.2	16.2	68.6	100%
Country average		17.2	11.2	71.6		18.0	13.9	68.2	
Country average excluding Australia, Norway and Netherlands		17.2	11.2	71.6		17.6	13.1	69.3	

Note: '..' indicates that data is unavailable or incomplete.

Source: data extracted from www.oecd.org/employment/database

workers in a UK local authority seeking to avoid compulsory redundancies in the context of neoliberal austerity. There is no OECD data on the prevalence of job redeployment, but there are reasons to believe that it may be important. In a number of countries, employment protection legislation means that companies are expected to exhaust opportunities for redeployment to a new role before making somebody redundant (OECD, 2020). In other cases, employers facing redundancy pressures may seek to avoid, or more likely reduce, redundancies by redeploying staff to new roles. A survey of around a thousand UK employers in autumn 2020 during the COVID-19 pandemic found that 37 per cent of employers were using redeployment as a means of avoiding or reducing redundancy (CIPD, 2020, p 4). Being able to successfully navigate job redeployment may therefore be particularly important in the context of the financial difficulties in the coming years. However, as we see from Chapter 3, older workers may often end up being marginalized in the context of redeployment under neoliberalism. It is furthermore argued that under the conditions of neoliberalism job redeployment is likely to be motivated by the needs of the organization rather than the older worker. This is further examined in Chapter 4, which explores why job mobility among manual workers in an organization in Sweden is not made available to older workers, despite the physical demands of the jobs.

Temporary employment

Moving into temporary employment is another way in which older people seek to extend their working lives, perhaps if other permanent work opportunities are unavailable. In Chapter 5 we explore the experiences of individuals doing temporary work in Belgium. As Table 1.4 shows, temporary employment among those aged 55 to 64 increased in Belgium overall between 2000 and 2019, although this was the result of men rather than women increasingly entering this form of employment. Indeed, overall the country averages show that temporary employment rose for men and declined for women. From the other countries examined in detail in this volume, however, it is clear that increases in temporary employment among older men *and* women occurred in Ireland and Italy. In 2019 temporary employment rates were comparatively high among older workers in fragmented welfare regimes of southern Europe, and in France. On the other hand, temporary employment was relatively low in the UK and Australia, and actually declined over the period in both countries. It should, however, be noted that in the UK employment protection legislation for those in 'permanent' jobs is relatively low (OECD, 2019), so there is less incentive to recruit temporary staff. This is likely to be reflected in the relatively high proportion of UK older workers recruited in the last five years (as

Table 1.4: Percentages of dependent workers aged 55–64 that are temporary, 2000 and 2019

		All			Men			Women		
		2000	2010	2019	2000	2010	2019	2000	2010	2019
Liberal	Australia	..	5.0	..	..	4.9	..	..	5.1	..
	Ireland	3.1	6.6	6.1	2.1	6.7	6.3	4.9	6.5	6.0
	United Kingdom	6.4	5.0	4.4	6.1	4.6	4.1	6.7	5.4	4.6
Conservative	**Belgium**	3.6	2.9	4.3	2.4	1.9	4.4	6.1	4.2	4.1
	France	5.7	8.7	9.0	5.4	8.4	8.8	6.0	8.9	9.1
	Germany	4.4	4.6	3.0	4.5	4.7	3.0	4.2	4.5	3.1
	Netherlands	6.4	6.8	7.1	5.0	6.3	7.1	9.1	7.5	7.1
Fragmented	Greece	7.5	7.7	8.5	6.7	6.1	8.4	10.1	11.0	8.7
	Italy	6.3	6.1	7.3	6.4	6.6	8.2	6.2	5.4	6.4
	Portugal	11.1	9.6	10.2	9.5	9.2	10.6	13.4	10.1	9.8
	Spain	13.2	10.2	13.2	12.4	9.4	12.6	15.4	11.4	13.8
Social democratic	Denmark	4.4	3.6	3.9	3.7	3.6	3.3	5.4	3.6	4.6
	Finland	6.1	7.5	8.3	4.9	7.0	7.1	7.1	7.9	9.2
	Norway	3.1	2.4	2.1	2.2	1.9	1.6	4.0	3.0	2.6
	Sweden	6.5	6.1	6.9	6.1	4.6	4.1	6.7	5.4	4.6
Country average		6.3	6.2	6.7	5.5	5.7	6.4	7.5	6.7	6.7

Note: '..' indicates that data is unavailable.

Source: data extracted from www.oecd.org/employment/database

per Table 1.3 earlier). Chapter 5 on Belgium shows that the older workers interviewed were taking temporary jobs because they were unable to find permanent positions, but to some degree they internalized and presented narratives about the need to be active.

Unemployment

Unemployment is another transition that older people may have to navigate their way out of in order to extend their working lives, and Chapter 6 examines the experiences of unemployed people in Italy. Unemployment, of course, fluctuates depending upon the underlying economic circumstances, so looking at unemployment levels in individual isolated years underplays how many older people may be affected at one point in time. Figure 1.1 therefore shows yearly unemployment levels for

Figure 1.1: Unemployment rates among those aged 55–64, 2000–19

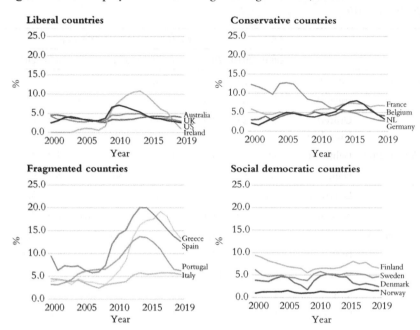

Source: data extracted from www.oecd.org/employment/database

those aged 55 to 64 between 2000 and 2019. In liberal and fragmented countries we can see significant peaks in employment following the financial crash in 2008. Interestingly, unemployment was lower in Italy than in other fragmented countries for most of this period. In conservative countries, we see modest increases in unemployment overall, comparing 2019 with 2000, with the exception of Germany, where the conditions of receiving unemployment insurance were tightened (Ebbinghaus and Hofäcker, 2013). Finally, in social democratic countries there is some variability in unemployment over the period, with particularly low rates in Norway where older inactive individuals tend to be in receipt of disability rather than unemployment benefits (OECD, 2013).

Considering the importance of examining long-term trends, Table 1.5 compares the unemployment rate in 2019 between those aged 25 to 54 and those aged 55 to 64. Looking at the country average, we can see that unemployment rates were slightly lower for the older group (5 per cent versus 6 per cent), with the biggest disparity in relation to lower unemployment rates among the older people in Italy, Portugal and Ireland. Generally speaking, countries with high unemployment among the younger group tended to have relatively high unemployment among those aged 55 to 64.

Table 1.5: Unemployment among those aged 25–54 and 55–64, 2019

		Unemployment rate		% of unemployed who are long-term unemployed (1+ years)	
		Aged 25 to 54	Aged 55 to 64	Aged 25 to 54	Aged 55 to 64
Liberal	Australia	4.0	4.0	24.8	35.2
	Ireland	3.9	1.0	..	..
	United Kingdom	2.9	2.9	28.6	39.9
	United States	3.1	2.6	13.9	18.0
Conservative	**Belgium**	4.8	4.1	46.2	64.7
	France	7.5	6.8	38.7	62.1
	Germany	3.0	2.7	38.2	55.1
	Netherlands	2.6	3.2	32.6	59.6
Fragmented	Greece	17.1	13.4	70.3	81.1
	Italy	9.8	5.4	58.3	63.3
	Portugal	5.7	6.2	..	..
	Spain	12.9	12.6	37.8	57.8
Social democratic	Denmark	4.4	2.4	..	..
	Finland	5.1	6.6	21.5	34.8
	Sweden	5.3	4.6	14.6	28.6
	Norway	3.2	1.6	29.1	52.8
Country average		6.0	5.0	35.0	50.2

Note: '..' indicates that data is unavailable.

Source: data extracted from www.oecd.org/employment/database

While younger people were generally marginally more likely to be unemployed, older people, on the other hand, were likely to find it harder to get another job, consistent with previous research evidence (Lain, 2016). The final two columns of Table 1.4 shows percentages of unemployed individuals who were long-term unemployed in 2019 (that is, for one plus years). As this demonstrates, in all countries older people were more likely to fall into this category, with a country average of 50 per cent of older unemployed individuals being out of work for a year or more, compared with 35 per cent for those in the younger category. Between the countries there was some variation in the proportion of unemployed individuals being out of work for a year or more, with this being particularly high in conservative and fragmented countries and lower in liberal and social democratic countries.

The experiences of unemployed older people in Italy discussed in Chapter 6 reflect the difficulties of getting another job in the context of long-term unemployment, but the narratives of interviewees reflected the perceived need to be active and entrepreneurial and take responsibility for managing their work transitions, consistent with a logic of neoliberal responsibilisation.

Working after pension age and transitions into retirement

The final two chapters focus on women and their employment beyond pension age and their expectations regarding the transition to retirement. Chapter 7 explores employment beyond state pension age among women in Germany and the UK. It is not easy to measure this with comparable statistics, because pension ages are rising, but statistics are still collected using fixed age-bands. However, Table 1.6 gives an insight in this regard by showing employment rates at age 65, historically (male) state pension age in many countries, in the period between 2000 and 2019. As this shows, employment among this age group rose among women and men in all the countries except Greece and Portugal, often doubling as a percentage. Despite their historical classification as being different 'types' of welfare states/labour markets, employment at age 65 rose significantly for women in both Germany and the UK (from 1.5 per cent to 5.5 per cent in Germany, and from 3.5 per cent to 8.2 per cent in the UK). As the chapter shows, motivations for working were fairly similar between the countries, reflecting a mix of financial need and a desire to be independent. In some cases this reflected a continuation of the job done immediately before pension age, and with policy changes to either abolish or raise mandatory retirement ages in some countries we may expect to see a further rise in this trend.

Finally, in Chapter 8 we explore the final work-related transition: from work to retirement, in Ireland. Measuring and comparing retirement transitions across countries is not straightforward, because individuals may leave work for reasons other than retirement – for example, ill health or unemployment – and *then* define themselves as retired. The OECD measures this using 'effective retirement ages', which represents the average age of withdrawal from the labour market for those over age 40 over a five-year period. Table 1.6 shows these statistics for the five-year period leading up to 2000, 2010 and 2018; we have called them 'effective exit rates' here to account for the fact that not everybody leaves for the purposes of retirement. While it is not a measure of retirement per se, it is a good measure of exit because it considers employment levels of individuals at younger ages. In the case of women in particular, increases in employment in older age may partly reflect the fact that more women are working at younger ages, rather than because women are working longer. We should, however, bear

Table 1.6: Employment rates at age 65+ by sex, 2000–19

		All			Men			Women		
		2000	2010	2019	2000	2010	2019	2000	2010	2019
Liberal	Australia	6.0	10.6	14.5	9.8	15.2	18.6	3.0	6.8	10.8
	Ireland	6.8	8.3	11.2	13.6	13.8	16.5	1.6	3.8	6.6
	United Kingdom	5.2	8.1	10.7	7.5	11.0	13.7	3.5	5.8	8.2
	United States	12.5	16.2	19.6	7.5	11.0	13.7	3.5	5.8	8.2
Conservative	**Belgium**	1.5	2.0	2.9	2.4	3.2	4.4	0.8	1.2	1.8
	France	1.3	1.5	3.3	2.1	2.2	4.5	0.8	1.0	2.4
	Germany	2.7	4.0	7.8	4.4	5.7	10.7	1.5	2.7	5.5
	Netherlands	3.2	5.7	9.1	5.5	9.1	13.2	1.5	3.0	5.4
Fragmented	Greece	5.2	4.0	3.7	8.3	6.3	5.6	2.8	2.1	2.2
	Italy	3.2	3.1	5.0	5.8	5.6	7.7	1.5	1.3	2.8
	Portugal	18.0	16.5	11.5	25.1	22.2	17.1	13.0	12.4	7.5
	Spain	1.6	2.0	2.4	2.5	2.6	3.2	0.9	1.5	1.8
Social democratic	Denmark	2.4	6.6	8.6	3.9	10.5	13.2	1.3	3.5	4.6
	Finland	3.7	7.8	11.2	6.3	11.0	14.7	1.6	5.0	8.1
	Norway	9.4	18.1	10.9	11.9	23.1	12.4	7.1	13.5	9.1
	Sweden	10.2	13.3	17.5	14.7	18.4	20.7	6.3	8.3	14.5
Country average		5.8	8.0	9.4	8.2	10.7	11.9	3.2	4.9	6.2

Source: data extracted from www.oecd.org/employment/database

in mind that the latest data period is from 2013 to 2018, so if long-term trends have continued we would expect additional increases in exit ages to have occurred since then.

As Table 1.7 shows, across the countries as a whole the average age of male and female exit increased by over two years over the period, from 62.1 to 64.5 for men and 61 to 63 for women. Increases in male exit age occurred across all of the countries, with the exception of Greece. As we might expect from earlier analysis, exit ages were relatively high in social democratic countries, at around 66 for men in the later period in Sweden and Norway and 64/65 for women. In conservative and fragmented welfare states exit ages there was obviously a general trend towards working later, but more variability than we might expect from predictions of welfare-state analysts, with comparatively high exit ages in Germany, the Netherlands and Portugal. Female exit ages actually marginally declined in Greece and Spain in the context of an overall increase in employment and relatively high unemployment.

Table 1.7: Average effective age of exit from work

		Men				Women			
		1995–2000	2005–10	2013–18	Change (years)	1995–2000	2005–10	2013–18	Change (years)
Liberal	Australia	62.0	64.5	65.3	3.3	59.6	62.7	64.3	4.7
	Ireland	65.2	63.0	65.6	0.4	66.0	64.0	64.1	–1.9
	United Kingdom	62.5	64.1	64.7	2.2	60.9	61.9	63.6	2.7
	United States	64.8	65.6	67.9	3.1	63.7	65.3	66.5	2.9
Conservative	**Belgium**	58.5	60.6	61.6	3.1	57.1	59.0	60.5	3.5
	France	59.0	59.3	60.8	1.8	58.6	59.5	60.8	2.2
	Germany	61.0	62.0	64.0	3.1	60.3	61.2	63.6	3.4
	Netherlands	60.6	62.9	65.2	4.6	58.7	61.4	62.5	3.8
Fragmented	Greece	63.2	61.9	61.7	–1.5	62.7	60.3	60.0	–2.7
	Italy	60.4	60.6	63.3	2.9	58.4	59.0	61.5	3.0
	Portugal	63.5	66.5	68.5	5.0	60.3	64.7	65.4	5.1
	Spain	61.6	62.3	62.1	0.5	61.8	63.0	61.3	–0.5
Social democratic	Denmark	63.4	64.0	65.1	1.7	59.8	61.8	62.5	2.8
	Finland	60.2	61.7	64.3	4.1	59.8	61.7	63.4	3.6
	Sweden	63.7	65.4	66.4	2.7	62.4	63.3	65.4	3.1
	Norway	64.0	64.1	66.1	2.1	63.7	63.8	64.1	0.4
Country average		62.1	63.0	64.5	2.4	2.4	62.0	63.1	2.2

Source: data extracted from www.oecd.org/employment/database

In liberal countries, male exit rates increased to around 65 in Australia and the UK, 65.6 in Ireland and almost 68 in the US. Interestingly, the growth in employment for men in Ireland was relatively modest as the exit age was already 65.2 in 2000 (the dip in exit ages in the middle period can be explained by very high unemployment; see Figure 1.1). Female exit ages were also high in 2000, at 66, albeit based on a relatively small proportion of women working at this time; this fell to 64.1 as overall employment levels of older women employment increased. The long-term, relatively late nature of exit in Ireland therefore makes it an interesting country to examine expectations about transitions to retirement among women in work. The chapter compares the experiences of low-paid care workers with better-paid and pensioned teachers. It finds that care workers had much greater expectations about needing to work up to, or even beyond, the state pension age of 66. This highlights the importance of recognizing the inequalities that are set to emerge as pressures for individuals to take financial responsibility for their own transitions to work intensify.

Outline of the book

Having set out recent changes with regard to extended working lives, in Part II we draw on qualitative research on older people's experiences of trying to navigate different types of transitions – within-organization job redeployment/mobility in the UK and Sweden, temporary employment in Belgium, unemployment in Italy, working beyond typical pension age in Germany and the UK, and expected transitions into retirement in Ireland. However, prior to this, in the next chapter we complete our discussion of the changing context by exploring the wider historical, labour market and policy changes that have shaped the need for extended working lives and job transitions in later life. In Part III we discuss the findings from the empirical chapters in light of the theoretical and policy context outlined in the first two chapters of the book.

References

Amable, B. (2003) *The Diversity of Modern Capitalism*, Oxford: Oxford University Press.

Baccaro, L. and Howell, C. (2017) *Trajectories of Neoliberal Transformation: European Industrial Relations since the 1970s*, Cambridge: Cambridge University Press.

Brunello, G. and Langella, M. (2013) 'Bridge jobs in Europe', *IZA Journal of Labor Policy*, 2(1): 1–18.

Buchholz, S., Rinklake, A., Schilling, J., Kurz, K., Schmelzer, P. and Blossfeld, H.-P. (2011) 'Aging populations, globalization and the labor market: comparing late working life and retirement in modern societies', in Blossfeld, H.-P., Buchholz, S. and Kurz, K. (eds) *Aging Populations, Globalization and the Labor Market: Comparing Late Working Life and Retirement in Modern Societies*, Cheltenham: Edward Elgar, pp 3–33.

Burnay, N. and Vendramin, P. (2020) 'Belgium', in Ní Léime, A., Ogg, J., Street, D., Krekula, C., Rašticová, M., Bédiová, M. and Madero-Cabib, I. (eds) *Extended Working Life Policies: International Gender and Health Perspectives*, Cham: Springer Open.

CIPD (Chartered Institute of Personnel and Development) (2020) *Labour Market Outlook Autumn 2020*, London: Chartered Institute of Personnel and Development.

Conway, E. and Monks, K. (2017) 'Designing a HR system for managing an age-diverse workforce', in Parry, E. and McCarthy, J. (eds) *The Palgrave Handbook of Age Diversity and Work*, London: Palgrave Macmillan, pp 585–606.

Earl, C. and Taylor, P. (2017) 'Reconceptualising work-retirement transitions: critiques of the new retirement and bridge employment', in Aaltio, I., Mills, A. and Mills, J. (eds) *Ageing, Organisations and Management*, London: Palgrave MacMillan, pp 323–44.

Ebbinghaus, B. (2006) *Reforming Early Retirement in Europe, Japan and the USA*, Oxford: Oxford University Press.

Ebbinghaus, B. and Hofäcker, D. (2013) 'Reversing early retirement in advanced welfare economies: a paradigm shift to overcome push and pull factors', *Comparative Population Studies*, 38(4): 807–40.

Esping-Andersen, G. (1990) *The Three Worlds of Welfare Capitalism*, Princeton, NJ: Princeton University Press.

European Commission (2011) *Commission Presents White Paper on Pensions* [online], available at: https://ec.europa.eu/commission/presscorner/det ail/de/MEMO_12_108 [accessed 9 April 2021].

European Commission (2012) *Guiding Principles for Active Ageing* [online], available at: https://data.consilium.europa.eu/doc/document/ST%2017 468%202012%20INIT/EN/pdf [accessed 9 April 2021].

Foucault, M. (1991) 'Governmentality', in Burchell, G., Gordon, C. and Miller, P. (eds) *The Foucault Effect: Studies in Governmentality*, Chicago IL: Chicago University Press, pp 87–104.

Foucault, M. (2008) *The Birth of Biopolitics: Lectures at the Collège de France, 1978–79*, New York: Palgrave.

Hall, P.A. and Soskice, D. (eds) (2001) *Varieties of Capitalism: The Institutional Foundations of Comparative Advantage*, Oxford: Oxford University Press.

Hasselhorn, H. and Apt, W. (eds) (2015) *Understanding Employment Participation of Older Workers*, Research Report, Berlin: Federal Ministry of Labour and Social Affairs (BMAS).

Hess, M. (2016) 'Germany: a successful reversal of early retirement?', in Hofäcker, D., König, S. and Hess (eds) *Delaying Retirement: Progress and Challenges of Active Ageing in Europe, the United States and Japan*, London: Palgrave.

Hilsen, A.I. and Midstundstad, T. (2015) 'Domain: human resource management and interventions', in Hasselhorn, H. and Apt, W. (eds) *Understanding Employment Participation of Older Workers*, Research Report, Berlin: Federal Ministry of Labour and Social Affairs (BMAS).

Institute for Fiscal Studies (2020) *The Coronavirus Pandemic and Older Workers*, IFS Briefing Note BN305 [online], available at: https://ifs.org.uk/uplo ads/BN305-The-coronavirus-pandemic-and-older-workers.pdf [accessed 9 April 2021].

Krekula, C. and Vickerstaff, S. (2020) 'The "older worker" and the "ideal worker": a critical examination of concepts and categorisations in the rhetoric of extending working lives', in Ní Léime, A., Ogg, J., Street, D., Krekula, C., Rašticová, M., Bédiová, M. and Madero-Cabib, I. (eds) (2020) *Extended Working Life Policies: International Gender and Health Perspectives*, Cham: Springer Open, pp 29–54.

Lain, D. (2016) *Reconstructing Retirement: Work and Welfare in the UK and USA*, Bristol: Policy Press.

Lain, D., Airey, L., Loretto, W. and Vickerstaff, S. (2019) 'Understanding older worker precarity: the intersecting domains of jobs, households and the welfare state', *Ageing and Society*, 39(10): 2219–41.

Laliberte Rudman, S. and Aldrich, R. (2021) 'Producing precarity: the individualization of later life unemployment within employment support provision', *Journal of Aging Studies*, 57(2): 1–9.

Lassen, A. and Vrangbæk, K. (2021) 'Retirement transitions in the 21st century: a scoping review of the changing nature of retirement in Europe', *International Journal of Ageing and Later Life* [advanced access], 15(1): 1–75.

Liff, R. and Wikström, E. (2020) 'Prolonged or preserved working life? Intra-organisational institutions embedded in human resource routines', *Ageing & Society* [online first], 1–19.

Lössbroek, J., Lancee, B., van der Lippe, T. and Schippers, J. (2021) 'Age discrimination in hiring decisions: a factorial survey among managers in nine European countries', *European Sociological Review*, 37(1): 49–66.

Macnicol, J. (2015) *Neoliberalising Old Age*, Cambridge: Cambridge University Press.

Mopact (2017) *Final Country Report: Italy* [online], available at: www.ffg.tu-dortmund.de/cms/de/Projekte/Abgeschlossene_Projekte/2017/MOPACT_-_Mobilising_the_Potential_of_Active_Ageing_in_Europe/MOPACT_WP3_Task5_2a_Final_Country_Report_Italy.pdf [accessed 9 April 2021].

Moulaert, T. and Biggs, S. (2013) 'International and European policy on work and retirement: reinventing critical perspectives on active ageing and mature subjectivity', *Human Relations*, 66(1): 23–43.

Ní Léime, A., Ogg, J., Street, D., Krekula, C., Rašticová, M., Bédiová, M. and Madero-Cabib, I. (eds) (2020) *Extended Working Life Policies: International Gender and Health Perspectives*, Cham: Springer Open.

Ogg, J. and Rašticová, M. (2020) 'Introduction: key issues and policies for extending working life', in Ní Léime, A., Ogg, J., Street, D., Krekula, C., Rašticová, M., Bédiová, M. and Madero-Cabib, I. (eds) *Extended Working Life Policies: International Gender and Health Perspectives*, Cham: Springer Open, p 1.

OECD (Organisation for Economic Co-operation and Development) (2013) *Norway: Working Better with Age*, Paris: OECD Publishing.

OECD (2017) *Pensions at a Glance 2017*, Paris: OECD Publishing.

OECD (2018a) *Ireland. Key Policies to Promote Longer Working Lives. Country Note 2007 to 2017*, Paris: OECD Publishing.

OECD (2018b) *Italy. Key Policies to Promote Longer Working Lives. Country Note 2007 to 2017*, Paris: OECD Publishing.

OECD (2018c) *Key Policies to Promote Longer Working Lives in Sweden*, Paris: OECD Publishing.

OECD (2019) *Pensions at a Glance 2019*, Paris: OECD Publishing.

OECD (2020) *Employment Outlook 2020*, Paris: OECD Publishing.

Palme, M. and Laun, L. (2018) *Social Security Reforms and the Changing Retirement Behavior in Sweden*, NBER Working Paper 25394, Cambridge, MA: National Bureau of Economic Research.

Pyysiäinen, J., Halpin, D. and Guilfoyle, A. (2017) 'Neoliberal governance and "responsibilization" of agents: reassessing the mechanisms of responsibility-shift in neoliberal discursive environments', *Distinktion: Journal of Social Theory*, 18(2): 215–35.

Rose, N. (1999) *Powers of Freedom: Reframing Political Thought*, Cambridge: Cambridge University Press.

Streeck, W. and Thelen, K. (eds) (2005) *Beyond Continuity: Institutional Change in Advanced Political Economies*, Oxford: Oxford University Press.

Street, S. and Ní Léime, A. (2020) 'Problems and prospects for current policies to extend working lives', in Ní Léime, A., Ogg, J., Street, D., Krekula, C., Rašticová, M., Bédiová, M. and Madero-Cabib, I. (eds) *Extended Working Life Policies: International Gender and Health Perspectives*, Cham: Springer Open.

Taylor, N. (2017) 'A job, any job: the UK benefits system and employment services in an age of austerity', *Observatoire de la Société Britannique*, 19: 267–85.

Vickerstaff, S. and Cox, J. (2005) 'Retirement and risk: the individualisation of retirement experiences?', *The Sociological Review*, 53(1): 77–95.

Wang, M., Penn, L., Bertone, A. and Stefanova, S. (2014) 'Bridge Employment in the United States', in Alcover, C., Topa, G., Parry, E., Fraccaroli, F. and Depolo, M. (eds) *Bridge Employment: A Research Handbook*. London: Routledge, pp 159–215.

Women and Equalities Committee (2018) *Older People and Employment*, Report [online], available at: https://publications.parliament.uk/pa/cm201719/cmselect/cmwomeq/359/35902.htm [accessed 17 September 2021].

2

The Social Construction of Work and Retirement: Changing Transitions and 'Work-endings'

Chris Phillipson

Introduction

A range of policy developments are influencing transitions from work to retirement, which focus on encouraging people to continue working into their 60s and 70s. The benefits of an extended working life (EWL) have been linked to improvements in personal health as well as offering benefits for mitigating the costs associated with population ageing (Altmann, 2015; International Longevity Centre, 2022). This development has been accelerated by reforms in the case of the UK such as the abolition of the default retirement age (DRA), and the raising of state pension age (SPA) for both genders to age 66, rising to 67 by 2028. Other Organisation for Economic Co-operation and Development (OECD) countries are following similar paths, with, for example, France, Germany and Spain increasing their SPA to 67 between 2023 and 2029.

The changes to pension ages underpin what is an increasingly complex pattern of withdrawal from later life working, with a weakening in the place of retirement as an institution within the life course (McDonald and Donahue, 2011; Phillipson, 2019). To summarize the argument developed in this chapter, the evidence suggests that the relatively orderly work-retirement transitions developed in the 1950s and 1960s, mainly limited to men in secure occupations, can now be seen as a temporary phase in the history of retirement. What came to be viewed as the norm in this period was the idea of a 'crisp' transition from employment to retirement at a standard age (for example 60 or 65). However, it is now possible to see this period as an exception in what has always been an unstable period, especially so for women, minority groups and those from manual occupations (Henkens et al 2018).

This chapter examines the various influences shaping the transition from work to retirement, with the argument built around the following sections: first, a summary of the apparent institutionalization of retirement in the 1950s and 1960s; second, changes affecting work and retirement in the 1970s and 1980s; third, the reconstruction of this period from the 1990s onwards, and the attempt to EWL into the late 60s and beyond; fourth, a review of the various forms of 'precarity' which have come to affect work-endings; finally, a concluding review of the implications for developing public policies in the field of work and retirement.

Transitions from work to retirement

In 1960, Donahue, Orbach and Pollack published a wide-ranging essay charting the rise of retirement, suggesting that it had now come to 'occupy a central place in Western society' (1960, p 330). The publication of the essay came at the mid-point of the growth of retirement during the period 1950–70, driven by the expansion of occupational pensions (especially for non-manual groups) and mandatory retirement ages (Atchley, 1982). Historians and sociologists have argued that this period may be seen as representing the 'coming of age' of retirement (Atchley, 1982), with its growth taking place across three dimensions: the increase in the proportion of people reaching retirement age; the decreasing significance of paid work after retirement, and the importance of income derived from state and occupational pensions (Graebner, 1980; Hannah, 1986; Phillipson, 2013).

For Donahue and her colleagues there could be little doubt that these changes were deep-rooted, leading to substantial claims on the priorities of social institutions. In this context, governments would, it was argued, be increasingly involved in expanding support for people after the cessation of paid employment. Writing from the perspective of the late 1950s, the researchers concluded that: 'the long-range development of our retirement system will undoubtedly tend more and more to assume entirely the character of a government function as it moves in the direction of providing an adequate economic base for the years in retirement' (Donahue et al 1960, p 353).

From a sociological perspective, two contrasting features emerged in the 1950s and the 1970s regarding the transition from work to retirement. First, leaving employment came to be viewed (in the case of men) as finishing at a fixed age, with retirement a 'reward [for] past service' (Graebner, 1980, p 269). Second, linked to this came a discussion about viewing retirement as a 'distinctive' phase in the life course, one which required a period of 'preparation' and 'planning' (Help the Aged, 1979; Phillipson, 1981). This approach subsequently evolved into the idea of 'the third age' (and associated theories of 'active' and 'successful' ageing) built around securing 'personal achievements' in retirement, these separate from those associated with the individual's work and occupational identity (Laslett, 1989; Gilleard and Higgs, 2005).

'De-institutionalizing' retirement

However, the initial phase in the development of retirement proved to be of relatively short duration, lasting little more than two decades (Graebner, 1980). Almost as soon as the outlines of a settled period had appeared, it became clear that long-term changes affecting working life were creating a range of instabilities in the transition from employment. Researchers began to draw a distinction between 'retirement' on the one side, and 'early exit' on the other. The former referred to entry into a publicly provided old-age pension scheme; the latter, early withdrawal from employment, supported through unemployment, disability or associated benefits (Kohli et al 1991). Rather than employment ending at a fixed chronological age, there was now a measure of ambiguity about when working life ended and retirement began. The previous template of a long working life followed by a short retirement (especially for working-class retirees), was being eroded: for a majority of workers through greater insecurity in the workplace; for a minority, through the attractiveness of a retirement cushioned by the safety net of an occupational pension (Phillipson, 2013).

Martin Kohli (1986) and Anne-Marie Guillemard (1989) came to view these changes as part of what they defined as the 'de-standardisation' of the life course (see also Ogg and Renaut, 2019). They argued that evidence that people were withdrawing from work at earlier ages confirmed the transformation in the type of retirement that had developed in the 1950s and 1960s. Guillemard (1989, p 177) took the view that the life course itself was becoming 'de-institutionalised': 'Along with the abandonment of conventional retirement, we also see the break-up of ... the three-fold model which placed the individual in a foreseeable life course of continuous, consecutive sequences of functions and statuses. As a consequence, an individual's working life now ends in confusion'.

The growth of 'early retirement'

The sense of 'confusion' highlighted by Guillemard was most clearly expressed with the increase in early retirement in the 1970s and 1980s. Older workers were progressively marginalized in the labour force, due to their concentration, in many cases, in contracting industries; the operation of schemes to promote worker redeployment or replacement; the pressure of mass unemployment; and views expressed by government and trade unions that older people had less need for a job as compared with what was a large cohort of younger workers (Laczko and Phillipson, 1991). For some groups, it could be argued that the push towards early retirement helped support the view that retirement could be a positive phase in the life course. Cribier (1981), for example, demonstrated a noticeable change among French retirees interviewed during the 1970s. The younger cohorts in her study were more likely to view retirement as a desirable goal, with early retirement seen as especially attractive – findings supported by research in the US (Atchley, 1971) and the UK (Phillipson, 1993). But early retirement also highlighted social class tensions in the opportunities available for people after a lifetime of employment. Bytheway (1986), in a study of Welsh steelworkers, found dissatisfaction being expressed with men feeling that their skills were wasted. Walker, Noble and Westergaard's (1985) research on the impact of redundancy among steelworkers in Sheffield found men who had taken the early retirement option to be evenly divided between those relieved to be leaving work and those expressing regret.

Guillemard (1986) related the problem of the early retired to ambiguities in their social position. She viewed them as entering an indeterminate social category – neither really unemployed nor actually retired. Very few, she suggested, accept the label 'senior citizen', yet society had no category or role in between that of worker or pensioner. The relevance of this observation became more acute in the 1990s and 2000s, given further changes in how the status of retirement in general, and early retirement in particular, was viewed. Concerns about the economic consequences of ageing populations and the associated costs of pensions and care services became prominent in the late 1990s and early 2000s (for example OECD, 2006). This was evidenced in pressures on individuals to remain in some form of work for as long as possible, illustrated by increases in pension ages across most OECD countries; the limiting of options to retire 'early' on the grounds of ill health; and cutbacks in disability and unemployment benefits. Such moves placed the emphasis on the responsibility of individuals to manage their own retirement but in the context of pressure to delay leaving work for as long as possible (Macnicol, 2015; Hofäcker et al 2016; Lain, 2016; Ní Léime and Loretto, 2017; Ní Léime and Ogg, 2019).

This outline of the main institutional changes affecting the move from work to retirement has focused largely on macro–level processes, notably those relating to the economy. However, from a sociological perspective, it is important to recognize the role of different actors within the periods of change identified – notably the state, employers, and individuals themselves. The next section of this chapter provides an overview of this issue, following the periods previously discussed.

Changing influences on retirement decisions

The periods outlined produced variations in the balance of forces influencing work-endings. In the first – from the 1950s through to the end of the 1960s – the state was largely dominant, reflecting the role of mandatory retirement and welfare provision regulating the passage from paid employment through to retirement (Kohli and Rein, 1991). Employers played an important, albeit secondary, role, illustrated by the growth (mostly for men) of defined benefit pension schemes in enabling continued employment (Hannah, 1986).

Over the course of the 1970s and 1980s, the state and employers played a more equal role shaping transitions from work. The former exercised influence in setting out the terms of the response to the challenge of finding employment for a (relatively) large cohort of younger workers (a product of the post-war baby boom). Early retirement came to be viewed as a 'bloodless' (Kohli and Rein, 1991, p 11) way of coping with structural unemployment in industries such as mining, shipbuilding and steel. But employers were crucial in the development of measures to facilitate early retirement and other pathways from employment. As a result, much of the decision-making power in the 1980s about retirement rested neither with the state nor with individuals but shifted to the discretion of employers (Guillemard and van Gunsteren, 1991). Individuals had some control over whether to stay at work or leave employment, especially if supported by an occupational pension. However, the decline in employment in many industrial countries suggests pressure to leave work, even if for some early retirement was an attractive prospect given the burden associated with many forms of employment (Sennett and Cobb, 1977).

From the 1990s, all three actors – the state, employers and individuals – became involved in shaping work-retirement transitions. The general context was one of governments encouraging people to work longer while shifting the burden of paying for a longer life onto the shoulders of individuals (Macnicol, 2015). At the same time, moves to EWL increased the influence of employers, for example in determining (late) career options; supporting flexible/partial retirement; providing training; and facilitating job redesign. For older workers, entering what Vickerstaff (2006, p 509) defined as the 'retirement zone', the ability to control 'work-ending' was subject to considerable variation according to class, gender, ethnicity, health, occupation, and related factors (see, further, Ní Léime et al 2017; Ní Léime and Ogg, 2019).

From a life course perspective, the broader picture was one of increased instability affecting the experiences of a variety of groups from midlife onwards. At the same time, the policy of EWL itself came under pressure: governments appeared committed to institutionalizing this approach, but in a context where a global pandemic, technological change and inequalities within the workforce provided an 'uncertain future' for many groups of workers. These factors contributed to what Lain et al (2019) identified as a form of 'precarity' affecting work–retirement transitions, an issue explored further in the next section (see also Standing, 2014; Kalleberg, 2018; Grenier et al 2020).

Precarious work-endings

A central argument of this chapter is that the development of policies to lengthen working lives – facilitated by changes to occupational and state pension systems – coincided with the onset of 'precarious' forms of employment affecting labour markets in industrial economies. Kalleberg (2018, p 201) suggests that:

> The idea of precarious work has gained wide currency among social theorists as a way of describing the condition of growing insecurity and uncertainty in contemporary capitalism that results from processes of globalization, technological change, the weakening of workers' power, and the political and cultural dynamics associated with neoliberalism. … This growth of precarious work represents a partial return to the market-mediated employment systems and relative lack of social protections that preceded the development of the Keynesian welfare state, and has created considerable uncertainty and insecurity about the future of jobs and careers. (See, further, Grenier et al 2020)

Standing (2011) links the growth of precarious forms of work to the impact of globalization and the fragmentation of traditional class identities (see, further, Savage, 2015). This he views as producing a distinctive social group – the 'precariat' – one which lacks various forms of labour-related security, including: labour market security, for example adequate income-earning opportunities; employment security, for example protection against arbitrary dismissal; and income security, for example assurance of an adequate stable income. Standing (2011) argues that a range of groups have joined the precariat, including women, minority ethnic groups and older people, with the last of these taking low-level jobs in later life, largely to supplement inadequate pensions and/or health insurance. Accordingly, certain groups of older people can find themselves in a 'precarity trap', forced to remain or re-enter the workforce in flexible and lower-income status positions. Older people with limited financial resources may themselves rely upon precarious workers as carers, and family networks may be reduced or drained by means of their own precarity (see, further, Lain et al 2019).

The growth of precarious working might be further viewed as a consequence of the type of work–retirement transitions which developed from the 1990s (Phillipson, 2002). These entailed a deinstitutionalization of retirement on the one side and a weakening of supports provided through the welfare state on the other. The assumption was that workers were entering a new period of choice and control, 'reinventing retirement' as a time where different combinations of work and leisure-orientated activities could be developed (Altmann, 2015). This was itself seen as fuelled by the rise of the baby-boom cohort, a group viewed as wanting a greater range of employment-related options in comparison with earlier cohorts (Lain et al 2019).

But the development of precarious employment complicates the idea of later life working constructed around a great degree of choice, underpinned by different forms of flexible employment. An alternative view would see this environment as an extension of Beck's (1992) 'risk society', with retirement reverting to a 'social risk' rather than a 'social right', but with the idea that encouraging longer working lives – through raising pension ages – can provide a secure bridge into older age. But the extent to which work is becoming less rather than more secure raises problems for this approach (Susskind, 2020). Taylor (2019) makes the point that the terms of an individual's labour market engagement is of critical importance. Yet, as he notes: 'many older people move into bridge forms of employment in contingent, non-core areas of the labour market with the attendant risks of poor health and injury associated with poor work organization, and a lack of adequate training' (Taylor, 2019, p 101). Moreover, 'rather than acknowledge the potential health and other risks associated with poor-quality, precarious or unwanted work, emerging narratives of working longer from a healthy aging perspective have generally ignored such issues' (Taylor, 2019, p 101; see also Parker et al 2020).

The problems facing older workers have been reinforced by the continuation of long-standing age discrimination within the labour market, for example in areas such as hiring, job progression and remuneration (Macnicol, 2015). A nationally representative survey commissioned by the Centre for Ageing Better (2021) found one third of workers aged 50–69 felt their age would disadvantage them in applying for jobs; a similar proportion were told that their application was unlikely to be successful as they were considered over experienced and/or overqualified. The research found that ageism operated at every stage of the recruitment process, from the initial wording for job advertisements through to the experience of being interviewed.

The trends outlined have assumed added importance given the move to raise pension and social security ages as a means of extending working life (or, more accurately, discouraging retirement). Over the course of the 1990s, and into the opening decades of the 2000s, a majority of OECD countries implemented a range of pension reforms, key to which to which were raising the age at which pensions could be drawn – typically from 65 to 67 but with later ages also planned (Axelrad and Mahoney, 2017). This was also linked with the abolition of mandatory retirement in a number of countries, giving people the theoretical right to continue working into their 60s, 70s and beyond. At the same time, as Vickerstaff and Loretto (2017, p 176) observe: 'Very little [was] typically said about the differential capacity of people to work or the ... neglected question of whether there [was] sufficient labour market demand to absorb extended working lives.' Ní Léime and Ogg (2019, p 2164) noted that: 'Extended working life policies have been introduced without adequate consideration of the gender implications for different groups of older workers – those in precarious and secure occupations, physically demanding or sedentary jobs.' Indeed, an emerging issue has concerned the extent to which a new 'zone of insecurity' has developed for people in their 50s and 60s, with increasing numbers stranded without access to suitable employment but deemed too young to draw a pension.

The OECD (2019a) found that in 26 (out of 36) member countries, one quarter of men still retired below the age of 60 in 2018, with the corresponding age often substantially lower in the case of women. While average effective retirement age (ERA) has risen in a majority of OECD countries since the late 1990s, it is still below the level it was 1980 in most (see, further, OECD, 2017). This suggests that delaying the point at which pensions can be drawn until people are in their late 60s (or 70 before full social security benefits are available in the case of the US) is likely to cause considerable hardship for many groups struggling to retain a hold in the labour market. This is especially true in the case of women, where the average gender gap in employment for OECD countries stood at 18 per cent for 55–64-year-olds in 2018, down by only three percentage points from ten years previously (OECD, 2019b). The experience of the UK is illustrative of the pressures affecting people faced with working longer in the context of precarious labour markets. Lain et al (2019, p 2225) argue that the UK is moving towards 'a "self-reliance" model where most individuals now have the theoretical right to continue working past 65, but [with] rapid state pension age increases [offering] little realistic alternative to employment'.

However, despite much being made of progress in achieving longer work lives (Department for Work and Pensions [DWP], 2017), a different picture emerges from examining trends in the *average age of exit* from the labour market (that is, the age at which people over 50 are most likely to leave the labour force). In the case of men, a high point was reached soon after the Second World War, with an average age of exit in 1950 of 67.2 years. The trend thereafter was downward to a low of 63.0 (in 1996), with increases thereafter but with virtually no movement since 2016 (65.2); 64.2 years in 2020. The figures for women have been influenced by the equalization of pension ages, with the average age of exit in 2019 64.3 years, compared with a previous high in 1950 of 63.9 years (DWP, 2020). Men's average age of exit increased by just seven months in the 11 years from 2008 to 2020. Leaving aside the exceptional years of full employment in a post-war economy, the average age of exit for men has fluctuated between 63 and 65 (for women 62 and 64) over a period of 60 years, but in a period characterized by a decline in the type of employment (that is, manufacturing) which sustained blue-collar employment and the entry of women into different forms of (largely) part-time work.

Inequality and extended working life

The figures presented suggest that, at least taking the example of the UK, extending working life into the late 60s and early 70s is likely to produce new inequalities at the end of working life, in particular for groups such as women, workers from minority ethnic groups and those in poor health (Grenier et al 2020). The extent of inequality arising from EWL, and the rapid reversal from early retirement, has been documented in a series of studies, notably in Germany, but also other European countries, for example those by Buchholz et al (2013), Hofäcker and Naumann (2015) and Hofäcker et al (2016). Hofäcker and Naumann (2015) make the point that early exit pathways, as developed in the 1970s and 1980s, were an important route for workers with low or limited skills, reducing the financial penalty associated with the loss of work. Closure of these pathways, however, has forced many to continue working longer – but mainly driven by financial need rather than any active choice to remain in the labour market. Hofäcker et al (2016, p 223) conclude from their survey of the labour market situation of older workers in 30 countries (drawing on data from the European Social Survey), that:

> recent policy developments create new risks such as old age poverty that mainly threaten low-skilled workers. ... As a result of anticipated benefit cuts for early pension entrance, these workers have to continue working although their chances of finding an adequate job is comparably low – either because of their individual health or because of their critical labour market situation.

Lain (2016, pp 138–40) found that financial, rather than intrinsic or social reasons, for working are *higher* among the poorest segments of the workforce than the richest, and highest among those with poor levels of health and education. Analysis of workers aged 65–67 in the 2008 US Health and Retirement Survey found that 84.2 per cent of those in the poorest wealth quartile said they would like to stop working but needed the money, with similar proportions echoing this among those below high school qualifications and those in poor/fair health. Lain and Phillipson (2019) argued, on the basis of this and other research, that it was reasonable to conclude that many individuals continue working even though they consider it to be detrimental to their health and well-being.

Finally, to what extent will changes to employment increase or decrease the demand for older workers? One neglected area in debates around EWL concerns the extent to which technological change is likely to change the terms of the debate about the extent to which later life employment can be achieved. Frey and Osborne (2013) predict in the case of the US that 47 per cent of jobs are at 'high risk' of being automated over the course of the 2020s, with similar estimates being made for Europe (Frey and Osborne, 2013; see also Srnicek and Williams, 2015; Avant, 2017). Frey (2019, p 350) suggests that: 'Unskilled work is not coming to an end [but] low-skilled jobs are more exposed to future automation.' However, Benanav (2019, p 12) notes a broader issue, namely that the impact of automation reflects the extent to which global capitalism is: 'failing to provide jobs for many of the people who need them'. He suggests that:

> There is, in other words, a persistently low demand for labour, reflected not in higher spikes of unemployment and increasingly jobless recoveries ... but also in a phenomenon with more generic consequences: declining labour shares of income. Many studies have now confirmed that the labour share, whose steadiness was held to be a stylized fact of economic growth, has been falling for decades. (Benanav, 2019, p 12; see also Blanchflower, 2019)

It is also the case that EWL has to be placed in a context where poor-quality work remains an issue for a substantial number of employees. Susskind (2020, pp 222–3) notes studies from the US which show that almost 70 per cent of workers are either 'not engaged' in or 'actively disengaged' from their work, while only 50 per cent 'get a sense of identity from their job'. And he cites the work of the late David Graeber (2018), who argued that people often find themselves trapped in what the researcher termed 'bullshit jobs', occupations which were essentially meaningless and psychologically destructive.

The impact of COVID-19, and the introduction of a source of insecurity for older workers (Commetti, 2021; Office for National Statistics (ONS, 2021), has raised the stakes in respect of extending working life: what sort of jobs will be available? What kind of security will they provide? And will they give meaning to people's lives? There are no obvious answers to any of these questions at the present time. What does seem clear is the potential for new inequalities affecting people in the transition from work to retirement, and the need for a fresh approach from public policy. This issue is examined in the concluding section of this chapter.

Conclusion

In December 1929, the *Birmingham Post* reported the following note left by an unemployed man who killed his wife and then committed suicide:

> I feel so terribly worried, I am writing this while I am able to do so, for at times I go so strange I hardly know what to do with myself. My inside trembles, my head aches and I go dizzy often on the verge of collapse, and even when crossing the road I fear I shall get knocked down. Sometimes I cross as in a dream. Therefore, if something happens it will not be the fault of the driver, but my own inability to get out of the way. (Cited in Phillipson, 1978, p 40)

The note was signed, 'Frank Thornby, age 62', with the footnote: 'Out of employment and can't get a job ... the younger men get the jobs'.

Frank Thornby can be seen as an early, and tragic, example of age discrimination – one which occurred during an early period of automation in the workplace. A century later, the pressures are similar but with greater numbers affected and different types of insecurities (or precarities) involved. Policies to EWL face a severe test of credibility, given an economic and social context vastly changed since their introduction. Extending employment into people's 60s (even 70s) was based on what now seem flawed assumptions about the potential demand for labour (and especially that of older workers). But these have become even more questionable given the employment crisis brought about by COVID-19. But the crisis has also exposed the way in which EWL was introduced without corresponding support in areas such as lifelong learning and training, or financial assistance for those involved in care for children or relatives, or acknowledgement of the problems facing those with long-term illnesses of various kinds.

The conjunction of failures of policy highlighted by the labour market crisis produced by COVID-19 is creating new tensions and pressures in work-endings – both paid employment and retirement can be said to be facing 'uncertain futures'. Working lives are increasingly ending in 'confusion', reflected in the reality of health inequalities and the pressures arising from COVID-19. Retirement will remain in some form or another, but its entry points will be increasingly blurred and uncertain for large numbers of workers. Indeed, we are likely to see increased stratification within retirement, with economic divisions based on unequal access to occupational pensions, large variations in health status, and healthy life expectancy between social classes (Parker et al 2020), and differences as well in responsibilities for caring for vulnerable groups within the community.

What sort of policies might be developed given the pressures and insecurities associated with work and retirement transitions? First, greater attention needs to be given to the way in which the raising of pension ages generates inequalities linked to contrasting experiences in respect of health, finances and social relationships. Many groups of workers are unlikely to benefit from a lengthy period of retirement (dying prematurely) or will have insufficient income to be able to leave what may be 'precarious work' in their 60s/early 70s. Others may choose to leave early or have a minimal EWL (because they have substantial pensions and savings) and will experience an active retirement supported by many years of 'healthy life expectancy'. This indicates new inequalities arising from longer working lives, with a redistribution of resources from the poor to the wealthy. The argument here is for a work and retirement policy which recognizes processes of cumulative advantage and disadvantage operating over the life course (Dannefer, 2003; Kendig and Nazroo, 2016). This point has been made by Berkman et al (2015, pp 44–5) where they argue that given divisions between groups (especially in terms of health):

> it is critical to create differentiated paths to retirement and labor-force exits depending upon health (which in turn depends on economic and social experiences earlier in life). ... This may mean the implementation of both a general retirement age that is indexed in some way to life expectancy and an early-retirement option based on the ability to work. For older workers in poor health, it is obviously better for their health and well-being not to have to work. This may mean that certain groups within the population – such as the less educated and those with very physically demanding jobs – may need the option to take an early path to retirement.

Second, there is a particular tension developing between EWL policies and pressures on women undertaking care responsibilities in later life. Ní Léime and Loretto (2017, pp 58–9) suggest that the 'individualised adult worker model has meant more work for women, who have tended to add paid work to existing care responsibilities, while men in many Western countries have decreased their amount of paid work, but only slightly increased care' (a situation further reinforced by COVID-19). This situation needs an urgent response in terms of action from employers and from public policy more generally. Relevant policies which will need to be implemented across all OECD countries pursuing EWL, including: carer's benefits to include paid leave and pension/social security credits for time spent caring for groups such as older people; public provision for childcare and elder care; and policies encouraging men to take a more equitable share in the unpaid work of caring (see, further, Vickerstaff et al 2017).

Third, the impact of COVID-19 is such that it will demand a re-think regarding the place of paid employment on the identities and expectations of older workers. The short- and medium-term outlook for many is certainly bleak in respect of access to secure employment. Gardiner et al (2020) note that longitudinal data collected during the first lockdown (over the period March–June 2020) indicates that more than half of under-25s and people 65 and over who were employed before COVID-19 have experienced furloughing or were out of work by June 2020, compared to less than one third of other age groups. The researchers also highlight the impact of the pandemic on the self-employed, among whom there is a disproportionate number aged 50 and over. These findings were confirmed in research on the effect of the pandemic in the period December 2020–February 2021, this confirming a continuing decline in the employment of older workers – especially those in the 50–54 and 65 plus age groups (ONS, 2021).

These findings underline the importance of Susskind's (2020, p 238) conclusion to his book *A World Without Work*:

> In the twenty-first century, we will have to build a new age of security, one that no longer relies on paid work for its foundation. And we have to begin this task today. Although we cannot know exactly how long it will take to arrive at a world with less work for humans to do, there are clear signs that we are on our way there. The problems of inequality, power, and meaning are not lurking in the distance, hidden out of sight in the remote future. They have already begun to unfold, to trouble, and test our inherited institutions and traditional ways of life.

In conclusion, there is much uncertainty about how work and retirement transitions will unfold over the next few decades. Of course, some retirees will continue to develop lifestyles reflecting an expansive 'third age', these driven by more prosperous and healthier groups reaching middle age. But retirement is still likely to be viewed with ambivalence at the level of the state – a potential burden on developing a productive economy (a view likely to be reinforced by the impact of COVID-19). All the more reason to address the issues raised by Susskind and other researchers. The danger is that inaction will lead to large numbers of people experiencing new forms of insecurity given continuing attempts to prolong working life. Conducting a debate and developing new research about ways to reconstruct the middle and later phases of the life course will continue to be a crucial area for economic and social policy.

References

Altmann, R. (2015) *A New Vision for Older Workers: Retain, Retrain, Recruit*, London: Department for Work and Pensions.
Atchley, R. (1971) 'Retirement and leisure participation', *The Gerontologist*, 11: 13–17.

Atchley, R. (1982) 'Retirement as a social institution', *Annual Review of Sociology*, 8: 263–87.

Avant, R. (2017) *The Wealth of Humans: Work and its Absence in the 21st Century*, London: Allen Lane.

Axelrad, H. and Mahoney, K. (2017) 'Increasing the pensionable age: what changes are OECD countries making? What considerations are driving policy?', *Open Journal of Social Sciences*, 5: 56–70.

Beck, U. (1992) *Risk Society: Towards a New Modernity*, London: Sage.

Benanav, A. (2019) 'Automation and the future of work – 1'. *New Left Review*, 119: 5–38.

Berkman, L.F., Boersch-Supan, A. and Avendano, M. (2015) 'Labor-force participation, policies and practices in an aging America: adaptation essential for a healthy and resilient population', *Daedalus*, 144: 41–54.

Blanchflower, D. (2019) *Not Working: Where Have All the Good Jobs Gone?*, Princeton, NJ: Princeton University Press.

Buchholz, S., Rinklake, A. and Blossfeld, H.-P. (2013) 'Reversing early retirement in Germany: a longitudinal analysis of the effects of recent pension reforms on the timing of the transition to retirement and on pension incomes', *Comparative Population Studies*, 38: 881–906.

Bytheway, W. (1986) 'Redundancy and the older worker', in Lee, R. (ed) *Redundancy Lay-offs and Plant Closures*, Beckenham: Croom Helm.

Centre for Ageing Better (2021) *Too Much Experience: Older Workers' Perceptions in the Recruitment Process*, London: Centre for Ageing Better.

Commetti, N. (2021) *A U-Shaped Crisis: The Impact of the COVID-19 Crisis on Older Workers*, London: The Resolution Foundation.

Cribier, F. (1981) 'Changing patterns of the seventies: the example of a generation of Parisian salaried workers', *Ageing & Society*, 1: 51–73.

Dannefer, D. (2003) 'Cumulative advantage/disadvantage and the life course: cross fertilizing age and social science theory', *Journal of Gerontology: Social Sciences*, 58: S327–37.

DWP (Department for Work and Pensions) (2017) *Fuller Working Lives: A Partnership Approach*, London: Department for Work and Pensions.

DWP (2020) *Economic Labour Market Status of Individuals Aged 50 and Over, Trends over Time: September 2020* [online], available at: www.gov.uk/gov ernment/publications/economic-labour-market-status-of-individuals-aged-50-and-over-trends-over-time-september-2020/economic-labour-market-status-of-individuals-aged-50-and-over-trends-over-time-septem ber-2020 [accessed 20 January 2021].

Donahue, W., Orbach, H. and Pollack, O. (1960) 'Retirement: the emerging social pattern', in *Handbook of Social Gerontology: Societal Aspects of Aging*, Chicago, IL: University of Chicago Press.

Frey, C.B. (2019) *The Technology Trap: Capital, Labour and Power in the Age of Automation*, Princeton, NJ: Princeton University Press.

Frey, C.B. and Osborne, M. (2013) *The Future of Employment*, Oxford: Oxford Martin Programme on Technology and Employment.

Gardiner, L., Gustafsson, M., Brewer, M., Handscomb, K., Henehan, K., Judge, L. and Rahman, F. (2020) *An Intergenerational Audit for the UK*, London: Resolution Foundation [online], available at: www.resolutionfoundation.org/publications/intergenerational-audit-uk-2020/ [accessed 30 January 2021].

Gilleard, C. and Higgs, P. (2005) *Contexts of Ageing: Class, Cohort and Community*, Cambridge: Polity Press.

Graeber, D. (2018) *Bullshit Jobs: A Theory*, New York: Simon and Schuster.

Graebner, W. (1980) *A History of Retirement: The Meaning and Function of an American Institution, 1885–1978*, New Haven, CT: Yale University Press.

Grenier, A., Phillipson, C. and Settersten, A. (eds) (2020) *Precarity and Ageing: Understanding Insecurity and Risk in Later Life*, Bristol: Policy Press.

Guillemard, A.-M. (1986) 'Social policy and ageing in France', in Phillipson, C. and Walker, A. (eds) *Ageing and Social Policy: A Critical Assessment*, Aldershot: Gower, pp 263–79.

Guillemard, A.-M. (1989) 'The trend towards early labour force withdrawal and the reorganisation of the life course: a cross-national analysis', in Johnson, P., Conrad, C. and Thomson, D. (eds) *Workers versus Pensioners: Intergenerational Justice in an Ageing World*, London: Centre for Economic Policy Research, pp 164–80.

Guillemard, A.-M. and van Gunsteren, H. (1991) 'Pathways and their prospects: a comparative interpretation of the meaning of early exit', in Kohli, M., Rein, M. and Guillemard, A.-M. (eds) *Time for Retirement: Comparative Studies of Early Exit from the Labor Force*, Cambridge: Cambridge University Press, pp 362–87.

Hannah, L. (1986) *Inventing Retirement: The Development of Occupational Pensions in Britain*, Cambridge: Cambridge University Press.

Help the Aged (1979) *The Time of Your Life*, London: Help the Aged.

Henkens, K., van Dalen, H., Ekerdt, D., Hershey, D., Hyde, M., Radl, J. et al (2018) 'What we need to know about retirement: pressing issues for the coming decade', *The Gerontologist*, 58: 805–12.

Hofäcker, D. and Naumann, E. (2015) 'The emerging trend of work beyond retirement age in Germany', *Zeitschrift für Gerontologie und Geriatrie*, 48: 473–9.

Hofäcker, D., Hess, M. and König, S. (2016) *Delaying Retirement: Progress and Challenges of Active Ageing in Europe, the United States and Japan*, London: Palgrave.

International Longevity Centre (2022) *Plugging the Gap: Estimating the Demand and Supply for Jobs by Sector in 2030*, available at: https://ilcuk.org.uk/plugging-the-gap/ [accessed 13 January 2022].

Kalleberg, A. (2018) *Precarious Lives: Job Insecurity and Well-being in Rich Democracies*, Hoboken, NJ: John Wiley.

Kendig, H. and Nazroo, J. (2016) 'Life course influences in later life: comparative perspectives', *Journal of Population Ageing*, 9: 1–8.

Kohli, M. (1986) 'The world we forgot: a historical review of the life course', in Marshall, V.W. (ed) *Later Life: The Social Psychology of Aging*, Beverly Hills, CA: Sage, pp 271–303.

Kohli, M. and Rein, M. (1991) 'The changing balance of work and retirement', in Kohli, M., Rein, M. and Guillemard, A.-M. (eds) *Time for Retirement: Comparative Studies of Early Exit from the Labor Force*, Cambridge: Cambridge University Press, pp 1–35.

Kohli, M., Rein, M. and Guillemard, A.-M. (eds) (1991) *Time for Retirement: Comparative Studies of Early Exit from the Labor Force*, Cambridge: Cambridge University Press.

Laczko, F. and Phillipson, C. (1991) *Changing Work and Retirement: Social Policy and the Older Worker*, Milton Keynes: Open University Press.

Lain, D. (2016) *Reconstructing Retirement: Work and Welfare in the UK and USA*, Bristol: Policy Press.

Lain, D. and Phillipson, C. (2019) 'Extended working lives and the rediscovery of the "disadvantaged" older worker', *Generations: Journal of the American Society on Aging*, 43: 71–7.

Lain, D., Airey, L., Loretto, W. and Vickerstaff, S. (2019) 'Understanding older work precarity: the intersecting domains of jobs, households and the welfare state', *Ageing and Society*, 39: 2219–42.

Laslett, P. (1989) *A Fresh Map of Life*, Cambridge: Cambridge University Press.

Macnicol, J. (2015) *Neoliberalising Old Age*, Cambridge, MA: Cambridge University Press.

McDonald, L. and Donahue, P. (2011) 'Retirement lost?', *Canadian Journal on Aging*, 30: 401–22.

Ní Léime, A. and Loretto, W. (2017) 'Gender perspectives on extended working life policies', in Ní Léime, A., Street, D., Vickerstaff, S., Krekula, C. and Loretto, W. (eds) *Gender, Ageing and Extending Working Life: Cross National Perspectives*, Bristol: Policy Press, pp 53–76.

Ní Léime, A. and Ogg, J. (2019) Gendered impacts of extended working life in the health and economic wellbeing of older workers, *Ageing and Society*, 39: 2163–70.

OECD (Organisation for Economic Co-operation and Development) (2006) *Live Longer, Work Longer*, Paris: OECD Publishing.

OECD (2017) *Pensions at a Glance 2017*, Paris: OECD Publishing.

OECD (2019a) *The Future of Work: Employment Outlook 2019*, Paris: OECD Publishing.

OECD (2019b) *Working Better with Age* Paris: OECD Publishing.

Ogg, J. and Renaut, S. (2019) 'The influence of family and professional lifecourse histories on economic activity among older French workers', *Ageing and Society*, 39: 2242–67.

ONS (Office for National Statistics) (2021) *Living Longer: Older Workers During the Coronavirus (COVID-19) Pandemic*, London: Office for National Statistics.

Parker, M., Bucknall, M., Jagger, C. and Willkie, R. (2020) 'Population-based estimates of healthy working life expectancy at age 50 years: analysis of data from the English Longitudinal Study of Ageing', *The Lancet Public Health*, 5: e395–403.

Phillipson, C. (1981) 'Pre-retirement education: the British and American Experience', *Ageing and Society*, 1: 393–413.

Phillipson, C. (1993) 'The sociology of retirement', in Bond, J., Coleman, P. and Peace, S. (eds) *Ageing in Society: An Introduction to Social Gerontology*, London: Sage, pp 180–99.

Phillipson, C. (2002) *Transitions from Work to Retirement: Developing a New Social Contract*, Bristol: The Policy Press/Joseph Rowntree Foundation.

Phillipson, C. (2013) *Ageing*, Cambridge: Polity Press.

Phillipson, C. (2019) '"Fuller" or "extended" working lives: critical perspectives on changing transitions from work to retirement', *Ageing and Society*, 39: 629–50.

Phillipson, P. (1978) *The Experience of Retirement: A Sociological Analysis*, PhD thesis, Durham: University of Durham, available at: http://etheses.dur.ac.uk/8072/1/8072_5072.PDF [accessed 20 July 2022].

Savage, M. (2015) *Social Class in the 21st Century*, London: Pelican Books.

Sennett, R. and Cobb, J. (1977) *The Hidden Injuries of Class*, Cambridge: Cambridge University Press.

Srnicek, N. and Williams, A. (2015) *Inventing the Future: Postcapitalism and a World Without Work*, London: Verso Books.

Standing, G. (2011) *The Precariat: The New Dangerous Class*, London: Bloomsbury.

Standing, G. (2014) *A Precariat Charter: From Denizens to Citizens*, London: Bloomsbury.

Susskind, D. (2020) *A World Without Work: Technology, Automation and How We Should Respond*, London: Allen Lane.

Taylor, P. (2019) 'Working longer may be good public policy, but it is not necessarily good for older people', *Journal of Aging & Social Policy*, 31(2): 99–105.

Vickerstaff, S. (2006) 'Entering the retirement zone: how much choice do individuals have?', *Social Policy and Society*, 5: 507–19.

Vickerstaff, S. and Loretto, W. (2017) 'The United Kingdom: a new moral imperative: live longer, work longer', in Ní Léime, A., Street, D., Vickerstaff, S., Krekula, C. and Loretto, W. (eds) *Gender, Ageing and Extending Working Life: Cross National Perspectives*, Bristol: Policy Press, pp 175–91.

Vickerstaff, S., Street. D., Ní Léime, A. and Krekula, C. (2017) 'Gendered and extended work: research and policy needs for work in later life', in Ní Léime, A., Street, D., Vickerstaff, S., Krekula, C. and Loretto, W. (eds) *Gender, Ageing and Extending Working Life: Cross National Perspectives*, Bristol: Policy Press, pp 219–42.

Walker, A., Noble, I. and Westergaard, J. (1985) 'From secure employment to labour market insecurity: the impact of redundancy on older workers in the steel industry', in Roberts, B., Finnegan, R. and Gallie D. (eds) *New Approaches to Economic Life*, Manchester: Manchester University Press, pp 319–37.

European Experiences of Older Worker Transitions

PART II

European Experiences of Older Worker Transitions

3

Job Redeployment of Older Workers in UK Local Government

David Lain, Sarah Vickerstaff and Mariska van der Horst

Introduction

As we saw in Chapter 1, in recent years financial pressures to work longer have increased considerably in the UK, with state pension ages rising fast and 'working age benefits' for unemployment and disability being further residualized. Mandatory retirement ages have also been abolished, in 2011, meaning that older people now have the theoretical right to continue working. It is important to note that these changes arguably reflect a longer-term political turn towards neoliberalism, the 'political rationality' that links 'a reduction in (welfare) state services and security systems to the increasing call for "personal responsibility" and "self-care"' (Lemke, 2001, p 203). A key turning point was the election of the conservative government under Margaret Thatcher in 1979 (Rose, 1999), which represented a decisive break from the immediate post-war period when an extensive welfare state appeared to be developing covering financial support from the 'cradle to the grave'. TH Marshall (2006 [1950], p 37) had famously described this as the development of 'social citizenship', or 'social rights', 'a universal right to real income that is not proportionate to the market value of the claimant'.

By the late 1980s the sociologist Gosta Esping-Andersen (1990) had labelled the UK a 'liberal' welfare state that was 'weakly decommodifying'. Individuals were said to be reliant on selling their labour as a 'commodity' to a high degree because cash benefits were meagre and relatively hard to obtain due to strict eligibility requirements. This approach was aimed at encouraging individuals to be self-reliant and to look to the private sphere to meet their welfare needs, with parallels to later arguments about neoliberalism (Rose, 1999). In the field of pensions, the real value of the 'basic' state pension fell over many years, and attempts to develop a supplementary 'State Earnings

Replacement Pension' were undermined after 1979 in favour of promoting private pension savings (Lain, 2016). Changes to state pensions since the early 2000s therefore have to be understood in this longer-term context of 'neoliberal responsibilisation' (see Chapter 1).

In parallel to the welfare state, the UK also has a relatively unregulated 'liberal market economy' (Hall and Soskice, 2001). This has meant that employers have a lot of discretion over how they utilize staff, a trend that is increasing across Organisation for Economic Co-operation and Development (OECD) countries but is at a particularly advanced stage in the UK (Baccaro and Howell, 2017). This makes it easy for UK employers to respond to financial pressures by making redundancies and redeploying staff to new roles. This affects not only those in the private sector, but also those working in the public sector that have been on the 'receiving end' of government budget cuts, or 'austerity', since the early 2010s.

In this chapter we explore the redeployment of UK older workers in one organization affected by austerity, a UK local government (LG) authority. It first situates the topic of job redeployment in the context of local government 'austerity' since the early 2010s. It then presents evidence from a qualitative case study of older workers experiencing job redeployment and job reconfiguration. The main argument is that under conditions of neoliberalism, job redeployment is likely to be focused on meeting the perceived needs of the organization rather than the worker. In this context, redeployment can arguably be detrimental to extended working lives rather than helpful as it ends up magnifying older worker marginalization that occurs as a result of underlying ageism.

Context of job redeployment under local government austerity

The use of job redeployment generally

There is currently little research on job redeployment in older age but historically it has been an important tool of management. As Phillipson (1982) pointed out, before the advent of retirement it was not uncommon for employers to transfer certain older workers in physically demanding jobs to 'light work duties' as they got older, as part of an implicit lifetime employment contract. Today, we often think about redeployment in benevolent terms. For example, Naegele and Walker (2006, p 19) include it in their 'guide to good practice in age management' and conclude that: 'Good practice in redeployment refers primarily to coordinating the demands of the workplace with the capacity of the (older) employees.' It is therefore seen as being a way in which the organization can compensate for the individual's changing work capacity as they age by moving them to new roles. However, it is questionable whether employee-focused redeployment is always beneficial in terms of extending working lives. Research by Herrbach et al (2009) found that moving French managers into new roles specifically *for* older workers increased their propensity to retire early, suggesting that it had worsened their self-image. There is also limited evidence that older people are outliers by typically favouring downsizing into low-paid, low-skilled jobs in older age (Inceoglu et al 2012; Lain, 2012). Furthermore, it is questionable how common job redeployment *in response to individuals'* needs really is in the context of the financial pressures facing organizations today. As Krekula's (2019) research in a Swedish steel foundry suggested, in an increasingly competitive environment we would expect there to be fewer 'lighter jobs' within organizations for older people to move into (see Chapter 4).

There is stronger evidence of redeployment being used to meet changing needs of organizations in the context of financial pressures. More than a third of UK employers surveyed during the COVID-19 pandemic anticipated using redeployment of staff as part of their strategy to respond to the financial pressures caused, often alongside redundancies (Chartered Institute for Personnel and Development [CIPD], 2020). Likewise, after the financial crash of 2008 employers appeared to increase workplace flexibility as a means of responding to declining demand for their goods and services (Beck, 2013).

Redeployment in local government under neoliberal austerity

In the context described earlier, UK local government authorities are an interesting example of redeployment under severe financial pressures, in this case from 'neoliberal austerity' in the form of significant budget cuts from central government since 2010 (Johnson et al 2019). This has resulted in the need for local authorities to cut staffing levels and to restructure their activities, which has, in turn, created pressures for greater staff flexibility (and, potentially, redeployment).

Austerity in the UK followed the financial crash of 2008, but it is important to see it as part of a wider trend towards neoliberalism (Grimshaw and Rubery, 2012). As Farnsworth and Irving (2018, p 461) point out, 'Austerity incorporates the neoliberal desire to shrink the (social welfare) state, deregulate labour markets and emphasise private markets as the drivers of growth.' As the governmentality perspective argues, the state does not have the capacity to exercise complete control over delivering such a transformational change; therefore, the state must 'govern at a distance' and ultimately get individuals to think and act in ways that are compatible with this aim. The situation with local government authorities is illustrative of this; local authorities are responsible for delivering local services in the UK that are funded to a significant degree by central government but are under local political control. Central government therefore cannot control the provision and organization of local services directly, but it can set the budgetary context. This means that local government authorities (and their employees) have to be more 'entrepreneurial' in delivering the services they can with the budgets they have.

Austerity therefore creates problems for all local government authorities. Historically they typically had 'psychological contracts' involving job security, stability and opportunities for development within a clear career framework (Lewis et al 2003); neoliberal austerity makes such organizational principles very difficult to adhere to. We would not expect local government authorities to respond to these neoliberal austerity pressures in exactly the same way because the political and local contexts are bound to vary to some degree (Newman, 2014). However, the responses to which local authorities gravitate are all likely to involve job reductions, reorganization and greater role flexibility for workers. According to Johnson et al (2019), some local authorities have gone down a more negative 'marketisation' path, by reducing costs, outsourcing services, holding down pay and conditions, using *compulsory redundancy* and *increasing staff flexibility*. Others were instead said to adopt a more positive 'political partnership' approach seeking 'to minimise [compulsory] job losses and outsourcing by utilising *voluntary redundancies* and *increased internal labour flexibility*' (Johnson et al 2019, p 18, emphasis added).

In this context of austerity, local authorities inevitably look for discourses that can be used to try and motivate people and shift their 'way of thinking' in the workplace (what Rose, 1999, refers to as 'translation'). In 2012, the CIPD, the leading HR and people management professional body, sought to identify such a post-austerity narrative in their report 'Leading Culture Change: Employee Engagement and Public Sector Transformation' (CIPD, 2012). Based on their interviews with Chief Executives and HR directors in ten local authorities (and other public bodies) they drew the following conclusion:

> Employers need to build a new psychological contract. There is widespread agreement that a new employment deal needs to be articulated that is underpinned by greater flexibility for individuals, skills and employability development opportunities, as well as good-quality people management and leadership to compensate for lower levels of reward and job security. (CIPD, 2012, p 2)

Interestingly, the narrative being presented has parallels with the 'appeal of freedom' narrative identified in the 'neoliberal responsibilisation' literature discussed in Chapter 1. According to Pyysiäinen et al (2017, p 216) an 'appeal of freedom' is one of two routes by which neoliberal responsibilisation occurs, that is, people 'come to see that they ought – naturally – to see themselves as responsible for their own fate, to actively assume responsibility for outcomes in relevant areas of their lives'. This is based on 'discourses that tap into and resonate with the subjects' desires of personal freedom, quality-of-life and fulfilment of selfrealisation potential' (Pyysiäinen et al 2017, p 219). In the context of austerity, individuals might have to work in a more uncertain environment, where job roles are less fixed and secure, for example, but the appeal of increased personal freedom implied by CIPD (2012) suggests that there are opportunities for those willing to take them.

We might expect HR managers in local authorities to embrace the kind of 'appeal of freedom' narrative identified by CIPD (2012). A problem, however, is that individuals might not be 'converted' to the neoliberal mentality; they might not 'buy into' this idea of personal freedom and self-actualization being available to them in the way presented by HR managers. Indeed, older workers may view their ability to benefit from development opportunities apparently on offer as being limited, given that managers often assume them to be 'on their way out' and 'less productive, more resistant to change, less open to training and development opportunities, less competent, more costly and more prone to illness' (Conway and Monks, 2017, p 587).

An alternative, second route to responsibilisation identified by Pyysiäinen et al (2017, p 216) is 'responsibilisation through threat to personal control'. Under conditions of uncertainty people may perceive their controllability over events as being threatened and react by striving to restore personal control; this is referred to as 'psychological reactance'. This might mean striving to take whatever opportunities are available in the organization, even if this represents a downward or detrimental movement within the organization or exit. As Pyysiäinen et al (2017, p 230) argues, 'even if autonomy and controllability in one's action situation would appear very limited ... one could still persistently continue to use one's actions as means to "fight back" and to prevent losing even the last remains of one's personal control over the situation'.

The suggestion, therefore, is that under neoliberal pressures discourses involving appeals to freedom are likely to be used by HR managers as a form of 'translation', that is, to shift ways of thinking in the organization that encourage individuals to take responsibility for their own transitions as a form of positive self-actualization. Older workers may not be 'converted' by this neoliberal mentality because it is unlikely to correspond to their experiences. Instead, their route to responsibilisation is likely to follow the route of 'psychological reactance' – seeking to restore control over their circumstances, even when this results in less desirable outcomes that involve redeployment and/or exit.

Case study and methods

In order to investigate redeployment in the context of austerity, and older worker and HR narratives and responses, this chapter examines a local government authority (LG) that fits the 'political partnership' post-austerity model of employment relations (as per Johnson et al 2019). LG experienced significant central government funding cuts, but worked with the local trade union to agree a non-compulsory redundancy deal. There was a 40 per cent drop in workforce numbers between 2010 and 2016, achieved largely through voluntary severance (a lump sum) and voluntary early retirement (a lump sum and the individual's pension from age 55). External recruitment effectively ceased in 2012. Service delivery had undergone significant change, resulting in organizational restructuring and job redesign. Many employees had to apply for reconfigured jobs, or enter a redeployment scheme and apply for alternative jobs within the local authority.

The research in LG followed a case study design (Yin, 2009). We draw on Marshall's (1999, p 380) definition of a case study as 'a study of one industrial or corporate setting, using a number of different research techniques, with the intent of assembling a comprehensive description of the setting in terms of a discrete number of research objectives'. Older workers (aged 50 plus) were interviewed, as were HR managers and line managers. This is different from the other chapters in this book, which focus exclusively on the perspectives of older people without reference to specific organizational contexts. In this chapter the perspectives of HR and line managers are important in terms of helping us construct a 'comprehensive description' of what appears to be happening at an organizational level.

A maximum variation sampling strategy (Patton, 1990) was used to achieve a diverse mix of interviewees. Following previous studies, older workers (n= 37) were defined as those aged 50 plus. Older worker interviewees were aged between 50 and 59 (n=28) and 60 and 64 (n=9), as employment beyond 65 was rare. Reflecting the local government workforce, they were similarly split by gender (20 female, 17 male), and worked in a diverse range of white collar (n=27), blue collar (n=6) and supervisory/managerial (n=4) jobs. HR managers were in senior positions and covered different dimensions/areas of HR, and line managers (n=9) were selected to cover the management of a diverse range of older workers.

Semi-structured interviews were conducted on a one-to-one basis. HR manager and line manager interviews explored the management of older workers in the changing context facing the organization. Older worker interviews explored their job (and how/if this had changed); their attitudes and expectations about extended working lives and the treatment of older workers (including themselves) in the organization. Interviews were recorded and transcribed verbatim. Thematic data analysis was conducted (Hennink et al 2011) to enable the experiences of participants to emerge from the data. An initial data coding framework was devised from the interview topic guide and from the process of open coding (Corbin and Strauss, 1990) a selection of interviews. Once the final coding protocol was established, all interviews were coded for key themes using the NVivo 11. Given the focus on marginalization, older interviewees were classified on the basis of the type of transition they had made in the post-austerity period (upwards, downwards, sideways or in the same or a reconfigured job) to enable between-group comparison (Hennink et al 2011). Older workers that remained in the same job were therefore included in the analysis, so we can compare their insights and experiences with those being redeployed. Pseudonyms have been given for all interviewees directly referred to. The ages of older workers are identified in brackets when they are first introduced in the text; line managers and HR managers are identified with 'LM' and 'HR' throughout.

Narratives of neoliberal responsibilisation from HR

All of the HR managers interviewed agreed that the biggest challenge facing the authority has been dealing with the financial pressures resulting from "severe spending cuts and the financial settlement" from central government (Fiona, HR). Central to much of the discussion was the redeployment scheme, which had been introduced as a result of jobs being disestablished and work and service delivery being reorganized. This aimed to match up employees with new and vacant jobs within the local authority. Clearly the redeployment scheme represented considerable uncertainty to individuals compared with the past. However, the narratives of HR managers appeared to demonstrate 'appeals to freedom' associated with neoliberal responsibilisation (Pyysiäinen et al 2017). They presented job redeployment as being potentially positive in terms of enabling individuals of any age to develop and progress: "it [the redeployment scheme] hasn't got anything to do with age, it is across the board for anybody who wants to either change a role, needs development, needs moving due to ill health, no longer have a job because the service is restructured. It's for all the scenarios" (Fiona, HR). The HR interviewees were positive about the development possibilities for redeployment, if only people would embrace it as enterprising and autonomous individuals:

'we have got a whole team dedicated to moving people around, and it's very proactive in terms of saying, you know, you can opt in to people to say, actually I'm ready for a change, you know, what's out there, and how can I develop myself? So wanting to move people *it's just whether people are up for that.*' (Amanda, HR, emphasis added)

'a vehicle driver who can no longer drive, we would find another role. There's only a slight problem, a lot of people would want the perfect role and it is about changing that expectation. If you can't do this job, you know, they want to dictate the hours, they want to dictate the location, they want to dictate the kind of job.' (Fiona, HR)

It is important to note that the message conveyed by HR was consistent with an 'age neutral' HR approach: "so long as people can be flexible and are willing to be flexible ... and you need to be delivering. So long as people can live with those two things age is irrelevant" (Amanda, HR). In the case of people finding it hard to adapt, this was represented as being related to the characteristics of the individuals, rather than a lack of support available. This was at times presented as relating to long job tenure, with HR careful to disassociate this from being an older worker:

'I think it's, you know, there are people in their late 30s who've still worked here for 20 years who could struggle with that just the same as someone who's 55.' (Amanda, HR)

'they might have been in the organization for 30, 40 years in a particular area of work, they've got a particular profession and training and skillset. And to then tell them they've got to completely move away from that to do something that's entirely different can be difficult.' (Craig, HR)

While Craig (HR) raised some challenges facing (older) workers with long tenure, he was also typical in referring to "people from different ages" who were moved to new jobs and "flourishing" and had asked why they were "scared" to move before.

Aside from the difficulties of individuals with long tenure being able to adapt to the changing situation, the problem of adaptation was primarily confined to the extreme situation of moving individuals from physically demanding manual work to white-collar employment, although it was unclear how common this had been. Amanda (HR), for example, highlighted the theoretical challenges of reskilling someone who worked on highways maintenance to work in administration. More generally, however, the larger constraints on people moving into new roles seemed to be what they saw as entrenched attitudes among some people about not wanting to change their work, and maybe not being entrepreneurial and responsibilized enough. There was relatively little discussion about a lack of support that might make it hard for older people to adjust, or worsening working conditions and work intensification:

'What we've tried to do we've tried to, in a way, balance the need for reductions along with a more balanced and humane approach to our workforce. And it's quite difficult and there's been a lot of dialogue with trade unions. And we've tried to maintain the level of terms and conditions whilst making the reductions. So in many situations I think the working arrangements for staff actually improved, that's my personal view, rather than having compulsory redundancies.' (Fiona, HR)

Clearly redeployment, and people applying for reconfigured job roles, was only part of the response to austerity, and the HR managers also discussed the use of voluntary severance or early retirement as a means of reducing staffing numbers. This was disproportionately taken by older employees, something that HR managers were keen to present as relating to a choice that older workers could take:

> 'In 2013–14 we shed about 800 people, 45 per cent of them were over 55. And that's just because … you know, either their service had completely gone or was changing in a way that they didn't particularly feel comfortable with and/or their personal circumstances including the offer that was available allowed them to say, "Actually I can make a choice here, you know, and I can choose to go." They weren't pushed out, it was … there wasn't any kind of particular aim to say we're to target the over 55s. … We actually did it on a basis of, we looked at people's skills. So we said, "You could be 95 but we need your skills."' (David, HR)

Overall, therefore, HR managers were positive about the response of the local authority to austerity and the introduction of the redeployment scheme, which was seen as offering opportunities for enterprising individuals to progress and adapt their work to their changing circumstances, irrespective of their age.

Difficulties of enacting the role of the enterprising, flexible redeployed older worker

Unmet demand for development

The evidence from the older worker interviews suggested that they had struggled to live up to the narrative presented by HR. This is not to say that they did not experience significant change. Around half of the 37 interviewees either moved to another job during the period of austerity (n= 13) or had their job significantly reconfigured such that additional roles or responsibilities were added (n=6). This meant that around half (n=18) were doing the same job, although it is possible that some of these individuals also had some degree of reconfiguration that was not picked up. Despite the amount of change and the HR emphasis on development, the 'appeal of freedom' side of the bargain, none of the 37 older workers appeared to have progressed up the hierarchy as a result of redeployment or applying for jobs that had arisen due to organizational restructuring. One interviewee had moved into a more professional role requiring significant training in her early 50s, but this had happened *before* the period of intensified neoliberal austerity pressures.

The lack of upward movement among older workers interviewed was not because aspiration to progress did not exist within the organization. A number of older individuals interviewed had made unsuccessful attempts to progress their careers. Mary (aged 56) was an older worker in a managerial position working in an area where a lot of restructuring had taken place; she recounted an experience of being unsuccessful in applying for a restructured job:

> 'So I didn't get that job, which would have been a promotion, and on that restructure there was quite a lot of feeling amongst the people over 50 that it was the people over 50 who didn't get the jobs.'
>
> [Interviewer] 'Is that right?'
>
> 'Yes. Over 55 in particular. So I mean there was no way you could prove it obviously, but a lot of people who ended up not with a job, or not with a job they originally wanted, were the older people. So I know one woman did mention it to a manager, but no one put an official complaint in.' (Mary, aged 56)

Mary was keen to emphasize that she thought the allocation of jobs on the basis of age was "a non-official policy" that they "would never admit to". This was partly because they were about to start a new round of voluntary retirement/voluntary severance opportunities. She goes on: "I think they [managers] always think people over 55 – I mean you don't get sacked, you are put in another job – but [managers think] it's an option for them [to go early] and that they tend to favour the younger people". Consistent with this, another older worker passed over for promotion revealed what appeared to be underlying assumptions held by some managers:

> 'I have heard someone who I thought should have known better saying, "Well, you know, they're 55, they'll be going soon." That shocked me and it worried me because not everyone can go at 55, 55 is very young. And that was from quite a senior person, a senior male.' (Annie, aged 56)

Older workers interviewed did not generally see themselves as being 'on their way out' as the aforementioned stereotype implies. Around two thirds of interviewees signalled no intention to take voluntary early retirement or severance, or to leave early. These workers had stayed thus far, and many financially needed to continue working due to modest pension accrual or domestic circumstances. Some of the interviewees therefore anticipated a further ten to 15 years of employment and were eager to progress.

While some older workers expressed a desire to progress, there were suggestions in some older worker interviews that opportunities for training and development were being denied to them because of their age:

> 'those of a similar age and my age, I don't feel that training opportunities are, erm, offered or encouraged as they are for maybe post-grads and the likes, to further their career. ... I paid for my own course that I did, erm, six, nine months ago now. Even though [LG] do actually promote and offer the course, they wouldn't give it to me, so I had to pay £800 to go on a five-day course.' (Steve, aged 56)

Interviews with line managers also hinted that training beyond the basics was informally rationed to younger staff in the context of the financial pressures; as one line manager reported:

> 'I will usually direct them [training opportunities] to, if you like, the up-and-coming staff rather than my long-standing and by default older members of staff. ... It's about their development, really. ... And you're talking about ... again, training, it's quite rare to get the funding to actually have anything meaningful to do. So if you're rationing something then you have to make some decisions about who's going to get the most out of it, which is harsh but that's the reality, really.' (Susan, LM)

Another line manager, Paul, made a broader claim about the lack of training and development opportunities available to older people:

> 'I think the ageism, which is evident and apparent in everyday life, takes place in [LG] in subtle and not so subtle ways. And I'm sure there will be lots of people who will say they haven't had access to training, or they're overlooked or treated seriously because they're seen as being on the their way out. Now that's, you know, I'm fairly convinced that's the position.' (Paul, LM)

Even when individuals invested in their own qualifications it did not necessarily translate into progression, as this older worker reported:

> 'I'm still in administration, secretarial and in my opinion, I don't think [LG] recognizes people that are a certain age with qualifications, but that's my opinion. 'Cause I've applied for jobs within [LG]. I consider [I] submitted a good application, and in my opinion they're not supposed to age discriminate but I think they do.' (Donna, aged 58)

To some degree, individuals seemed to display initiative and entrepreneurialism by taking their training and development into their own hands. However, the fact they had to do this and its limited impact on job opportunities reflected the fact that older workers were constrained from having the degree of freedom to develop presented in the HR narratives.

Moving downward

With older workers being unable to 'don the mantle' of autonomous individuals embracing opportunities for development, those experiencing a lot of change arguably responded through 'psychological reactance' (Pyysiäinen et al 2017; see Chapter 1). In other words, they saw the austerity pressures as being beyond their control, and failed to buy into the 'appeals to freedom' narrative of HR. However, they assumed responsibility over their situation, despite the fact that it is not of their own making, and in the context of great uncertainty acted in ways that sought to bring about some control. In some cases, this had meant individuals taking lower-level roles in LG.

In the HR interviews downward movements into lower-level roles was presented as being the result of autonomy and choice. For example, Craig (HR) highlighted a case of an older employer with a health condition voluntarily downsizing into a lower role "that has less responsibility, less physical activity". From our interviews, there was only one individual, Greg (aged 64), who had voluntarily moved to a lower-grade role, however. Greg had done this by taking flexible retirement – he had taken his pension and moved down four grades in order to remove himself from a very stressful job with long hours. This had in part been motivated by a serious health event, and a discussion with his doctor:

> 'He [the doctor] asked how stressful work was [and] … I said, "It is quite stressful," and he said, "You need to step back and have a look [at the situation]." Now he didn't advise me to take flexible retirement, I hadn't actually heard about it at that stage, but certainly it was a contributing factor in making my decision.' (Greg, aged 64)

Greg was very happy to have made this move to a lower-level role, and he had engineered it, so we might interpret this as being a positive example of redeployment. At the same time, however, it is noteworthy that this individual saw the stressfulness and hours of his former job as being inevitable, and he interpreted it as being his responsibility to respond to the situation by moving to a lower-level job. In the case of this individual, it was also important to note that he was in a financial position to make this move.

The remaining individuals downsizing into lower-level roles (around five in number) had attempted to get jobs at the same, or even higher, level and had been unsuccessful. These individuals were generally unhappy in their new jobs, but most were financially unable to leave, and saw the prospects of getting a job elsewhere as being low. Some felt that age discrimination was an issue, others were uncertain or interpreted it as being part of the wider context in which the organization was operating. One older interviewee, Jeremy (aged 60), was formerly in a professional/managerial role but he had dropped two grades in the restructuring; he was uncertain about whether age had influenced his treatment, but elsewhere in the interview argued, "I definitely got this feeling as though that as you got older you tend to get sidelined." This individual did not want to stop working, and felt unable to leave as he saw little prospect of getting another job. He had applied unsuccessfully for training that others had received but attempted to rationalize it to himself, reporting, "well, I'm over 60 now, you know". Moving to a lower-level role had not meant moving into a role with less pressure, as HR had implied, however; as Jeremy reported, "I'm constantly busy, under pressure, hitting deadlines".

There was no suggestion that individuals had been specifically instructed to take a lower-level job. However, in a stressful and uncertain context, in which they had lost their previous jobs and been unsuccessful in getting new roles at (at least) the same level, they had reluctantly taken it upon themselves to take a lower-level job. Rich (aged 56) had previously worked in an outdoors job that had been disestablished, but in the context of uncertainty felt compelled to take a lower-paid job he disliked. He was able to do this because individuals moving to lower-level roles have their pay protected for three years. However, after this period of pay protection had ended his pay dropped. He decided to take early retirement as he would be able to live on his pension income. He had previously enjoyed his job, and would have continued working if he had kept it. Rich described what he called a "black cloud", related to "cuts and the fact that for the first time ever you haven't got a job for life. You haven't got a secure place of work and anything could happen". His decision to go can be interpreted as an attempt to restore control over an uncertain set of circumstances, a form of psychological reactance:

'So the offer [voluntary early retirement] was made. I never thought I really would apply for it but then looking at it, I almost feel I got little option. I may well be wrong, but I feel as though I could a bit of a fool if I carry on and it goes pear-shaped, whereas at least if I take this option I know exactly where I stand. I have the facts and figures and I know that I am not being transferred to a job that I really don't want to do.' (Rich, aged 56)

The HR interviews had implied that redeployment was a positive choice and a way for individuals to develop themselves, but older workers did not see it that way. With the exception of the individual voluntarily moving down a number of grades due to stress and ill health, the movements made by individuals interviewed were in response to restructuring. Debbie (aged 57) had dropped to a lower grade and was keen to progress, but she saw the scheme as closed – you have to decide to change jobs (and get your manager's permission to enter the scheme) *before* you get to see what opportunities are on offer, limiting opportunities to move back upwards once you move down. Debbie noted how the scheme could be improved:

> 'If [redeployment] had that kind of facility within it, which it doesn't, which is about career discussions and stuff like that [it would be better]. You know, sideways moves, what else can you do, or about whatever may [be] becoming available. ... You've only got two options, you're either in it or you're not in it. If you're not in it, you don't get access to what's becoming available.' (Debbie, aged 57)

Arguably, the relative 'closure' of the system was unlikely to be accidental, however – it enabled the redeployment scheme to focus on the primary function it had been set up to deal with: labour resourcing in the context of radical restructuring.

Sideways moves at the same level

Most of those that had managed to successfully move sideways into roles at the same level elsewhere in the organization appeared to be broadly satisfied with their role (five of the 37 interviewees). These individuals had typically moved at earlier stages of their career, and this new role was either similar to previous roles or significantly utilized things they had done in the past. There was no indication that individuals in this category had received, or needed, training, in order to carry out their new role. This was important because there was very little training offered or available because of the budget cuts. What was generally available mainly appeared to be short generic courses on using basic computer software, and, as we saw earlier, additional discretionary training appeared to be sometimes rationed to younger staff.

Some of those that had successfully navigated the redeployment system to get another job at the same level were positive about it. For example, one older manager had managed to move from one managerial position to another, and was particularly enthusiastic (with parallels to the HR interviews):

> 'So basically to me it's [redeployment] is like a big agency but it belongs to us. And basically they look for a job that's in the [LG] for you, you

know, to try and align you to somewhere like that. And at the same time you can go into learning new things and new skills, which has been again quite easy for me because. I'm easy, flexible, not bother me. But I'm quite a good believer in that. And again it doesn't matter if you're older or you're younger or whatever. It makes no difference, you know.' (Linda, aged 62)

The aforementioned individual therefore partly attributed her ability to move to her own flexibility, and implies that such a mindset is important. Despite the reference to acquiring new skills there was little indication that she had required training in order to make this move, however.

The one individual making the move into a significantly different role was much less happy. Carol (aged 55) was a manager whose previous job had been eradicated in the restructuring process, and immediate jobs available to her were at a lower level. She held out against taking a lower-level job by covering periods of maternity leave, something she found very uncertain and stressful because she was unsure whether she would be made redundant and end up without a job. Carol explains:

'it was very unsettling ... we were going to be restructured and I didn't actually get a job. ... I was appointable but there was only four jobs and I was fifth ... so for a long time I didn't actually have a permanent job but I stayed within the team covering maternity leave because, you know, I think I was shell-shocked really, couldn't believe it had happened. Not that I thought I was better than the other people [who got the jobs in my area] but it was like what am I going to do, I've been here 30 years ... will I get made redundant, you know, it was very unsettling. And then finally I did get a job on the team, but I had to work for it, you know, have a proper full interview and fill in all the forms and do tests.' (Carol, aged 55)

Clearly it would have been the easier option, and perhaps the path expected of her, to take a demotion. Having taken responsibility for the role at her level she was now struggling because she lacked the technical understanding of the work and was reliant on asking more junior members of staff for help. When asked if there was training provided in order to take on the role, Carol replied: "Not really, no, and we're subject to constraints of the budgets, so what's more likely to happen is ask one of your colleagues and like they will go through, and I try and make notes". She was now considering leaving via voluntary early retirement because she was unable to cope in her new work, although she worried about the prospect of being able to get another job if she left. This was therefore arguably another example of an older worker taking responsibility for their predicament by leaving.

Reconfigured jobs

A number of the interviewees had not been redeployed but the job that they were doing had been reconfigured, for example with additional roles or responsibilities added (around six individuals). These individuals were unhappy with their situation, and as a result of severe work intensification and their new roles wanted to leave. Karen (aged 55), for example, had worked in a specialist role, but with reorganization was unhappy with changes to her job, as she explains:

> 'Because each of us had our own specialist knowledge, but then they didn't want us to have specialist knowledge, they just wanted us to work everywhere. Which is a great idea, it's like hot-desking, it sounds great – it's rubbish. ... Across the board people are incredibly stressed, incredibly unhappy with the work.' (Karen, aged 55)

Karen said that they had received "a small amount of training" and she had struggled to adapt to the new aspects of the job and was now planning to leave.

Not all older workers in reconfigured jobs were in a financial position to leave. Mark (aged 57), for example, was in a professional/managerial role and had seen the scope of his work expand dramatically, leading to high levels of stress among himself and his colleagues: "Before all the austerity measures came, all the cuts, was yeah, I was prepared to work on, you know, 'cause I like working for [LG]. ... But now with, you know, there's so much pressure on you I'd rather just get out." Mark was unable to leave via the early retirement scheme because his skills were needed, and it would not be approved. He reported: "they've said to us, 'You can apply but you'll be refused early retirement', basically, so there's no get-out clause at the moment". The level of work and stress had a negative effect on his mental health, resulting in him and some of his colleagues seeking professional medical help. However, access to the redeployment scheme to move into another role on the basis of ill health and so on would be blocked, as Mark explained, "to go on to the [redeployment scheme] ... your boss and his bosses have got [to] let you go. So if they're not letting you retire earlier they're not going to let you do that". This therefore was counter to the impression given by HR of redeployment being a means of meeting individuals' needs.

Those experiencing less change

Around half of the interviewees had remained in the same job, with little in the way of obvious job reconfiguration. This included jobs that were essential and hard to reconfigure. Some of these required specialist knowledge, experience or qualifications that made redeployment of other staff to the role, or job reconfiguration, difficult. Others were elementary, routine jobs where the individual worked on their own and efficiency savings would be difficult.

Some individuals experiencing limited change were interested in leaving via voluntary retirement/severance, and others ruled it out. However, individuals in these jobs were less dissatisfied with their changing treatment by the organization, and perhaps had a lack of awareness of the challenges faced by colleagues in other parts of LG (given the dispersed nature of the workforce). These individuals had therefore experienced fewer pressures from neoliberal austerity and consequently perhaps provided a partial window onto how employees were treated in the past.

Pete (aged 55) was an example of an older worker doing an elementary job. He was not in a financial position to take early retirement and had not appeared to really consider this option. He did not mind working, was grateful to have a job with a pension and liked to keep busy. When asked if he would like the option of being deployed to a less physically demanding job when he reached his early 60s, Pete indicated that he did not think this was a feasible or desirable option:

'I mean I don't like driving [as an alternative], I don't like driving about, I've never worked in an office, I've always been outside, always been a grafter if you want to rephrase, always worked manual, you know, I could never work ... don't work on computer or anything, no, I have trouble with a mobile phone, that's enough, you know what I mean, I couldn't work ... being sat in there [inside] doing all that, I'd rather be grafted, I'd rather be out working, you know what I'm meaning, that's what I've always done.' (Pete, aged 55)

Pete was happy to continue working as he had been, at least until state pension age (67 in his case) if he was able to. In this regard he was assuming individual responsibility for his fitness:

'I go over gym, try and keep fit, you know, no I don't smoke, I might go out once a week but like I say this week I won't go out 'cause I'm [working] on Thursday, Friday, Saturday, Sunday, yeah, me health's okay, you know. Everything just like I say, I just carry on working till, you know, until I'm not fit enough to do it.'

Another older worker, Tom (aged 62), was in a professional role and was planning to leave via voluntary early retirement in his early 60s. He expressed some desire to continue working due to intrinsic value attributed to his work: "So in one sense I would like to continue because I like what I do, and I'm very wrapped up in it." However, as Tom got older he found work more tiring: "when I get home at night I'm completely shattered". This did not appear to be because of a change in the nature of the work, which was always demanding, but due to the physical ageing process. This individual did not want to reduce his hours rather than retire – he would rather just stop working. The examples of Pete and Tom therefore highlight the limits of using redeployment of older workers to new roles, or reducing their hours, as a means of extending working lives. Pete and Tom both wanted the continuity of doing their current work until they left.

This does not imply that older workers were entirely happy with their working lives. Sharon (aged 57), for example, complained about the changing ethos of local government and wanted to leave:

> 'I think they've changed a lot recently. … I do consider myself to be a public servant and I think that's been eroded a bit now because of the fact that [LG] has to get funding going with private industry and we're sort of having to compete in that world, if you get what I mean, where money is so important. It wasn't in the past; it was people and that's where my heart lies. … It's sort of [become] more get up and go, get in there with the big boys, join the rat race type of thing.' (Sharon, aged 57)

Despite this, and some other general complaints about aspects of their work (including unmet aspirations for growth discussed earlier), older workers experiencing the least change were arguably in a better position to extend their working lives than those being redeployed or having their jobs reconfigured. This cannot simply be stereotyped as older people naturally being unable to adapt to change. One older worker discussed earlier, Karen, was planning to leave due to the reconfiguration of her job but nevertheless had plans to develop her own business in a different area once she had left via voluntary early retirement. However, the 'appeals to freedom' articulated by HR with regard to redeployment were difficult for older workers to live up to in the context of the local government, given the uncertainty and lack of real opportunities available to them.

Conclusion

It is often assumed that job redeployment is a positive tool for extending working lives, and certainly historically, before the advent of retirement, it was used in organizations to move people in physically demanding employment to 'light work' prior to the development of retirement (Phillipson, 1982). There is little evidence that redeploying staff to new roles specifically in line with their changing preferences and needs is now common, however. Indeed, given the increasing financial pressures under which organizations operate, it is likely that the availability of lighter jobs for older workers who want them are rare. In this context, when organizations do redeploy staff, it is likely to be in response to financial pressures and motivated by meeting the perceived organizational needs, rather than supporting older people and other groups to continue working.

This chapter examined the impact of job redeployment on older workers in a UK local government authority facing financial pressures from neoliberal austerity in the form of budget cuts from central government. In this local authority work and service provision had been reorganized in response to these pressures, and a redeployment scheme was introduced to move people to new and vacant roles. This context created a huge amount of uncertainty for workers, and in response HR managers drew on a narrative of 'appeals to freedom' identified in the neoliberal responsibilisation literature (Pyysiäinen et al 2017). According to this, redeployment was presented as an opportunity for people of all ages to adapt their employment in response to their changing circumstances and developmental preferences, *for those willing to be flexible and take responsibility for managing their circumstances.*

The analysis in this chapter showed that, in reality, older workers found it hard to live up to the ideal of enterprising, flexible redeployed workers presented by HR. There appeared to be minimal 'real' opportunities for older workers to progress in their careers and budget cuts meant that training beyond the basics was being informally rationed to younger workers in some cases. A number of older workers found themselves losing their previous jobs due to restructuring, and struggled to get jobs even at an equivalent level, with the suggestion being made by a number of interviewees that older people were discriminated against due to the (inaccurate) stereotype that they were 'on their way out' after age 55. In this context, older workers ended up participating in their own marginalization by taking jobs at lower levels in order to restore some control in an uncertain context, a form of 'psychological reactance' (Pyysiäinen et al 2017) that did not require management to direct older workers to take low-level jobs.

The redeployment scheme was not therefore, arguably, an effective way of 'coordinating the demands of the workplace with the capacity of the (older) employees' (Naegele and Walker (2006, p 19). Almost all of the redeployment of interviewees appeared to be as a result of restructuring, rather than in response to older workers' changing needs. One might argue that this was simply just not 'best practice' in job redeployment, but this response ignores the progressive intentions of the organization and the financial context within which it, and many other organizations, operate. In this context, it is fair to conclude that under neoliberalism, job redeployment is likely to be predominantly used to meet the needs of the organization rather than the worker. This means it is likely to often be detrimental to extending working lives humanely, because it ends up magnifying older worker marginalization.

References

Baccaro, L. and Howell, C. (2017) *Trajectories of Neoliberal Transformation: European Industrial Relations since the 1970s*, Cambridge: Cambridge University Press.

Beck, V. (2013) 'Employers' use of older workers in the recession', *Employee Relations*, 35(3): 257–71.

CIPD (Chartered Institute for Personnel and Development) (2012) *Leading Culture Change: Employee Engagement and Public Service Transformation*, London: Chartered Institute for Personnel and Development.

CIPD (2020) *Labour Market Outlook Autumn 2020*, London: Chartered Institute for Personnel and Development.

Conway, E. and Monks, K. (2017) 'Designing a HR system for managing an age-diverse workforce', in Parry, E. and McCarthy, J. (eds) *The Palgrave Handbook of Age Diversity and Work*, London: Palgrave Macmillan.

Corbin, J.M. and Strauss, A. (1990) 'Grounded theory research: procedures, canons, and evaluative criteria', *Qualitative Sociology*, 13(1): 3–21.

Esping-Andersen, G. (1990) *The Three Worlds of Welfare Capitalism*, Princeton, NJ: Princeton University Press.

Farnsworth, K. and Irving, Z. (2018) 'Austerity: neoliberal dreams come true?', *Critical Social Policy*, 38(3): 461–81.

Grimshaw, D. and Rubery, J. (2012) 'Reinforcing neoliberalism: crisis and austerity in the UK', in Lehndorff, S. (ed) *A Triumph of Failed Ideas: European Models of Capitalism in the Crisis*, Brussels: European Trade Union Institute.

Hall, P.A. and Soskice, D. (eds) (2001) *Varieties of Capitalism: The Institutional Foundations of Comparative Advantage*, Oxford: Oxford University Press.

Hennink, M., Hutter, I. and Bailey, A. (2011) *Qualitative Research Methods*, London: Sage.

Herrbach, O., Mignonac, K., Vandenberghe, C. and Negrini, A. (2009) 'Perceived HRM practices, organizational commitment, and voluntary early retirement among late-career managers', *Human Resource Management*, 48(6): 895–915.

Inceoglu, I., Segers, J. and Bartram, D. (2012) 'Age-related differences in work motivation', *Journal of Occupational and Organizational Psychology*, 85(2): 300–29.

Johnson, M., Rubery, J. and Grimshaw, D. (2019) 'Public sector employment relations after the crisis: a comparative case study analysis of UK local authorities', *Economic and Industrial Democracy* [online first], 1–23.

Krekula, C. (2019) 'Time, precarisation and age normality: on internal job mobility among men in manual work', *Ageing and Society*, 39(10): 2290–307.

Lain, D. (2012) 'Working past 65 in the UK and the USA: segregation into "Lopaq" occupations?', *Work, Employment and Society*, 26(1): 78–94.

Lain, D. (2016) *Reconstructing Retirement: Work and Welfare in the UK and USA*, Bristol: Policy Press.

Lemke, T. (2001) ' "The birth of bio-politics": Michel Foucault's lecture at the Collège de France on neo-liberal governmentality', *Economy and Society*, 30(2): 190–207.

Lewis, P., Thornhill, A. and Saunders, M. (2003) *Employee Relations: Understanding the Employment Relationship*, Harlow: Pearson Education.

Marshall, T.H. (2006 [1950]) 'Citizenship and Social Class', in Pierson, C. and Castles, F.G. (eds) *The Welfare State Reader*, Cambridge: Polity.

Marshall, V. (1999) 'Reasoning with case studies: issues of an aging workforce', *Journal of Aging Studies*, 13(4): 377–89.

Naegele, G. and Walker, A. (2006) *A Guide to Good Practice in Age Management*, Dublin: European Foundation for the Improvement of Living and Working Conditions.

Newman, J. (2014) 'Landscapes of antagonism: local governance, neoliberalism and austerity', *Urban Studies*, 51(15): 3290–305.

Patton, M. (1990) *Qualitative Evaluation and Research Methods* (2nd edn), Beverly Hills, CA: Sage.

Phillipson, C. (1982) *Capitalism and the Construction of Old Age*, London: Macmillan.

Pyysiäinen, J., Halpin, D. and Guilfoyle, A. (2017) 'Neoliberal governance and "responsibilization" of agents: reassessing the mechanisms of responsibility-shift in neoliberal discursive environments', *Distinktion: Journal of Social Theory*, 18(2): 215–35.

Rose, N. (1999) *Powers of Freedom: Reframing Political Thought*, Cambridge: Cambridge University Press.

Yin, R.K. (2009) *Case Study Research*, Thousand Oaks: Sage.

Time, Precarization and Age Normality: On Internal Job Mobility among Men in Manual Work in Sweden

Clary Krekula

Introduction

Since the end of the 1990s, there has been a rapid increase of policies supporting extended working life (Phillipson, 2019). The policies have tended to focus on individuals, and the debate has to a great extent described older people as the problem. Their participation in working life and current retirement trends are described as problematic as well as self-serving, uninformed and outdated, and as a threat to welfare provision and benefits (Krekula and Vickerstaff, 2017). Many governments have therefore focused on trying to persuade older workers to make 'wiser' decisions and delay their retirement, for example, by creating favourable conditions for those who are able and willing to continue working (Krekula et al 2017a), by making work pay through tax incentives (Vickerstaff and Loretto, 2017) and by narrowing gateways to early exit (Smeaton and White, 2016) (see Chapter 1).

The description of extended working life as a simple matter of older workers' individual choice is contradicted by research which shows that work content factors influence labour market participation in later life (Pohrt and Hasselhorn, 2015; Smeaton and White, 2016). The description is also debatable in view of research on work ability, that is, the balance between the demands of work and the resources of the individual, which, together with motivation and the opportunity to work, is described as intermediate steps to early retirement (Takala and Seitsamo, 2015). Research has also shown that ageism, for example in the form of discrimination, negative attitudes and a stereotypical picture of older workers (for the concept, see Butler, 1969; Wilkinson and Ferraro, 2002), forces people out of working life (Ilmarinen, 1997; 2006; Bennington, 2001). Regardless of whether the categorization 'older workers' is applied to middle-aged people, to elderly people or to people over the age of 50, older workers are discursively described as having a subordinated position in work organizations (Riach, 2009; Fevre, 2011; Krekula and Vickerstaff, 2017).

Age-based marginalization affects individuals' well-being and their will to work. Research shows, for example, that perceived ageism affects subjective health (Cadiz, 2010; World Health Organization, 2015), and that older workers are more prone to staying in workplaces that are less ageist (Cadiz, 2010). Behind the rhetoric about self-serving, uninformed and problematic older workers, there are thus well-documented organizational practices which create age-based marginalization and limit older people's participation in working life. The necessary conditions for extended working life need to be explored in a broader political and social context, and the debate needs to be based on knowledge of how age-based marginalization and the organizational practices of the workplace relate to retirement decisions (Hasselhorn and Apt, 2015; Krekula and Vickerstaff, 2017; Phillipson, 2019).

This chapter is a contribution to this debate by highlighting conceptions of the age at which employees are expected to change work station and duties in workplaces with physically demanding jobs. On the basis of qualitative interviews with men aged 56–74 in an industrial company and on the assumption that temporality makes up a fundamental dimension of an organization, the presence of temporal norms related to internal work mobility is identified. By showing that the temporal order (Zerubavel, 1981) affects older workers' possibilities to stay at work, the chapter problematizes the notion that working life in physically demanding workplaces can be extended through shifting work tasks. The chapter also illustrates that the temporal norms related to internal work mobility at an early stage influence individuals to plan for limitations that they fear will arise as a result of ageism in the future.

Literature survey

In a context of considerable economic decline in the industrial sector in Organisation for Economic Co-operation and Development (OECD) countries from the end of the 1970s to the early 1990s, policies at the time aimed to facilitate early retirement, and research focused on the characteristics of early exit. Against the backdrop of population ageing, more recently the focus has shifted, both in policies and in research, to analyze the possibility of people extending their working lives into their 60s and 70s (Van Dalen and Henkens, 2002; Phillipson, 2019). When extended working life is currently implemented in many countries, it takes place in a context with a gap between what older adults want and need and what they are offered by policy makers and employers (James et al 2016), where opportunities for full-time employment are restricted (Phillipson, 2019), labour force participation rates for prime working-age men, that is, 25–54, have been falling (Dvorkin and Shell, 2015) and employments with uncertain pension terms and guaranteed hours are on the increase (OECD, 2015).

At the same time, retirement is transforming from being a shift from full-time work to full and permanent retirement into a process of stages over several years (Sonnega et al 2016). Cahill et al (2015, p 385) refer to the process as the 'do-it-yourself' approach to retirement, including phased retirement from full-time to part-time work to full retirement, and transitions from a full-time career job to another, shorter duration job to full retirement, for example intermediate jobs or 'bridge jobs'. Research also indicates the existence of 'unretirement', in which workers return either to full- or part-time work after full retirement (Maestas, 2010). According to Kail and Warner (2013), to a great extent unretirement means that men resume full-time work and women return to part-time work.

Research indicates a number of factors that affect older workers' participation in working life, namely health, economic incentives, physical and psychosocial work environment, family/leisure, rate of work and working hours, the competence and skills of senior staff, work satisfaction and attitudes to older employees (Nilsson, 2016). At a general level, the reason for people retiring has been described as an interaction between (a) 'push' factors, for example no appreciation of or demand for older workers; (b) 'pull' factors, for example voluntary retirement for assumed economic reasons; and (c) 'jump' factors, for example retirement as a way of ageing with pleasure (Lund and Villadsen, 2005; Thorsen et al 2012).

Research indicating that marginalization and exclusion of the elderly are obstacles to older people's participation in the labour market (Ilmarinen, 1997; 2006; Bennington, 2001; European Commission, 2009) is also central to the present study. In the same vein, research also suggests that opportunities for development are associated with remaining at work or late retirement (Thorsen et al 2012).

Marginalization of older workers also emerges in studies showing that long-term unemployment increases with age (Henkens et al 1996; Schwartz and Kleiner, 1999); that older workers have the lowest re-employment probabilities (Yearta and Warr, 1995; Loretto et al 2000; Chan and Stevens, 2001; Kalavar, 2001; Gee et al 2007); that older people are not invited to job interviews (Benedick et al 1999; Nelson, 2005; Neumark, 2009); and that they have high probabilities of part-time employment while suffering the largest wage losses (Hirsch et al 2000; Bennington, 2001). However, the quality of life at work seems to affect men and women's retirement planning differently (Larsen, 2008). Ageism, lack of recognition and lack of development opportunities are associated with older male workers' retirement plans (Thorsen et al 2012). Perceived ageism is described as a significant factor for retirement before the average retirement age among men, but not among women (Soidre, 2005).

Concurrent with the ongoing debate on extended working life, research shows that older employees experience a growing discontent with work demands and the nature of work (Smeaton and White, 2016). This is in harmony with studies of work factors in relation to the employment participation of older workers, where heavy physical work demands have consistently been associated with disability retirement (Lund and Villadsen, 2005; Pohrt and Hasselhorn, 2015). It is also argued that work ability declines with age, especially in jobs with physically demanding tasks, and that some older workers are stuck in jobs that are physically demanding, which has been explained by their low levels of education (Takala and Seitsamo, 2015). Further, the quality of an individual's working life may affect women and men differently. Blekesaune and Solem (2005) found that among men, both disability and non-disability retirement were related to low autonomy in job tasks, and they argue that hard physical work is not generally associated with early retirement among men, as the case is for women. According to Ilmarinen and Ilmarinen (2015), the physical and mental work environment, working hours, work organization, the work community and work tasks, as well as management, are central factors influencing older employees' participation at work. Although these issues related to quality at work, the duties offered to older employees and the importance of avoiding being 'stuck in' heavy tasks are highlighted in research, systematic knowledge of how these factors are handled in the work organization and their consequences for extended working life is lacking.

In the light of research mentioned earlier on work quality, occupational transitions and internal job mobility, that is, switching tasks in the same workplace, have been designated as factors promoting working at an older age. In a study of later-life occupational transitions (Sonnega et al 2016), it was found that most career changes were made between closely related occupations. The researchers also found that occupation workers are most likely to move into jobs that tend to be seasonal or have low barriers to entry, and that employees in physically demanding jobs are less likely to have switched to a different type of job by age 66.

While work mobility in younger ages is associated with career development (Rosenfeld, 1992; Bidwell and Briscoe, 2010), changes of occupation at older ages tend to involve a reduction in wages (Groot and Verberne, 1997; Johnson and Kawachi, 2007; Sonnega et al 2016). Changing jobs is also linked to health, and studies show that downward occupational mobility in middle age has deleterious effects on women's health in later life (Wilkinson and Ferraro, 2012).

Research on internal job mobility among older people indicates that such transition above all means movement towards lower–status tasks, and it is difficult to find studies which look at promotion ladders among older people. This can be seen as an expression of the recurrent descriptions of ageing workers' bodies as 'at–risk' bodies (Katz, 2000), which is rationalized by the conflict between biological ageing processes and work requirements. Riach (2007) argues that the overall construction of a category of 'older workers' takes place by essentializing older workers' characteristics. When older workers are aligned with particular jobs, it comes down to work tasks which, rather than being based on knowledge or professional skills, are easier and less demanding. Overall, and from a critical age perspective (Krekula and Johansson, 2017), this research shows that internal job mobility does not constitute a unique and homogenous phenomenon, but rather it has different meanings and consequences depending on age.

Theoretical frames

The analysis focuses on the organizing of age and time and how it is connected to age relations at work and to older workers' participation in working life.

Organizing refers here to the overarching processes in which people cooperate to create shared understanding of given situations (Weick, 1969; Czarniawska, 2014). Age is a key organizing principle with great impact because it is often seen as neutral (Fineman, 2011; Krekula and Johansson, 2017). This starting point means that age, regardless of whether it is conceptualized as a resource or marginalization, is viewed as embedded in practices, that is, as a contextual doing (Laz, 1998; Calasanti, 2003; Krekula, 2009; Krekula and Johansson, 2017; Krekula et al 2017b; 2018).

Organizing is closely connected to constructions of social categorizations and privilege relations. Everyday organizing such as designing the work environment and access to tools are examples of subtle forms of pressure as individuals act in accordance with what a system requires (Foucault, 2004). Organizing age is based on age coding; distinctive practices associating a context or a phenomenon – such as internal job mobility with demarcated ages (Krekula, 2009). Coding means that some age groups are systematically favoured at the expense of others in different contexts, and that age normality is created in the form of limited age groups, and their actions assume a taken–for–granted position as an unproblematized norm (Krekula and Johansson, 2017; Krekula et al 2017b; 2018).

Brekhus (1996; 1998) argues that (age) normalities are created through actors viewing one part of a dichotomy (old/young, man/woman) as epistemologically unproblematic. By labelling some categorizations with an attribute (older workers), the categorizations are marked as distinctive, while the unmarked part of the compound (workers) is simply generic. In the analysis of how job mobility is related to the construction of age normality and marginalization, respectively, the binary marked/unmarked age is used in this chapter. Unmarked age here represents an unproblematized generic position, against which the marked age is constructed as a deviation (Krekula and Johansson, 2017; Krekula et al 2017b; 2018).

Organizing also takes place in terms of time (Zerubavel, 1981; Adam et al 2008; West-Pavlov, 2012), and then often through subtle aspects. Zerubavel (1987) provides examples of time being used as semiotic codes signifying priority and respect, without the need for verbal articulation. For example, making people wait, or giving them limited access to time in public environments, signals low priority (Zerubavel, 1987; Krekula et al 2017b). These non-verbal temporal practices are also active in the processes that create age normality (Zerubavel, 1981; Krekula et al 2017b). Krekula and Johansson (2017; see also Krekula et al 2017b) use the concept norma-/temporality to describe power practices based on this link between temporal organizing and construction of normality, and argue that the one cannot be understood without the other.

Temporal disciplining is also exercised through social activities structured by temporal regularity such as rigid sequential structures, fixed durations, standard temporal locations and uniform rates of recurrence (Berger and Luckmann, 1967; Zerubavel, 1981; West-Pavlov, 2012). There are several forms of temporal patterns in societal organizing. While the concept 'socio-temporal order' describes temporal regulation of social entities such as families, professional groups, complex organizations and even entire nations, the 'bio-temporal order' concerns temporal regularities involving living entities, for example duration of pregnancy periods and age-related physical changes (Zerubavel, 1981, p 2).

Temporal organization in working life has been illustrated with the concept 'career timetable', that is, age-graded career steps which individuals are expected to follow (Lawrence, 1988). In an article on mobility in industrial companies, Martin and Strauss (1956) argue that the speed at which individuals move along specific career lines tends to follow fairly identifiable timetables, which enable individuals to predict their chances of advancement to higher levels. Lawrence (1988) argues that, while being ahead of the timetable is seen as positive, being behind is regarded as negative. A number of studies support this thesis, and show that individuals who have been promoted at the expected pace are described as being 'on time' or 'on schedule', while individuals who have been promoted faster are seen as 'ahead of time', 'ahead of schedule' or on the 'fast track'. Conversely, those who have been promoted later than expected are 'behind time', 'behind schedule', 'dead wood' or 'old timers' (Cleveland et al 1997; Shore et al 2003; Quintens and Matthyssens, 2010; Lawrence, 2011). This dichotomization of on- and off-time (Zerubavel, 1981) shows that temporal regularity is based on assumptions about norms and deviation.

The analysis of the statements made on extended working life in the collected material is based on the assumption that political steering towards extended working life contributes to increasing individualization of working-life risks and to limiting security in respect of pensions (Lewis and Giullari, 2005; Krekula et al 2017a). Standing (2011) discusses these processes in terms of the concept of the precariat, which he describes as the growing group of people in the labour market with insecure working conditions who lack basic rights and have few opportunities to make a career. According to him, the ageing population is an important factor in the growth of the precariat since older workers constitute a growing source of cheap labour, thereby also forming a group at risk of ending up in the precariat.

Butler (2015) and Lorey (2015) argue that precarization means more than insecure jobs and the lack of security provided by waged employment. It should rather be understood as a general experience of living with the unforeseeable. It means that everyone is affected by the processes of precarization, and that they are the rule rather than the exception. Because insecure experiences are evident in all areas of life, a new form of disciplining is created, and precarization becomes a particular form of exploitation that characterizes contemporary society. Precarity is a basic dimension of a neoliberal governance through social insecurity. Lorey (2015) uses the concept of 'governmental precarisation' as a framework for these processes. This perspective on precarization emphasizes that it is important, although not sufficient, to display the consequences of political governance towards extended working life by identifying particularly exposed groups. In addition, the range of practices also needs to be problematized through identifying the processes in, for example, work organizations that normalize and trivialize the precarization in the wake of policies on extended working life.

Context, material and method

Sweden, the national context of this chapter, has a high proportion of older people in the population. In 2015, 19.8 per cent of the population were 65 plus (Statistics Sweden, 2016). In the same year, the average retirement age was 64.6 for women and 64.4 for men (Swedish Pensions Agency, 2016). In the age group 55–64, 71.5 per cent of the women and 76.3 per cent of the men were employed in 2014 (Eurostat, 2016), which is a high number from an international perspective, clearly exceeding the 50 per cent recommended by the European Union (European Commission, 2009).

The average retirement age in Sweden for men in the occupational group discussed in this chapter, that is, manual workers in the metals industry, is 64.1. This is somewhat lower than the age of 65, still regarded as the 'normal retirement age', and it is almost three years below the current highest retirement age of 67, which is seen as necessary in order to qualify for a reasonable pension (Andersson, 2015). This retirement pattern corresponds with a study on retirement-age preferences of women and men aged 55–64 years in Sweden (Soidre, 2005), which showed that qualified blue-collar workers had a significantly greater preference for early retirement than upper-rank white-collar workers.

The present study is part of a major research project on organizing age in work organizations, for which data were collected through interviews, observations and text analysis in the context of two case studies (Yin, 2009). This chapter is based on data from one of the cases, namely a large international steel company with a branch in Sweden. The company was chosen because it offered rich material in terms of age coding and age organizing due to its many varied units and a great number of employees of different ages. This was a male-dominated organization.

The policy discourse on extended working life has, to a great extent, been based on a homogeneous image of a generic, individualized 'adult worker' (Lewis, 2002; 2007; Hasselhorn and Apt, 2015; Krekula and Vickerstaff, 2017). This chapter focuses on the interviews conducted with men in order to contextualize the results and contribute to complexifying the homogeneous presentations. It also focuses on the fact that there were very few older female members of staff, which is why I do not discuss results in terms of 'older workers', but delimit to (older) men in manual work.

The material analyzed consists of interviews with 11 men between the ages of 56 and 74. They worked as foundry men, fitters, welders, economists and education managers. The latter occupational groups were included to, in the first stage of the study, enable a broad and overall picture of the internal mobility that is viewed as possible and expected within the work organization in question.

Because of the great economic fluctuations in the industry over the last decades, and several bankruptcies and new ownerships, many of the employees, including some of the men interviewed, were not employed by the company but by a staffing agency.

Respondents were partly recruited through so-called snowball sampling (Creswell, 1998). At interviews we asked for further people aged 50 plus, and for special groups such as unretired people, older people employed via a staffing agency, and people whose duties involved a great deal of travelling or strenuous physical work. Some respondents were recruited in connection with observations made. The ambition was to ensure variation in terms of age, duties and experience of being employed at the company.

The interviews, conducted by the author and a project colleague, lasted around 60 minutes and took place in the company's offices during the respondents' workday. All interviews were digitally recorded and transcribed verbatim.

The overall topic of the interviews was age in relation to power, status and career prospects, and descriptions of the respondents' working-life transitions and retirement plans. Respondents were first asked to outline the organization and its different units schematically. The sketches gave us an idea of the company from their perspective, and also served as a basis for talking about their units, their relocations, and their expected and unusual moves within the organization. In short, it served as a trigger of memories and as a point of departure for our discussions (Pink, 2001).

The empirical analysis was an interpretative process carried out in several steps. A thematic analysis was made of passages in the transcribed material (Guest et al 2012), illustrating the reasoning connected to the meanings of age, work mobility and future work. Data collection and analysis aimed to clarify the processes in question from the respondents' perspectives (Blaikie, 2007). In practice, this meant that the analysis was approached with the concepts of age and time, while social security and precarization were introduced into the process when the central role of these concepts emerged.

Temporal regimes creating age normality and disciplining

In previous research, work mobility among older workers has mainly been related to the inability to carry out physically strenuous work (for example, Ilmarinen and Ilmarinen, 2015; Takala and Seitsamo, 2015). Also policies have stressed the possibility of being given less strenuous tasks as a crucial factor for extended working life (SOU, 2013). While these studies have discussed the nature of work in relation to older workers, social organizing of work mobility and its significance to extended working life has received less attention. In this section, I problematize the organizing of work mobility by showing the presence of temporal norms creating age normality and affecting the employees' behaviour and their movements between different units in the workplace.

Temporal regimes creating age normality

In the empirical material, there are recurring descriptions of how transitions between different units and work tasks are expected to take place at a given age and after having done something else for a certain period of time. The data also show that the opportunity to change work tasks varies with the different units in the company and that some transitions are seen as highly unlikely, as expressed in the following statements: "The typical age to become project manager is 35 because by then you have acquired experience in construction"; "I don't think it's common for someone to move from the foundry to other units in the company"; and "You are probably not recruited to Start-up from administration or HR [Human Resources]". Overall, these statements show that there is a predominant and shared perception of when and how employees are expected to change units and work tasks.

Perceptions of when transitions are assumed to be possible and appropriate are expressed in terms of best age for transitions, which creates a dichotomy of transitions as being on-time or off-time. In this respect, the statements harmonize with studies of career timetables (Lawrence, 1988; 2011; Cleveland et al 1997; Shore et al 2003; Quintens and Matthyssens, 2010). In the present material, however, not only career-making, that is, promotion ladders, is discussed, but also horizontal moves to other units with similar status. Expressed differently, the career timetables identified do not only apply to upward career mobility but also to relocation generally in the organization.

A suggested age for expected and appropriate transitions is gradually established through statements indicating when transitions by younger and older employees are off-time, for example, in the following statement on a career move being overdue: "At 40–45 you start to think that it's a little too late to move from engineer to project manager." When the younger age groups are described as being off-time, it is particularly in relation to the idea that people can be prematurely promoted to a managerial position. This is illustrated by statements such as: "Sara was her age, between 35 and 40, when she got the production job. It's pretty early in the tech unit."

The age at which movement is assumed to be on-time is not specified directly in terms of chronological age, but emerges, as in the quotations earlier, through the narratives of its opposites, that is, transitions considered to be off-time, that is, too early or too late. Categorizations of on- or off-time are thus relationally constructed. From a constructivist and critical perspective on age, in which age is seen as contextually and relationally constructed (Krekula, 2009; Krekula et al 2017b), the processes can be understood as a concurrent construction of age normality, for example, unmarked age, because their transitions are described as expected, unproblematic and generic. Consequently, the description of other transitions as being off-time represents a marking of corresponding age groups (Krekula and Johansson, 2017; Krekula et al 2017b). The temporal orders on which the dichotomy of on-/off-time is based can therefore be understood as a temporal regime, and as examples of the form of power that has been referred to as norma-/temporality (Krekula and Johansson, 2017).

Some of the interviewees also mentioned how painful it can be to deviate from the temporal expectations. In the following quotation, a respondent describes what it was like to become a manager ahead of schedule:

'I was 25 at the time and too young to make that kind of career move. It was tough because I got very difficult tasks from the start, and it was at a time when everything was supposed to move to computers. The old-timers who were supposed to support the CEO [Chief Executive Officer] were so critical of me: "What could a young engineer have to teach us?" It was so tough that I cried a lot in the beginning.'

The quote illustrates that work transitions off-time can be openly criticized, evoke strong emotions and affect individuals' well-being, all of which indicate that temporal orders also constitute social norms. As such, they express social values about what is seen as normal and what is seen as deviant. As indicated earlier, the temporal norms enforce social control through sanctions, thus producing shame (Heller, 1985; Scheff, 1990; Krekula, 2009). When individuals comply with the norms about when and how to move within the work organization, it is an example of temporal adaptation to temporal norms, which has been described as a formal pattern of social organizing (Zerubavel, 1981).

Disciplining through fear of ageism

The empirical material also indicates that there is a fear of ending up in a situation when it is too late to entertain the idea of moving to another unit or tasks at all. As a 74-year-old man put it: "I'm surprised that some people haven't moved – that they stay. They have worked so long now that they couldn't even get a job as a financial manager at a company." The fear of being off-time and finding that it is too late to change units can also affect individuals' behaviour, as in a 63-year-old man's quotation reflecting on starting his present job: "I was at a suitable age when I began working here. However, I thought I was a little bit too old because it was the last chance to change jobs completely because otherwise I would have been 50 plus and that would have been difficult. That's what I thought then." In this reasoning, the respondent relates to a conception of a best-before-age to start over in a new unit; in his case before the age of 50. He states that he planned his job change so that it would take place before he became 'too old' to get the opportunity, thus illustrating a fear of age being an obstacle to career moves, which is supported by research showing that older people are discriminated against in recruitment processes (Benedick et al 1999; Kalavar, 2001; Nelson, 2005; Gee et al 2007; Neumark, 2009). Fear of age discrimination made this respondent take action before he was too old. In the words of Foucault (1991), this can be an expression of disciplining, where temporal norms and worries about ageism are internalized and lead to the attempt to harmonize behaviour and the norm.

Overall, the aforementioned results display the central role of socio-temporal orders in work organizations. They illustrate that the internal work mobility is regulated by normative assumptions on temporality, for example that they are based on temporal regimes. They also show that conceptions of career moves as being on- or off-time are constructed in conjunction with age-normality constructions, and that the temporal order constitutes a disciplining element for the employees; it makes individuals plan for avoiding future job limitations as a result of ageism. This disciplining can thus be seen as an example of the 'governmental precarisation' that Lorey (2015) describes as governing through social insecurity.

Changing corporate strategies with prevailing social insecurity

In parallel with the temporal orders described earlier, where transitions within the organization at certain delimited ages are seen as expected, other movements appear to be outside the socio-temporal order. This section deals with workplace mobility involving a change from physically strenuous tasks to less physically demanding tasks, which I discuss in relation to established temporal orders and vulnerability to insecurity.

Individualization of the risks of working life

The analyzed data provide several examples of respondents describing many of their work tasks as heavy and difficult to combine with a long working life. For example, people stated, "I don't know if we should be doing this when we're over 60, it's too heavy"; "In heavy industry, you can feel it's hurting"; and "If you think that an industrial worker should work until he is 67, you don't know the reality of this job." These quotes indicate an apparent need for less physically strenuous tasks if working at an older age should be possible. This relates to studies showing that both preferred retirement and the actual average retirement age are lower among occupational groups in physically demanding work (Soidre, 2005; Andersson, 2015), and to research pointing to the difficulties of maintaining work ability in jobs with physically demanding tasks (Pohrt and Hasselhorn, 2015; Takala and Seitsamo, 2015).

When the respondents talked about internal mobility, these transitions towards physically easier tasks were not mentioned. However, the theme was commented on when we explicitly asked them about the opportunities for older workers to get other work tasks, and then the answers varied greatly. Someone said that he had made that type of transition, others questioned whether the company had so-called 'retreat positions', while some thought that the option existed since they had heard about employees who had been given easier tasks when unable to perform their normal duties. A 56-year-old foundry repair man, for example, said: "If you cannot manage because the work is too heavy, I think 'the Company' will take care of it. I have noticed that some people have gotten easier tasks as they get older."

The many different types of answers and levels of uncertainty about which transitions can actually be made indicate that they are in the form of individualized arrangements and not based on formal routines, if at all possible. There are no established practices expressing that the company values the competences of older employees. The demand for tasks adapted to the individual is left to the individual to handle. The comments indicate that these types of transitions are not socially expected or recognized. Using Zerubavel's (1981) terminology, they can be described as a bio-temporal order construction with a focus on physical bodies, rather than as incorporated in the socio-temporal order with its relation to social structures and processes in the organization. Social processes are, in other words, redefined as a matter of individual physical bodies.

The analyzed material further shows that the exclusion of alternative tasks from the socio-temporal order has emerged over time, as expressed in the following:

> 'If you're working here, there aren't that many alternatives but we follow the rules of "the Company". We cannot offer someone an easier position before retirement the way we used to do. All those types of jobs have been removed. When I was younger there were lots of such jobs. If my body says, "No", there's not much I can do, unfortunately. If that's the case, in the end you'll have to stop working because we don't have those types of jobs any more. We're a joint-stock company and if one thing crashes everything crashes. We went bankrupt in the past and 100 people lost their jobs, 30 got to stay. There's no room in the budget for easier jobs, so you have to bring it up with the HR department. ... It's hard to find retreat positions today. It used to be easier, and people could do more simple things like sweeping the floors or cleaning.' (Man, 59 years old, foreman at the foundry)

The quotation suggests that it has been possible to get physically easier work tasks but that this no longer applies for economic reasons. The absence of formal routines supporting older employees corresponds with previous reports showing that the majority of employers in most countries lack measures to retain and recruit older workers (Walker, 2005; Van Dalen et al 2009; Jensen and Møberg, 2012). The argument that this is due to economic reasons projects the company as an anorectic organization where staffing is continuously reduced in relation to the demand of the products in question. On the basis of descriptions of downsizing as a globally established practice since the 1980s (Radnor and Boaden, 2004; Tyler and Wilkinson, 2007), this can be seen more as a manifestation of contemporary corporate strategies than as a characteristic feature of this company.

In the earlier quotation, it is further stated that tasks previously allocated to older employees were simple tasks like cleaning and sweeping the floors, which is tantamount to downward mobility and not a way to take advantage of the professional skills developed during a life of work experience. This is a trend also noted in previous studies (Riach, 2007; Wilkinson and Ferraro, 2012). The reason that the company previously offered other tasks to older workers was not therefore that there was a different and more positive view of their competences than today, or that active efforts were made to benefit from their knowledge and experiences.

Taken together, the results indicate an individualization of risks for older workers in this company, where the employer's previous responsibility for supporting older workers' continued participation in the workplace through reallocation of tasks, based on a socio-temporal order over time, has been turned into a problem for the individual, and justified on economic grounds.

Manifestations of precarization

The results also show that for some groups of employees there is an added element of insecurity in terms of employment and work tasks.

In the narratives of the respondents employed by staffing agencies there is a recurring theme of lack of support in the organization and of being in a situation of having to have the strength to perform tasks, as in the following statements: "There are no retreat positions for those of us who come from staffing agencies" and "Those who work on the assembly line, they are being looked after, of course. But those of us with temporary positions, we don't have a line of retreat. Yes, I know that there are different types of jobs for employees and people from staffing agencies." A further example of the perceived absence of support for this group is the following:

'I actually don't know what the situation is like today with retreat positions. Back in time, you would always get easier work tasks when you got older. But I don't think it's like that any more. Nowadays, I think they will take you to an old people's home if you can't manage. It's a little bit more like that now. At least if you're hired through a staffing agency.' (Man, 63 years old, fitter and welder)

The quote indicates that those who are hired through staffing agencies only have a place in the organization as long as they can perform what they have been hired to do. The phrase "if you can't manage" suggests that the responsibility for future work rests with the individual, as discussed earlier.

Some of the staff in this company were in charge of installing the machines that the company manufactures on site in other countries, which meant that they were expected to have around 150 travelling days per year, which was considered difficult to combine with family life and also entails vulnerability if they should be taken ill abroad. Stories were told about employees changing jobs when they or a family member were ill. This type of work also meant insecurity about future work, not least among workers employed for limited periods and jobs. A travelling consultant, employed through a staffing agency, described the situation in this way: "If I can't travel any more, I will have to find another job. After all, my job is to travel."

For the staffing agency, and other temporary employees, insecurity was related to whether or not there would be a continued need of their services. A 63-year-old man gave an example of this when reflecting on how long he was planning to work: "I plan to continue working until they don't want me any more."

The empirical material displays the respondents' general sense of insecurity concerning working at an older age with physically demanding jobs in this company without formal procedures supporting elderly people who have difficulty handling their tasks and where the need to get other tasks is presented as an individual problem. Results also indicate that precarization is expanding in different degrees among various employee groups. For staffing agency employees, insecurity also included narrowly defined tasks and periods of employment, and the knowledge that there may be no work beyond the fixed-term employment.

Conclusion

This chapter has looked at work mobility among men in physically demanding workplaces, and its temporal organizing. By problematizing the work mobilities that are regarded as possible, expected and coveted, I have pointed to the presence of temporal regimes and their key role in the work organization and to the employees' opportunities to continue working at an older age. Together, the results show the need for more thorough studies of how work ability relates to the physical aspects of the workplace as well as to its social organizing, including temporal practices. They also show the fruitfulness of bringing time and temporality into socio-gerontological studies and into sociology of age (Krekula and Johansson, 2017).

Drawing on the idea of temporal organization as a power practice, I have illustrated that internal work mobility is surrounded by normative assumptions, which, if violated, also affect individuals' well-being. Consequently, I have referred to the assumptions as temporal regimes and shown that they create an age normality against which the older workers are marked as problematic in terms of mobility in the organization. The chapter thus contributes to research on age relations and sheds light on the fruitfulness of identifying age groups that constitute age normality and the practices and discourses that produce age normality through concurrent marking of other age groups (Krekula et al 2017b). The study also supports previous arguments that age-based privileges are constructed through notions of time (Krekula and Johansson, 2017; Krekula et al 2017b) and contributes to such research by illustrating the disciplining that is formed through the expectation of timing transitions with temporal norms in the workplace. By demonstrating how the temporal processes relate to disciplining the employees, the chapter also contributes to placing the debate on extended working life in a contemporary social analysis. The results illustrate that the local socio-temporal order make up a disciplining element of the employees as they, from an early stage of their working life, are pressured to plan and act to create a safer future for themselves. In this material, two aspects of disciplining appear: in relation to feared ageism and to expected physical limitations. The results display the place ageism has in work organizations. The processes discussed here, in which fear of ageism creates disciplining, emphasize the central position which ageism can have in neoliberal governance by creating social insecurity among older workers (cf Butler, 2015; Lorey, 2015).

The study also shows that over time insecurity has been individualized and that this change is not based on a changed perception of elderly people, but rather on developed economic corporate strategies. When alternative tasks are offered to older workers, it represents a downward mobility, as shown by previous studies (Riach, 2007; Wilkinson and Ferraro, 2012). Organizing in the studied work organization, in other words, is narrowly based on the notion that older workers' bodies, knowledge and skills are problematic, that is, a marking of old age. This supports Standing's (2011) claim that older workers run a greater risk of precarization, emphasizing that this ultimately depends on the organizing of work on the basis of younger ages as the norm. These results indicate that we need more knowledge of the organizing of workplaces and age normality related to older workers' well-being and retirement strategies.

Earlier, we have also seen that individualization of risk in old age is highly related to the use of staffing agencies and the dismantling of corporate responsibility. Against the backdrop of increasing insecure employment in terms of pension and guaranteed hours (OECD, 2015), the results are noteworthy. They indicate a need to highlight company strategies and what they mean from an age perspective; not least to older workers. Extensive research has shown that the political ambition to implement extended working life has different consequences for groups of elderly people, and that, for instance, gender (Loretto and Vickerstaff, 2013), socio-demographic variables and sectoral composition of the economy (Phillipson and Smith, 2005) and care of next of kin (Lewis, 2007; Dewilde, 2012) are central factors. In addition, this study shows that the varying employment terms and vulnerability of older workers are also created through local practices and routines in work organizations. Like other studies (Hasselhorn and Apt, 2015; Krekula and Vickerstaff, 2017; Phillipson, 2019), this study shows the need to introduce organizational practices and corporate strategies in the debate on extended working life.

At the overall level, the study points to the importance of workplace organizing to the political initiatives for extended working life. Against the background of the mechanisms of workplace organizing, the policies describing older workers' retirement trends as self-serving and problematic (for a discussion, see Krekula and Vickerstaff, 2017) appear as simplified and uninformed about workplace terms for older workers. The rhetoric contributes to concealing the central role that organizational processes play in creating insecurity among older workers, and in normalizing social insecurity related to extended working life.

References

Adam, B., Whipp, R. and Sabelis, I. (2008) 'Choreographing time and management: traditions, developments, and opportunities', in Whipp, R., Adams, B. and Sabelis, I. (eds) *Making Time. Time and Management in Modern Organizations*, New York, NY: Oxford University Press, pp 1–30.

Andersson, R. (2015) 'Vem kan Jobba till 67? En Rapport om Medelpensioneringsåldern i olika LO yrken' [online], Stockholm: The Swedish Trade Union Confederation (LO), available at: www.lo.se/home/lo/res.nsf/vRes/lo_fakta_1366027478784_vem_kan_jobba_till_67_pdf/$File/Vem_kan_jobba_till_67.pdf [accessed 27 September 2021].

Benedick, M. Jr., Brown, L.E. and Wall, K. (1999) 'No foot in the door: an experimental study of employment discrimination against older workers', *Journal of Aging & Social Policy*, 10: 5–23.

Bennington, L. (2001) 'Age discrimination: converging evidence from four Australian studies', *Employee Responsibilities and Rights Journal*, 13: 125–34.

Berger, P.L. and Luckmann, T. (1967) *The Social Construction of Reality*, Harmondsworth: Penguin.

Bidwell, M. and Briscoe, F. (2010) 'The dynamics of interorganizational careers', *Organization Science*, 21: 1034–53.

Blaikie, N. (2007) *Approaches to Social Enquiry. Advancing Knowledge*, Cambridge: Polity.

Blekesaune, M. and Solem, P.E. (2005) 'Working conditions and early retirement. A prospective study of retirement behavior', *Research on Aging*, 27: 3–30.

Brekhus, W. (1996) 'Social marking and the mental coloring of identity: sexual identity construction and maintenance in the United States', *Sociological Forum*, 11: 497–522.

Brekhus, W. (1998) 'A sociology of the unmarked: redirecting our focus', *Sociological Theory*, 16: 34–51.

Butler, J. (2015) 'Foreword', in Lorey, I., *State of Insecurity. Government of the Precarious*, London: Verso Futures, pp vii–xi.

Butler, R.N. (1969) 'Age-ism: another form of bigotry', *The Gerontologist*, 9: 243–6.

Cadiz, D.M. (2010) *The Effects of Ageism Climates and Core Self-evaluations on Nurses' Turnover Intentions, Organizational Commitment, and Work Engagement*, Ann Arbor, MI: Portland State University.

Cahill, K., Giandrea, M. and Quinn, J. (2015) 'Retirement patterns and the macroeconomy, 1992–2010: the prevalence and determinants of bridge jobs, phased retirement, and reentry among three recent cohorts of older Americans', *The Gerontologist*, 55: 384–403.

Calasanti, T. (2003) 'Theorizing age relations', in Biggs, S., Lowenstein, A. and Hendricks, J. (eds) *The Need for Theory: Critical Approaches to Social Gerontology*, Amityville, NY: Baywood, pp 199–218.

Chan, S. and Stevens, A.H. (2001) 'Job loss and employment patterns of older workers', *Journal of Labor Economics*, 19: 484–521.

Cleveland, J., Shore, I. and Murphy, K. (1997) 'Person and context oriented perceptual age measures', *Journal of Organizational Behavior*, 18: 239–51.

Creswell, J.W. (1998) *Qualitative Inquiry and Research Design*, London: Sage.

Czarniawska, B. (2014) *A Theory of Organizing*, Cheltenham: Edward Elgar Publishing.

Dewilde, C. (2012) 'Lifecourse determinants and incomes in retirement: Belgium and the United Kingdom compared', *Ageing and Society*, 32: 587–615.

Dvorkin, M. and Shell, H. (2015) *A Cross-country Comparison of Labor Force Participation*, Federal Reserve Bank of St. Louis Economic Synopses 17 [online], available at: https://research.stlouisfed.org/publications/econo mic-synopses/2015/07/31/a-cross-country-comparison-of-labor-force-participation/ [accessed 27 September 2021].

European Commission (2009) *Dealing with the Impact of an Ageing Population in the EU*, Brussels: European Commission [online], available at: www. cedefop.europa.eu/en/news-and-press/news/dealing-impact-ageing-pop ulation-eu-2009-ageing-report [accessed 27 September 2021].

Eurostat (2016) *Employment Statistics* [online], available at: http://ec.eur opa.eu/eurostat/statistics-explained/index.php/Employment_statistics [accessed 27 September 2021].

Fevre, R. (2011) 'Still on the scrapheap? The meaning and characteristics of unemployment in prosperous welfare states', *Work, Employment and Society*, 25: 1–9.

Fineman, S. (2011) *Organizing Age*, Oxford: Oxford University Press.

Foucault, M. (1991) *Discipline and Punish: The Birth of the Prison*, London: Penguin Books.

Foucault, M. (2004) *Society Must Be Defended: Lectures at the Collège de France, 1975–76*, New York, NY: Picador.

Gee, G., Pavalko, E.K. and Long, J.S. (2007) 'Age, cohort and perceived age discrimination: using the life course to assess self-reported age discrimination', *Social Forces*, 86: 265–90.

Groot, W. and Verberne, M. (1997) 'Aging, job mobility, and compensation', *Oxford Economic Papers*, 49: 380–403.

Guest, G., MacQueen, K.M. and Namey, E.E. (2012) *Applied Thematic Analysis*, London: Sage.

Hasselhorn, H.M. and Apt, W. (2015) *Understanding Employment Participation of Older Workers: Creating a Knowledge Base for Future Labour Market Challenges*, Research Report. Berlin: Federal Ministry of Labour and Social Affairs (BMAS) and Federal Institute for Occupational Safety and Health (BAuA) [online], available at: www.jp-demographic.eu/wp-content/uplo ads/2015/07/JPIUEP_Brochure.pdf [accessed 27 September 2021].

Heller, A. (1985) *The Power of Shame: A Rational Perspective*, London: Routledge & Kegan.

Henkens, K., Sprengers, M. and Tazelaar, F. (1996) 'Unemployment and the older worker in The Netherlands: re-entry into the labour force or resignation', *Ageing and Society*, 16: 561–78.

Hirsch, B.T., MacPherson, D.A. and Hardy, M.A. (2000) 'Occupational age structure and access for older workers', *Industrial and Labor Relations Review*, 53: 401–18.

Ilmarinen, J. (1997) 'Aging and work – coping with strengths and weaknesses', *Scandinavian Journal of Work, Environment and Health*, 23: 3–5.

Ilmarinen, J. (2006) 'The ageing workforce – challenges for occupational health', *Occupational Medicine*, 56: 362–4.

Ilmarinen, J. and Ilmarinen, V. (2015) 'Work ability and aging', in Finkelstein, L.M., Truxillo, D.M., Fraccaroli, F. and Kanfer, R. (eds) *Facing the Challenges of a Multi-age Workforce: A Use-inspired Approach*, New York, NY: Routledge, pp 134–56.

James, J.B., Matz-Costa, C. and Smyer, M.A. (2016) 'Retirement security: it's not just about the money', *American Psychologist*, 71: 334–44.

Jensen, P.H. and Møberg, R.J. (2012) 'Age management in Danish companies: what, how and how much?', *Nordic Journal of Working Life Studies*, 2: 49–65.

Johnson, R.W. and Kawachi, J. (2007) *Job Changes at Older Ages: Effects on Wages, Benefits, and Other Job Attributes*, The Urban Institute, The Retirement Project Discussion Paper 07-03 [online], available at: http:// webarchive.urban.org/UploadedPDF/311435_Job_Changes.pdf [accessed 27 September 2021].

Kail, B.L. and Warner, D.F. (2013) 'Leaving retirement: age-graded relative risks of transitioning back to work or dying', *Population Research and Policy Review*, 32: 159–82.

Kalavar, J.M. (2001) 'Examining ageism: do male and female college students differ?', *Educational Gerontology*, 27: 779–811.

Katz, S. (2000) 'Busy bodies. Activity, aging and the management of everyday life', *Journal of Aging Studies*, 14: 135–52.

Krekula, C. (2009) 'Age coding: on age-based practices of distinction', *International Journal of Ageing and Later Life*, 4(2): 7–31.

Krekula, C. and Johansson, B. (2017) 'Introduktion', in Krekula, C. and Johansson, B. (eds) *Kritiska Åldersstudier*, Malmö, Sweden: Studentlitteratur.

Krekula, C. and Vickerstaff, S. (2017) '*Theoretical and conceptual issues in the extending working lives agenda*', in Ní Léime, A., Street, D., Vickerstaff, S., Krekula, C. and Loretto, W. (eds) *Gender, Ageing and Extended Working Life: Cross-national Perspectives*, London: Policy Press, pp 27–52.

Krekula, C., Engström, L.-E. and Alvinius, A. (2017a) 'Sweden: an extended working life policy which neglects gender and health considerations', in Ní Léime, A., Street, D., Vickerstaff, S., Krekula, C. and Loretto, W. (eds) *Gender, Ageing and Extended Working Life: Cross-national Perspectives*, Bristol: Policy Press, pp 157–74.

Krekula, C., Arvidson, M., Heikkinen, S., Henriksson, A. and Olsson, E. (2017b) 'On grey dancing: constructions of age-normality through choreography and temporal codes', *Journal of Aging Studies*, 42C: 38–45.

Krekula, C., Nikander, P. and Wilinska, M. (2018) 'Multiple marginalisations based on age. Gendered ageism and beyond', in Ayalon, L. and Tesch-Roemer, C. (eds) *Contemporary Perspectives on Ageism*, New York, NY: Springer, pp 33–50.

Larsen, M. (2008) 'Does quality of work life affect men and women's retirement planning differently?', *Applied Research in Quality of Life*, 3: 23–42.

Lawrence, B.S. (1988) 'New wrinkles in the theory of age: demography, norms, and performance rating', *Academy of Management Journal*, 31: 309–37.

Lawrence, B. (2011) 'The Hughes Award Lecture: who is they? Inquiries into how individuals construe social context', *Human Relations*, 64: 749–73.

Laz, C. (1998) 'Act your age', *Sociological Forum*, 13: 85–113.

Lewis, J. (2002) 'Gender and welfare state change', *European Societies*, 4: 331–57.

Lewis, J. (2007) 'Gender, ageing and the "new social settlement": the importance of developing a holistic approach to care policies', *Current Sociology*, 55: 271–86.

Lewis, J. and Giullari, S. (2005) 'The adult worker model family, gender equality and care: the search for new policy principles and the possibilities and problems of a capabilities approach', *Economy and Society*, 34: 76–104.

Loretto, W. and Vickerstaff, S. (2013) 'The domestic and gendered context for retirement', *Human Relations*, 66: 65–86.

Loretto, W., Duncan, C. and White, P.J. (2000) 'Ageism and employment: controversies, ambiguities and younger people's perceptions', *Ageing and Society*, 20: 279–302.

Lorey, I. (2015) *State of Insecurity. Government of the Precarious*, London: Verso Futures.

Lund, T. and Villadsen, E. (2005) 'Who retires early and why? Determinants of early retirement pension among Danish employees 57–62 years', *European Journal of Ageing*, 2: 275–80.

Maestas, N. (2010) 'Back to work: expectations and realizations of work after retirement', *Journal of Human Resources*, 45: 718–48.

Martin, N.H. and Strauss, A.L. (1956) 'Patterns of mobility within industrial organizations', *The Journal of Business*, 29: 101–10.

Nelson, T.D. (2005) 'Ageism: prejudice against our feared future self', *Journal of Social Issues*, 61: 207–21.

Neumark, D. (2009) 'The age discrimination in employment act and the challenge of population aging', *Research on Aging*, 31: 41–68.

Nilsson, K. (2016) 'Conceptualisation of ageing in relation to factors of importance for extending working life – a review', *Scandinavian Journal of Public Health*, 44: 490–505.

OECD (Organisation for Economic Co-operation and Development) (2015) *Employment Outlook 2015*, Paris: OECD Publishing.

Phillipson, C. (2019) ' "Fuller" or "extended" working lives? Critical perspectives on changing transitions from work to retirement', *Ageing and Society*, 39: 629–50.

Phillipson, C. and Smith, A. (2005) *Extending Working Life: A Review of the Research Literature* (Research Report No. 299), London: Department for Work and Pensions [online], available at: http://dwp.gov.uk/asd/asd5/rpo rts2005-2006/rrep299.pdf [accessed 27 September 2021].

Pink, S. (2001) *Doing Visual Ethnography: Images, Media and Representation in Research*, London: Sage.

Pohrt, A. and Hasselhorn, H.M. (2015) 'Work factors', in Hasselhorn, H.M. and Apt, W. (eds) *Understanding Employment Participation of Older Workers: Creating a Knowledge Base for Future Labour Market Challenges*, Research Report, Berlin: Federal Ministry of Labour and Social Affairs (BMAS) and Federal Institute for Occupational Safety and Health (BAuA), pp 48–9.

Quintens, L. and Matthyssens, P. (2010) 'Involving the process dimensions of time in case-based research', *Industrial Marketing Management*, 39: 91–9.

Radnor, Z.J. and Boaden, R. (2004) 'Developing an understanding of corporate anorexia', *International Journal of Operations & Production Management*, 24: 424–40.

Riach, K. (2007) ' "Othering" older worker identity in recruitment', *Human Relations*, 60: 1701–26.

Riach, K. (2009) 'Managing "difference": understanding age diversity in practice', *Human Resource Management Journal*, 19: 319–35.

Rosenfeld, R.A. (1992) 'Job mobility and career processes', *Annual Review of Sociology*, 18: 36–61.

Scheff, T.J. (1990) *Microsociology: Discourse, Emotion, and Social Structure*, Chicago, IL: The University of Chicago Press.

Schwartz, D.A. and Kleiner, B.H. (1999) 'The relationship between age and employment opportunities', *Equal Opportunities International*, 18: 105–10.

Shore, L.M., Cleveland, J.N. and Goldberg, C.B. (2003) 'Work attitudes and decisions as a function of manager age and employee age', *Journal of Applied Psychology*, 88: 529–37.

Smeaton, D. and White, M. (2016) 'The growing discontents of older British employees: extended working life at risk from quality of working life', *Social Policy and Society*, 15: 369–85.

Soidre, T. (2005) 'Retirement-age preferences of women and men aged 55–64 years in Sweden', *Ageing and Society*, 25: 943–63.

Sonnega, A., Helppie McFall, B. and Willis, R.J. (2016) *Occupational Transitions at Older Ages: What Moves are People Making?*, Michigan Retirement Research Center, Working Paper WP 2016-352 [online], available at: https://papers.ssrn.com/sol3/papers.cfm?abstract_id=2902 736 [accessed 27 September 2021].

SOU (2013) Åtgärder för ett Längre Arbetsliv. Slutbetänkande av Pensionsåldersutredningen, 2013:25, Stockholm: SOU.

Standing, G. (2011) *The Precariat. The New Dangerous Class*, London: Bloomsbury Academic.

Statistics Sweden (2016) Äldre i Befolkningen [online], available at: www.scb.se/sv_/Hitta-statistik/Statistik-efter-amne/Befolkning/Befolkning ens-sammansattning [accessed 19 September 2018].

Swedish Pensions Agency (2016) *Medelpensioneringsålder och Utträdesålder*, 2016:3, Stockholm: The Swedish Pensions Agency.

Takala, E.-P. and Seitsamo, J. (2015) 'Work ability', in Hasselhorn, H.M. and Apt, W. (eds) *Understanding Employment Participation of Older Workers: Creating a Knowledge Base for Future Labour Market Challenges*, Berlin: Federal Ministry of Labour and Social Affairs (BMAS) and Federal Institute for Occupational Safety and Health (BAuA), pp 52–5.

Thorsen, S., Rugulies, R., Løngaard, K., Borg, V., Thielen, K. and Bjorner, J.B. (2012) 'The association between psychosocial work environment, attitudes towards older workers (ageism) and planned retirement', *International Archives of Occupational and Environmental Health*, 85: 437–45.

Tyler, M. and Wilkinson, A. (2007) 'The tyranny of corporate slenderness: "corporate anorexia" as a metaphor for our age', *Work, Employment and Society*, 21: 537–49.

Van Dalen, H.P. and Henkens, K. (2002) 'Early-retirement reform: can it and will it work?', *Ageing and Society*, 22: 209–31.

Van Dalen, H.P., Henkens, K. and Schippers, J. (2009) 'Dealing with older workers in Europe: a comparative survey of employers' attitudes and actions', *Journal of European Social Policy*, 19: 47–60.

Vickerstaff, S. and Loretto, W. (2017) 'The United Kingdom – a new moral imperative: live longer, work longer', in Ní Léime, A., Street, D., Vickerstaff, S., Krekula, C. and Loretto, W. (eds) *Gender, Ageing and Extended Working Life: Cross-national Perspectives*, Bristol: Policy Press, pp 175–92.

Walker, A. (2005) 'The emergence of age management in Europe', *International Journal of Organisational Behaviour*, 10: 685–97.

Weick, K.E. (1969) *The Social Psychology of Organizing*, New York, NY: McGraw-Hill.

West-Pavlov, R. (2012) *Temporalities*, New York, NY: Routledge.

Wilkinson, J.A. and Ferraro, K.F. (2002) 'Thirty years of ageism research', in Nelson, T.D. (ed) *Ageism: Stereotyping and Prejudice Against Older Persons*, Cambridge, MA: MIT Press, pp 339–58.

Wilkinson, L.R. and Ferraro, K.F. (2012) 'Does occupational mobility influence health among working women? Comparing objective and subjective measures of work trajectories', *Journal of Health and Social Behavior*, 53: 432–47.

World Health Organization (2015) *World Report on Ageing and Health*, Luxembourg: World Health Organization [online], available at: http://apps.who.int/iris/bitstream/10665/186463/1/9789240694811_eng.pdf [accessed 27 September 2021].

Yearta, S.K. and Warr, P. (1995) 'Does age matter?', *Journal of Management Development*, 14(7): 28–35.

Yin, R.K. (2009) *Case Study Research: Design and Methods*, London: Sage.

Zerubavel, E. (1981) *Hidden Rhythms: Schedules and Calendars in Social Life*, Berkeley, CA: University of California Press.

Zerubavel, E. (1987) 'The language of time: toward a semiotics of temporality', *The Sociological Quarterly*, 28: 343–56.

5

Temporary Older Workers in Belgium as a Demonstration of a Paradoxical Situation

Nathalie Burnay

Introduction

In terms of public policy, the Belgian institutional system was historically designed to strongly adhere to the Bismarckian model, which is close to the continental model described by Esping-Andersen (1990) (see Chapter 1). It has functioned through a generous redistribution of income over the life course via cash benefits, the bulk of which (more than 70 per cent at present) are derived from the world of work. It has therefore been designed to protect individuals from large reductions in income when they become excluded from the labour market, either temporarily or permanently (as in the case of retirement). It has undoubtedly been generous, but it has favoured the model of the *male breadwinner* by providing assistance differentially according to gender: cohabitants, predominantly women, systematically receive less generous benefits than heads of household, predominantly men.

In this context, public policy has aimed at increasing employment rates among older workers since the early 2000s. The argument put forth is primarily economic, based on the sustainability of the social welfare system. Indeed, employment rates for seniors in Belgium are still among the lowest in industrialized countries, although they have increased significantly in recent years, albeit to a higher degree among women than men. In 2018, the employment rate among workers aged 55 to 64 years was 50.3 per cent in Belgium, compared to 58.7 per cent for the European Union as a whole. Moreover, the Belgian employment market is also characterized by a high proportion of part-time work at all stages of professional life, including at the end of career. This is particularly true among women: at present, one in two women over 50 years old in Belgium is in part-time employment compared to 13.3 per cent for men in the same age group.

The measures taken by the federal and regional authorities in recent years regarding the end of working life are directly influenced by this objective of increasing employment rates, and clearly subscribe to the paradigm of 'active ageing' (see Chapter 1). This approach is defined as 'helping people stay in charge of their own lives as long as possible as they age and, where possible, [helping them] to contribute to the economy and society' (European Commission, nd). In fact, the extension of professional careers is its primary concern. In terms of employment, it involves the development of national or regional policies to maintain older people in the workforce through a variety of measures, both incentive (for example supplementary training, combating discrimination against seniors) and dissuasive (for example suppression of mechanisms for early departure from the workforce, penalties for ceasing professional activity before the retirement age). The latter are far more numerous and significant, as in most Western countries.

Historic perspective and paradigm shift

For Peter Hall (Hall, 1993), any change in public policy can be categorized according to its degree of importance. He defines three orders of change, with differing effects on the social welfare system. While the first two orders concern only more or less important adjustments to the instruments of social policy, the third order corresponds to a true paradigm shift as defined by Kuhn (Kuhn,1962):

> First and second order change can be seen as cases of 'normal policymaking,' namely of a process that adjusts policy without challenging the overall terms of a given policy paradigm, much like 'normal science.' Third order change, by contrast, is likely to reflect a very different process, marked by the radical changes in the overarching terms of policy discourse associated with a 'paradigm shift. (Hall, 1993, p 279)

In Belgium, there was a real paradigm shift in the early 2000s.

In the mid-1970s, the Belgian social model was affected by the economic crisis. It was shaped by the politically assured desire to encourage early exit from the labour market to support the hiring of young workers (Sanderson, 2015). During the 1970s and 1980s, the rate of unemployment evolved within a context of major industrial upheaval and of large-scale restructuring and downsizing. The government policy to deal with the rising unemployment from about 1975 strongly favoured the young unemployed to the detriment of the older unemployed and even older workers (Simoens, 1980). The government encouraged people over 50 to leave the labour market through early retirement schemes, unemployment payment programmes, medical retirement and career breaks. Additionally, the reinterpretation of certain regulations regarding poor working conditions allowed others to leave work.

In the historical neo-institutionalist paradigm (Stone, 1992; Béland, 2002), the analytical focus is placed on the difficulty of implementing substantial reforms of the retirement system and the powerful resistance encountered by the model of maintaining older people in the workforce. The concept of 'path dependence' (Pierson, 2000) provides an insight into these forms of resistance to change. From a more sociological perspective, normative frameworks are identified as true obstacles to attempted change. Guillemard (2003) speaks of a veritable culture of early retirement in countries like Belgium, France and Germany, demonstrating how today's normative frameworks were shaped by decisions made in the 1970s and how they have become very difficult to change. International comparisons are used to consolidate these reflections by showing how public policies concerning the end of working life stem from differing conceptions of the welfare state (Ney, 2005; Guillemard, 2010). The development of a political model characterized by 'marginalisation and relegation' (Guillemard, 2003) has consequences for the resolution of conflicts generated, for example, in the case of large-scale lay-offs, but also for the way in which early retirements are handled. This approach creates a feeling in the individual that the process is normal and they start to anticipate retirement as a result. We then see a whole culture of early retirement developing as norms and values evolve, which are associated with the age of the employee. Social norms develop alongside the practice of early retirement, which is more and more common, as well as the perceived legitimacy of these practices. The creation of acknowledged procedures and practices seals the social contract between the state, the worker (and their union) and the employer.

However, despite the strength of the path of dependency, we can see a real change in the social perception and the place of workers linked to their age (Sanderson and Burnay, 2017), which ultimately leads to a shift of paradigm. Indeed, for 20 years now, international organizations have been concerned about the viability of pension systems and their ability to achieve their objectives. In Belgium, like in the European Union, the government introduced, in the beginning of the 2000s, a series of measures aimed at encouraging older people to remain in or to re-enter the labour market. In fact, these transformations obviously raise questions about the relationship between older workers and social justice and correspond with the expansion of liberalism. Justice, within this context, demands that economic rewards and societal resources are linked to ambition, effort and prudent exercise of individual choice, rather than, for example, to the citizen status

(Armstrong, 2006 quoted by Brodie, 2007). This model also assigns personal responsibilities rather than collective solutions to social problems (Beck and Beck-Gernsheim, 2002; Brodie, 2007).

Nevertheless, if on the one hand seniors are increasingly obliged to remain in the job market, on the other hand they can encounter real difficulties in doing so. These difficulties include collective redundancies focused on seniors, indirect discrimination in the workplace, difficulties in returning to the workforce and lack of training towards the end of working life (Burnay, 2011). Older workers are thus put in a paradoxical situation, accentuated by an end of career that is increasingly punctuated by health problems (de Zwart et al 1997; Jolivet and Volkoff, 2016), notably related to a harshening of working conditions (Carayon and Zijlstra, 1999; Askenazy et al 2007; Barnay, 2016).

It is in this difficult context, where the older worker is caught between strategies of inclusion and exclusion, that our research is situated. Although the situation of working for a temporary employment agency at the end of a career is still relatively rare, albeit growing, it illustrates the difficulty that older workers experience in responding to policies that extend the working life. The purpose of this chapter is to show how this increase in temporary workers is the result of the contraction of the labour market and the evolution of public policies.

Evolution of temporary workers in Belgium

Although working for a temporary employment agency at the end of a career is still fairly uncommon, it highlights the difficulties older workers experience when confronted with policies that extend the working life. Moreover, temporary employment also reveals significant normative transformations concerning the organization of work. By temporary work, we mean situations where an individual is employed by an agency to work temporarily in a business or an industry. In Belgium, only approved temporary employment agencies can supply workers to businesses and industries. The use of temporary employment among young workers is also legitimized in the wider objective of eventually achieving stable and long-term employment contracts.

The sector of temporary employment agencies in Belgium has been growing steadily for more than 20 years (with the exception of a significant decrease during the 2008 financial crisis), and it accounts for an expanding part of the Belgian economy. According to the annual reports of Federgon (the federation of human resources service providers), more than 580,000 people – approximately one in eight economically active people in Belgium – did at least one day of work for a temporary employment agency in 2015, for a total of 197 million hours worked (Federgon, 2018). Sixty per cent of employees in the sector are men and 40 per cent are women (Conseil supérieur de l'emploi, 2015). In terms of income, the volume of activity in the sector more than doubled between 1998 and 2012 (Valenduc, 2012).

If working for temporary employment agencies is seen primarily as a path to integration into the workforce for young people, it is also a form of employment that is increasingly being performed by seniors. In 2003, 7.8 per cent of workers in the sector were aged 45 years and above. Ten years later, in 2013, the figure had reached 15 per cent (Forem, 2013). In 2016, 16.7 per cent of temporary workers were over the age of 45 (Federgon, 2017), of whom 45 per cent had a very low level of qualification, but approximately 20 per cent had a very strong educational background. Approximately 25 per cent had held a permanent position before turning to temporary work. The percentage of temporary workers aged over 45 has continued to rise in recent years, reaching 19.3 per cent in 2020 (Federgon, 2022). This significant increase, coupled with the toughening of policies concerning end-of-career employment, means that examining senior temporary work is essential to understand the present professional realities of older workers in Belgium.

Data

This chapter is based on a qualitative analysis of semi-directed interviews carried out in Wallonia (the southern French-speaking part of Belgium). The main purpose is to understand the social contexts and the life experiences of the individuals interviewed as well as the meaning they give to their actions. We assume that the results would have been similar in Flanders and Brussels because the work constraints and opportunities affecting older workers are still very comparable, even though employment policies are now regionalized.

Sampling method

The data collected are based on 36 semi-structured interviews conducted between March 2014 and September 2015. In general, the interviews lasted between 45 and 90 minutes. They were conducted by two researchers (master's level) under the supervision of the author in two temporary employment agencies:

- an agency oriented more towards providing temporary jobs to unskilled workers; and
- an agency oriented towards better-educated and more highly skilled temporary workers.

Initially, the personnel of the temporary employment agencies contacted the interviewees to obtain their consent to participate in the study. Subsequently, the researchers contacted the interviewees directly to set up an appointment. The interviews were conducted at the agencies (but without the presence of the agency personnel) or at the interviewees' homes. The interviews were recorded with the consent of the interviewees. All names have been modified in order to guarantee the interviewees' anonymity.

The interview grid was tested beforehand by researchers and was adapted according to the feedback received in order to optimize it for the working environment of this specific population. Once the interview grid was stabilized, no further changes were made; thus, the 36 interviews were conducted using the same interview grid. Interviews took the form of a conversation that covered all of the topics in the interview guide, while guaranteeing the interviewee maximal freedom of expression. Several team meetings were also organized in order to ensure a degree of consistency among the interviews collected and reliability of the interview guide. Each interview was transcribed in its entirety to permit the closest possible analysis of its discourse. The researchers also used an interview notebook to record remarks or observations regarding the interview situation.

The sample was constructed based on criteria of gender and age and it included 20 men and 16 women between 45 and 67 years of age. The double principle of diversification of profiles and saturation of data was respected (see Table 5.1). The interview grid included the following themes:

- socio-demographic and professional characteristics;
- professional and family history;
- commitment to work and meaning of work;
- representations of temporary work;
- construction of temporalities;
- work-life balance;
- age and its inscription in the life course.

Table 5.1: Socio-demographic profile of the sample of temporary workers

		Number of interviews	
		Men	**Women**
Age	From 45 to 50	3	5
	From 51 to 55	7	5
	From 56 to 60	5	4
	Over 60	5	2
Educational level	Low level	8	4
	Intermediate level	6	7
	High level	6	5
	Total	20	16

This research is based on an inductive process and a thematic qualitative analysis. The main objective is to understand the social contexts and life experiences of the respondents and the meaning they give to their actions.

Findings

You are too old!

Many authors have called attention to the presence of discrimination against older workers in the job market. The term 'ageism', which first appeared in the United States in 1969, is defined as the process through which prejudices and discrimination form against individuals simply because they are older. At the professional level, two kinds of discrimination based on age can be identified: direct and indirect discrimination (Leleu, 2001).

Direct discrimination refers to measures that target older workers solely because of their age. For example, one would speak of direct discrimination when age limits appear in offers of employment or training, or when retirement age is imposed as a limit after which it is forbidden to work. In Belgium, an anti-discrimination law was enacted in 2003 (the law of 25 February 2003) which introduced mechanisms to protect workers. In the recruitment of personnel, for example, it is prohibited to fix a maximum age limit after which candidates will no longer be considered for hiring. However, direct discrimination is still present in the labour market, even if it is more hidden than before.

Indirect discrimination refers to measures that, although they are not explicitly linked to age, affect older workers disproportionately and negatively in comparison to other age groups (Drury, 1993). Stereotypes or prejudices that may influence the selection of a candidate for employment are considered as forms of indirect discrimination, since they may affect the attitudes and behaviour of the people at whom they are directed as well as those of the people holding them. These forms of discrimination remain operative (Drury, 1993) even when governments attempt to fight them through legislation.

Indirect discrimination is difficult to identify in a company's daily functioning. Nevertheless, a link can be established between discriminatory actions and representations of the senior. Many investigations of the social stereotypes concerning older workers have been carried out since the first American studies in the 1950s (Kirchner et al 1952). These mental images condition our individual representations of reality, thereby affecting the decisions we make. A number of different studies have been able to demonstrate how our representations of the senior are structured negatively: older workers are seen as being in poorer physical and mental health (Taylor and Walker, 1994; Gaillard and Desmette, 2010), being slower to accept change (Taylor and Walker, 1994; McGregor and Gray, 2002), and having difficulty in relating to young people (Taylor and Walker, 1994; Hassell and Perrewe, 1995), in learning (Itzin and Phillipson, 1993; Loretto and White, 2006; Cheung et al 2011), and in mastering new technologies (Van Dalen et al 2010). They are also seen as having fewer or outdated skills and competencies (Maurer et al 2008) and as being less interested in new challenges (Kluge and Krings, 2008).

Interviews of temporary workers approaching retirement age revealed the indirect discrimination that they suffered, but also direct discrimination despite the fact this is illegal. These people were aware of how their age constituted a significant barrier to their entry into the workforce, particularly when they only had a low educational level, or their skills were not in demand. They understood that employers refused to hire them because of their age, whether or not this was explicitly stated. They were well aware that their advancing age was against them, hindering their professional development:

'Yes, you see, I, that's how it is. Like, at the beginning, I didn't find [work], because I, after all, there's still a certain barrier with age, once you're 50 or older. In fact, recently, I [tried] again, I replied to an offer on the Internet, for a job, um, half-time, which suited me, here in Wavre, very close to home, 200 m from home, and they didn't want to accept me because I'm 54 years old. Too old.' (Paul, 54 years old, intermediate level education)

'And, um … it's already very difficult, when you're middle-aged, after 50 years, they penalize us too because they think of us as very elderly: "Finding work is difficult at your age, you won't be able to find work." And, um, I think that at that point there are a lot of people who give up, but the morale counts.' (Pierre Olivier, 52 years old, high level education)

'Oh, there's still disappointment when you make it that far into the interview, when you get through a first preselection interview and then they tell you okay, you'll go on to a second interview, and then during the second interview they tell you that anyway the problem is your age. Well, now, I've got used to the idea; there's nothing to be done about it, so, wanting … it's not that I want to be, that's not what I want to say, but the fact is, well, it's something that I know. My handicap is age, and my advantage is my practical knowledge.' (Sonia, 48 years old, high level education)

These results are consistent with the analysis of the Federal Centre against Discrimination (Unia). In the 2017 report, there were more than 500 open files regarding discrimination in the labour market in Belgium, 27 per cent of which concerned age (Unia, 2018). In addition, this trend has been increasing significantly over the last few years: there were 57 files in 2013 compared to 108 in 2017. These results do not necessarily mean that the situation has deteriorated, but perhaps also that seniors are more confident about making age discrimination complaints to this federal centre. In 2012, research by Unia, in partnership with the University of Leuven, demonstrated the strength of discrimination that occurs in the hiring process in Belgium. Researchers responded to 854 job advertisements. For each post, two CVs were sent, one for a 47-year-old candidate and the other for a 35-year-old. Results showed the eldest applicant had been invited to an interview seven to eight times less than the youngest (Unia, 2019). These Belgian analyses highlight the persistence of age discrimination in the labour market, not only during the hiring process but also throughout the individual's career. They are consistent with an important scientific literature on this phenomenon (Loretto and White, 2006; Kluge and Krings, 2008; Cheung et al 2011; Abrams et al 2016).

Reactions to such discrimination are multiple and depend on the resources that can be mobilized by the individual, family configurations and the symbolic weight of work in the life course. Three different reactions can be identified.

Some workers have experienced a very precarious life course. They have few qualifications and have never managed to enter the labour market on a long-term basis. Without temporary work, these workers would be unemployed. They are too young to leave the labour market, but they do not have the skills to get a permanent job. They are stuck between two statuses, and temporary work is therefore the only way of staying in the labour market; working is particularly important in a male breadwinner model society where employment is a source of social identity, especially for men. Indeed, not having a job is not only a financial problem, but also more a problem of personal and social identity. In this model, only the job allows one to define oneself positively. In this sense, discrimination against them complicates their already fragile situation:

> 'It's a matter of pride! It's, look, at no matter what country, finally in no matter what culture, African or other, he who doesn't work is the laughing stock of the others. It's really a matter of pride, that is to say that when you work it's your money that you earn, you deserve it, and so you don't let yourself be pushed around in life by people who'll tell you all kinds of rot.' (Serge, 60 years old, low level education)

For others, especially women, discrimination affects their investment in their work. They will gradually refocus their symbolic investment on the private sphere, abandoning their professional careers. They will accept temporary employment 'missions' when these are not too restrictive in terms of the organization of their lives. They can take time for themselves, but above all they will rebuild their identity through care activities, within the family or in charitable associations:

> 'My mum is seriously ill, and my mother-in-law is also seriously ill. And I'm very lucky, thanks to temp work, I can take care of these two ladies who have done so much for me, for my husband, and for my children. And temp work gives me a freedom that I didn't know about when I started.' (Anne, 56 years old, intermediate level education)

For highly skilled or highly educated workers, indirect discrimination is particularly difficult to capture. For some temporary agency workers, this type of employment is the result of a choice, a form of freedom, the possibility of changing jobs, of not feeling trapped in a long-term contract. They have built their entire career in temporary employment, but indirect discrimination also affects them. They like the challenge, but they are aware that discrimination against them is becoming an increasing problem for them. Age restricts the choice of temporary employment missions. These are shorter, fewer and less interesting:

> 'I'm a professional temp [laughs]. And several times I've done long missions and they've offered me a permanent contract after, and I've refused it. Companies don't always understand, eh? "Aren't we good to you?" or "Doesn't what you're doing interest you?" or, um. ... But it's no, but I don't have, I don't feel ready, it's been years that I haven't felt ready to sign a contract, to commit myself. I want to continue to progress, I want to continue to study and to evolve. ... However, now, it's more difficult for me to have new missions and new opportunities. Sometimes, I feel that I'm over.' (Ingrid, 56 years old, high level education)

You have to be active!

Until 2000 and the radical change of public policies, older unemployed people who tried to remain in the labour market found that they had fulfilled their moral contract with society through their many previous years of work; the weight of their professional careers legitimized their abandonment of the search. Society as a whole, through a form of collective responsibility, acknowledged their difficulty in finding work, thereby permitting them to stop trying (Burnay, 2000). Moreover, the public authorities also recognized this near impossibility of returning to the workforce. For example, a special status of 'older unemployed person' was created in 1985, conferring specific rights to unemployed people over 45 years old: these included increased indemnities and exemption from the requirement to present themselves at the unemployment office. This status corresponded in fact to a form of early retirement.

Twenty years later, public policies have undergone fundamental changes, and the pressure exerted by international bodies to increase employment rates among older people has intensified. Early retirement programmes have been substantially reduced, and the dominant paradigm is now one of extending the working life (see Chapter 1). This paradigm shift has manifested itself not only through the restriction of options for early departure from the workforce, but also – and more importantly – through a change in the perceived responsibility for failure. Over the past 20 years, there has arguably been a shift from a collective responsibility ("there isn't enough work for everyone, so it's legitimate that you're not finding work") to an individual responsibility ("it's your fault if you don't find work"). In this context, we observe the emergence of the concept of *employability*: the jobseeker must do everything possible to reintegrate into the workforce (additional training, internships, precarious jobs, and so on). Like unemployed people, older workers must now demonstrate that they are active and that they are truly making an effort to find or keep a job, although indirect discrimination continues to limit their real prospects.

This reversal could explain why the number of temporary workers is significantly increasing in Belgium. Older people have to find a job even in the face of strong stereotypes which ultimately prevent the return to the labour market in the form of a stable job. The only solution is to agree to remain in a precarious status!

In the interviews, many temporary workers expressed their difficulty in finding a stable job due to their age. Often, temporary work is the only means of returning to the labour market:

'That's what's great and difficult at the same time with temping because you're doing jobs you would never have done otherwise. Especially when you're looking for work and you need it to pay your rent and the various expenses.' (Serge, 54 years old, low level education)

'It was the only way to work at the time. So, it's true that at my age I didn't have much chance of finding a stable job, and when I had that opportunity through this person, for him, it was the only solution that was interesting for him, it was to hire me as a temporary worker. It was almost a week from time to time. Obviously this formula suited me because it was always better than nothing.' (Philippe, 56 years old, low level education)

'I accepted to get my head out of the water and not to stay inactive because I know the spiral. I mean, the spiral in a theoretical way. I was out of work for several weeks.' (Monique, 52 years old, intermediate level education)

You are too expensive!

While discrimination continues to be widespread, with age remaining a significant barrier to employment, a new argument has been introduced in recent years, especially by employers' representatives: the cost of labour. In Belgium, salaries increase substantially with age for workers with the status of employees (though not for blue-collar workers). For public employees, for example, a system of grades based on seniority is used to define salaries. In general, when workers change jobs, there are numerous legal constraints that oblige employers to consider their seniority in their previous positions. Hence, it is considerably more expensive for an employer to hire an older worker compared to a younger one. The increasing number of people nearing retirement age resorting to temporary work is directly affected by this constraint: as seniority is not recognized in the same way in temporary work, a senior worker is less expensive in this setting. The advantage for employers is twofold: increased flexibility at a lesser cost:

'I don't really feel it directly. They don't give me any clear reaction to that; employers can't decently do that, they can't discriminate, you see. But you do feel it, there's always an excuse, whatever it might be, and uh, it's always geared towards, um, "You see, we found someone who has a better profile than you," there's always … sometimes they tell me, "You see, in terms of price you're too expensive," but there's not much of that. Employers really have prejudices about workers more than 50 years old, there's a whole list of them.' (Sarah, 58 years old, high level education)

'There are companies that don't want to hire [people] over 50 years because that's too expensive in terms of, um, future pensions, what. And the social contributions cost more for the boss for [people] over 50 than … that's why they came up with the "Activa plans" [encouraging employers to hire long-term unemployed and older people] and everything that goes with them, eh. Precisely to, um … to compensate, what. And so, there, I did feel that.' (Paul, 54 years old, intermediate level education)

The challenge for employers is therefore to break this very strong link between seniority and salary. Thus, in its 2018 annual report, the High Council on Employment (Conseil supérieur de l'emploi)[1] wrote:

While the elimination of the incentives for early departure permits the limitation of the transition to inactivity, it is nevertheless insufficient for maintaining or creating employment opportunities for those aged over 55 years. To do that, it is necessary to preserve their employability, that is to say to ensure the congruent evolution of their productivity and of their salary costs. In Belgium, there is a largely constant positive relationship between salary progression and age [for workers with the status of employees, as this is not the case for blue-collar workers], while in other countries a plateau is reached more rapidly. The ageing of their personnel may therefore pose a problem to Belgian firms in terms of competitiveness and productivity. To avoid this problem, salary progression over the course of a career should depend exclusively on criteria of competencies acquired rather than on considerations of seniority. (Conseil supérieur de l'emploi, 2018, p 16)

This lengthy citation is a clear illustration of what will be at stake in the future Belgian employment policy: the end of the link between seniority and salary. The argument advanced is based on the valorization of work performed – of merit – regardless of age. However, this reasoning also leads to a reduction in the social protection of older people, with the risk of salaries diminishing as retirement approaches.

Conclusion

Public policy developed since the early 2000s in Belgium has fundamentally changed the view of retirement in society and by extension the associated models or norms, thus creating, alongside the then established systems, new approaches which are seen as just as legitimate. Indeed, the recent transformations of the public policies towards older workers fall within the framework of the neoliberal conception and especially the expansion of individualization (see Chapter 1).

From this perspective, individuals are obliged to find a job, even if they are at the end of their career. Failure to meet this requirement is an individual responsibility. Unemployment is then read as an individual inability to activate yourself, to adapt your employability to the constraints of the market. This is obviously a denial of the structural constraints of the labour market, its evolution in the context of globalization and financialization of the economy. In this neoliberal ideology, older workers are faced with two consequences.

First, the risks of the precarious existence increase if the government modifies the conditions for early retirement to raise the level of employment. Second, individualization is increasingly embedded in strategies for public policy reform, which both promote the illusion of choice and have designed the shape of citizens into self-sufficient market actors who provide for their needs and those of their families (Brown, 2005 quoted by Brodie, 2007). This definition obviously fits with the evolution of the older workers' status in Belgium.

Older workers therefore find themselves in a paradoxical position where they are pushed by the political authorities to remain in the labour market but are also victims of forms of discrimination that exclude them from the labour market. Temporary employment is often likely to be the only solution offered to them to combine these contradictory imperatives. Indeed, discrimination against older workers is still relevant in Belgium, particularly for those trying to reintegrate into the workforce after a temporary hiatus. Their chances of finding stable jobs clearly depend on their own competencies and qualifications, but also on external factors over which they have little control. The near disappearance of early retirement has resulted in a financial and symbolic pressure on seniors, pushing them to register with temporary employment agencies.

These forms of discrimination against older workers are linked to negative stereotypes that are well established in companies, but also, and in Belgium in particular, to the increase in salary costs at the end of career. There is a risk that the wages of older workers will be reduced in order to increase the employment rate of this age category. But without fighting against the very present social stereotypes, the risk is a reduction in wages without any real change to the professional situation of older workers and thus contributes to making their situation more precarious.

Belgian statistics continue to show that the great majority of older workers are in stable employment, with more than 90 per cent of those aged 50–65 in permanent positions (Desmette and Vendramin, 2014). However, this is undoubtedly more due to generation than age. The risk of further deterioration in the situation of older workers is significant, given the evolution of the job market and the employment policies enacted by the Belgian authorities. This is a question not only of individual responsibility or lack of initiative, but also of structural conditions that transcend individual destinies. In this way, temporary workers highlight a paradoxical situation for older workers and emphasize the real risk of a deterioration of the living conditions at the end of career.

Note
[1] Council created in 1995, presided by the Federal Minister of Employment, which provides advice and recommendations concerning employment policy. It comprises experts of the employment market.

References

Abrams, D., Swift, H.J. and Drury, L. (2016) 'Old and unemployable? How age-based stereotypes affect willingness to hire job candidates', *Journal of Social Issues*, 72: 105–21.

Armstrong, C. (2006) *Rethinking Equality: The Challenge of Equal Citizenship*, Manchester: Manchester University Press.

Askenazy, P., Carron, D., de Coninck, F. and Gollac, M. (2007) *Organisation et Intensité du Travail*, Octares: Toulouse.

Barnay, T. (2016) 'Health, work and working conditions: a review of the European economic literature', *The European Journal of Health Economics*, 17: 693–709.

Beck, U. and Beck-Gernsheim, E. (2002) *Individualization: Institutionalized Individualism and its Social and Political Consequences*, London: Sage.

Béland, D. (2002) 'Néo-institutionnalisme historique et politiques sociales: une perspective sociologique', *Politique et Sociétés*, 21: 21–39.

Brodie, J. (2007) 'Reforming social justice in neoliberal times', *Studies in Social Justice*, 1: 93–107.

Brown, W. (2005) *Edgework: Critical Essays on Knowledge and Politics*, Princeton, NJ: Princeton University Press.

Burnay, N. (2000) *Chômeurs en fin de Parcours Professionnel*, Paris-Lausanne: Delachaux et Niestlé.

Burnay, N. (2011) 'Ageing at work: between changing social policy patterns and reorganization of work time', *Population Review*, 50: 150–65.

Carayon, P. and Zijlstra, F. (1999) 'Relationship between job control, work pressure and strain: studies in the USA and in the Netherlands', *Work and Stress*, 13: 32–48.

Cheung, C., Kam, P.K. and Man-hung Ngan, R. (2011) 'Age discrimination in the labour market from the perspectives of employers and older workers', *International Social Work*, 54: 118–36.

Conseil supérieur de l'emploi (2015) *Rapport 2015*, Brussels: Conseil supérieur de l'emploi.

Conseil supérieur de l'emploi (2018) *État des Lieux du Marché du Travail en Belgique et dans les Régions*, available at: https://cse.belgique.be/sites/defa ult/files/content/download/files/cse_rapport_juin_2018.pdf [accessed 24 May 2022].

Desmette, D. and Vendramin, P. (2014) 'Bridge employment in Belgium: between an early retirement culture and a concern for work sustainability', in Alcover, C.M., Topa, G., Parry, E., Fraccaroli, F. and Depolo M. (eds) *Bridge Employment – A Research Handbook*, London: Routledge, pp 70–89.

de Zwart, B., Broersen, J., Frings-Dresen, M. and van Dijk, F. (1997) 'Repeated survey on changes in musculoskeletal complaints relative to age and work demands', *Occupational and Environmental Medicine*, 54: 793–9.

Drury, E. (1993) *Discrimination Fondée sur l'Âge Exercée Contre les Travailleurs Âgés de la Communauté Européenne. Une Analyse Comparative*, Brussels: Eurolink Age.

Esping-Andersen, G. (1990) *The Three Worlds of Welfare Capitalism*, Princeton, NJ: Princeton University Press.

European Commission (nd) *Active Ageing* [online], available at: https://ec.eur opa.eu/social/main.jsp?catId=1062&langId=en [accessed 26 March 2019].

Federgon (2017) *Tout le Monde à l'Emploi … une Priorité pour les Labour Market Makers!* [Annual Report, 2016] [online], Brussels: Federgon, available at: https://federgon.be/fileadmin/media/pdf/fr/federgon_-_rapport_annu el_2016.pdf [accessed 13 June 2019].

Federgon (2018) *Les Caractéristiques du Profil des Intérimaires*, Brussels: Federgon.

Federgon (2022) *Répartition par âge des Intérimaires – Données 2020*, Brussels: Federgon, available at: https://federgon.be/fr/centre-de-connaissances/ chiffres/ [accessed 6 January 2022].

Forem (2013) *Analyse du Marché de l'Emploi. Intérim: du Travail à l'Emploi?*, Brussels: Forem.

Gaillard, M. and Desmette, D. (2010) '(In)validating stereotypes about older workers influences their intentions to retire early and to learn and develop', *Basic and Applied Social Psychology*, 32: 86–98.

Guillemard, A.-M. (2003) *L'Âge de l'Emploi. Les Sociétés à l'Épreuve du Vieillissement*, Paris: Armand Colin.

Guillemard, A.-M. (2010) *Les Défis du Vieillissement. Age, Emploi, Retraite. Perspectives Internationales*, Paris: Armand Colin.

Hall, P. (1993) 'Policy paradigms, social learning, and the state: the case of policymaking in Britain', *Comparative Politics*, 25: 275–96.

Hassell, B. and Perrewe B. (1995) 'An examination of beliefs about older workers: do stereotypes still exist?', *Journal of Organizational Behaviour*, 16: 457–68.

Itzin, C. and Phillipson, C. (1993) *Age Barriers at Work*, London: Metra.

Jolivet, A. and Volkoff, S. (2016) 'Vieillir (mais) travailler', *Vie Sociale*, 3: 85–100.

Kirchner, W., Lindbom, T. and Paterson, D. (1952) 'Attitudes toward the employment of older people', *Journal of Applied Psychology*, 36: 154–6.

Kluge, A. and Krings, F. (2008) 'Attitudes toward older workers and human resource practices', *Swiss Journal of Psychology*, 67: 61–4.

Kuhn, T. (1962) *The Structure of Scientific Revolutions*, Chicago, IL: The University of Chicago Press.

Leleu, M. (2001) *Stéréotypes et Travailleurs Âgés. Le cas de la Belgique et des Pays Limitrophes: Luxembourg, Pays-Bas, Genève*, Rapport pour le Bureau International du Travail, Luxembourg: ILO.

Loretto, W. and White, P. (2006) 'Employers' attitudes, practices and policies towards older workers', *Human Resource Management Journal*, 16: 313–30.

McGregor, J. and Gray, L. (2002) 'Stereotypes and older workers: the New Zealand experience', *Social Policy Journal of New Zealand*, 18: 163–77.

Maurer, T.J., Barbeite, F.G., Weiss, E.M. and Lippstreu, M. (2008) 'New measures of stereotypical beliefs about older workers' ability and desire for development: exploration among employees age 40 and over', *Journal of Managerial Psychology*, 23: 395–418.

Ney, S. (2005) 'Active ageing policy in Europe: between path dependency and path departure', *Ageing International*, 30: 325–42.

Pierson, P. (2000) 'Increasing returns, path dependence, and the study of politics', *The American Political Science Review*, 94: 251–67.

Sanderson, J.-P. (2015) 'Vieillissement de la population et retraites en Belgique, 19ème-20ème siècles', *Revue Belge d'Histoire Contemporaine*, 4: 1–15.

Sanderson, J.-P., and Burnay, N. (2017) 'Life courses and ends of career: towards de-standardization? An analysis of the Belgian case', *Journal of Population Ageing*, 10: 109–24.

Simoens, D. (1980) 'Hoe pijnloos is de crisis? Kritische analyse van de ontwikkeling van de wetgeving over de sociale zekerheidsprestaties (1976–1979)', in Simoens, D., de Broeck, G. and van Langendonck, J. (eds.) *Crisiswetgeving en Sociale Zekerheid*, Antwerp: Kluwer, pp 70–82.

Stone, A. (1992) 'Le «néo-institutionnalisme». Défis conceptuels et méthodologiques', *Politix*, 5: 156–68.

Taylor, P. and Walker, A. (1994) 'The ageing workforce: employers' attitudes towards older people', *Work, Employment and Society*, 8: 569–91.

Unia (2018) *Rapport Annuel – Chiffres 2017*, Brussels: Unia.

Unia (2019) *Trop Jeune, trop Vieux, Unia Combat la Discrimination Fondée sur l'Âge*, Brussels: Unia.

Valenduc, G. (2012) *L'Emploi Intérimaire, Entre Risque de Précarité et Opportunité d'Insertion*, Note d'éducation permanente de l'ASBL Fondation Travail-Université (FTU), No. 2012 – 11 novembre 2012 [online], available at: www.ftu-namur.org/fichiers/2012_11_Emploi%20interim.pdf [accessed 26 September 2021].

Van Dalen, H.P., Henkens, K. and Schippers, J. (2010) 'Productivity of older workers: perceptions of employers and employees', *Population and Development Review*, 36: 309–30.

6

Attempted Transitions from Unemployment in Italy

Emma Garavaglia

Introduction

Italy was one of the European Member States to be affected the most by the 2008 financial crisis. The first signs of the recession appeared in the second quarter of 2008, and the enormous impact this had on employment quickly became clear: since the crisis outbreak, about 1.2 million workers lost their jobs (Istat, 2018). The crisis especially hit young people, defined as a lost generation in the labour market (Gabriel et al 2013), but it also weakened the employment condition of groups of workers who, in the past, tended to emerge unscathed by economic recessions. In particular, middle-aged or older men with uninterrupted careers in the same company who – thanks to the rigid employment protection legislation were traditionally protected – have been facing an increased risk of job loss (López-Andreu, 2019). In this regard, the 2008 credit crunch also exacerbated the tendency, already apparent since the early 2000s, to dismiss managers and executives due to restructuring processes (Unioncamere, nd).

A significant number of studies explore the experience of job loss among managerial and professional employees (Gabriel et al 2013). However, with few remarkable exceptions (Mendenhall et al 2008; Garrett-Peters, 2009; Riach and Loretto, 2009; Gabriel et al 2013; Gray et al 2015; Raito and Lahelma, 2015), the literature appears to lack studies that focus on late-career unemployment and attempted transitions out of unemployment among this group of workers – despite age-related issues having progressively become central in the public and political debate on employment.

A rapidly ageing population is said to make older workers crucial for maintaining the sustainability of social security systems and guaranteeing personal and family well-being (Eurostat, 2019). Notwithstanding its popularity among policy makers, the prospect of working longer raises a few controversial issues that relate, among others, to the opportunities for older people to make genuine choices around work. These opportunities are affected by the number of jobs available to them, as well as the policies that regulate work and the welfare state (Lain et al 2018).

As far as the Italian situation is concerned, a persistent lack of job opportunities still poses a major problem, across generations. This increases the risk that policies designed to extend working life might reduce the opportunities available for younger workers, thereby sustaining the widespread idea of an intergenerational conflict in the labour market and society at large (Marcaletti, 2013). Overall, in a country that is home to one of the world's oldest populations, older workers' labour market inclusion appears to be both a relevant and controversial topic, and one which still requires a long-term comprehensive policy strategy (Franco and Tommasino, 2020).

Starting from this premise and drawing on data collected through 15 in-depth interviews (Legard et al 2003), this chapter explores the experience of unemployment and attempted transition out of unemployment among upper-level managers in Italy who lost their job while in their 50s.

The chapter commences with a brief description of the institutional context in which Italian older workers experience labour market mobility and, in particular, the body of policies and processes that are likely to influence late-career employment transitions. It proceeds to describe the research design before drawing upon the interview materials to examine how participants interpret the experience of job loss and unemployment and how they react to it. Findings show the huge obstacles older workers face when trying to re-enter the labour market, especially related to suffered and self-imposed age discrimination (Duncan and Loretto, 2004; Macnicol, 2006). In the discussion, the chapter reflects on the strategies participants adopt in order to make sense of difficult and frustrating experiences and find a new place in the world of work. This shows how common discourses about ageing and work in contemporary labour markets (Lane, 2011; Thomas et al 2014) seem to limit the options available to react to the situation.

The context of attempted late-career transitions from unemployment in Italy

Italy is home to one of the world's oldest populations (Eurostat, 2019). As of 1 January 2019, 22.9 per cent of the population is aged 65 plus and 7.2 per cent is aged 80 plus; the largest proportion of older people per total population in Europe. Conversely, the number of residents aged 15 or under has progressively declined and is currently 13 per cent of the total population (compared to 17 per cent in 1990) (Eurostat, 2020a).

As in most European countries, the age composition of the population is linked to the fertility fluctuation that took place in the second half of the 20th century: the so-called 'baby boomers' are now transitioning into old age, while a significant proportion of the working-age population comprises the 'baby bust' cohort – the generation following the baby boomers who had very low fertility rates (Mazzola et al 2016). These circumstances, the progressive increase in life expectancy at birth (83.4 in 2018) and the constant decrease in fertility rates (1.28 in 2018) have contributed to a progressive increase in the older population, which is expected to reach 250,000 individuals by 2050 (Eurostat, 2020a). This is notwithstanding the mitigation effects of the positive net migration flows, which have been sustaining the working-age population and fertility levels over the last 30 years (Mazzola et al 2016).

As in most developed countries, the rapid ageing of the population raises concerns especially regarding the economic growth and the sustainability of the social security system (Eurostat, 2019). In Italy, the weight of public expenditure on old-age benefits is particularly relevant: pension spending amounts to 16.2 per cent of the GDP; together with Greece, it is the highest in the Organisation for Economic Co-operation and Development countries (OECD, 2015). Public pensions, combined with means-tested benefits for low earners and survivors, achieve almost universal coverage of the population aged over 65 (Floridi, 2020). The increase in the number of pensioners and the decrease in the number of contributors are clearly threatening the sustainability of the system.

The main response of the Italian government to the challenges posed by the ageing of the population has been a number of reforms of the pension system (Franco and Tommasino, 2020), which culminated in the last so-called Fornero Reform that was passed in December 2011 during the technocratic government of Monti. The reform accelerated the introduction of a Notional Defined Contribution system – in line with the previous Dini reform (1995). It also increased the minimum pension age (irrespective of sector or gender), which is scheduled also to further increase linked to life expectancy, with narrowed the opportunities for early retirement (Giuliani, 2020). Notwithstanding some shortcomings pointed out by scholars (Giuliani, 2020), the reform has contributed to the prolongation of work careers, increasing the average effective age of labour market exit for both men (62 years) and women (61 years), although it still remains lower than the OECD average (OECD, 2017).

Nevertheless, neither the 2011 reform, nor the related or subsequent labour market policy interventions have succeeded in raising older workers' employment to intended levels (OECD, 2019). In fact, although in Italy the employment rate of older workers has constantly increased over the last 20 years, for both genders, it is still well below the corresponding EU28 level (60.0 per cent in 2019). The total employment rate of workers aged 55–64 was 27.3 per cent in 2000 and reached 54.3 per cent in 2019 – women maintain a negative gap of around 20 percentage points with respect to men (Eurostat, 2020b). Moreover, since the 2008 economic crisis older workers have faced an increasing risk of job loss and unemployment (Jin et al 2016). Traditionally, the strict Italian employment protection legislation has favoured the so-called 'insiders', workers with a stable contract who enjoy favourable employment conditions: typically, middle-aged or older men employed full-time by large companies (Jessoula et al 2010). The crisis and the following austerity period caused the risks to spread to core workers, not least also due to the increase in employers' ability to hire and fire, guaranteed by labour market reforms that (at least partially) embraced liberalization pressures (López-Andreu, 2019).

Even though Italian older workers are still less frequently separated from a permanent job than their younger counterparts, their probability of becoming unemployed has almost doubled since the 2008 economic crisis (Jin et al 2016). Moreover, after losing a job, older workers tend to experience longer unemployment periods and their probability of falling out of the labour market altogether is higher (Stier and Endeweld, 2015). Their professional experience does not improve their chances of re-employment. When they succeed in finding a new job, both earnings and working conditions tend to deteriorate, especially if the spell of unemployment is very long (Frosch, 2006; Jin et al 2016). The barriers that Italian older workers face when trying to revive their career can be attributed, on the one hand, to the generalized persistent scarcity of job opportunities and, on the other, to the lack of a comprehensive strategy to promote active ageing (Franco and Tommasino, 2020). Despite the last pension reform which successfully intervened on the side of the so-called 'pull factors' (Walker, 2006) by reducing the possibilities of choosing to retire early,[1] other relevant variables were systematically ignored.

The most important factor that is ignored by policy is the lack of public care services. Within a familistic system, older adults – especially women – often have to manage complex care responsibilities, with critical consequences for their effective participation in the labour market (Checcucci et al 2020). Also, the lack of policies or services specifically aimed at sustaining older workers' employability, both on the side of the government and companies – and reflected in the low levels of older workers' training participation[2] – helps to explain why displaced older workers are very likely to become inactive after experiencing unemployment (Checcucci et al 2020). Added to this, it is important to consider the lack of labour market policies ensuring that an increasing labour supply of older workers is met by an adequate demand, especially in a context where the idea of an intergenerational conflict in the labour market is still common (Marcaletti, 2013).

Methods

This chapter is the product of qualitative research based on 15 in-depth interviews (Legard et al 2003) with upper-level managers aged between 52 and 65 years who lost their job when they were in their 50s. The research was carried out in 2016, in Milan. Participants were recruited through purposive sampling (Hood, 2007). Access was gained via (a) a training course for unemployed managers and professionals who wished to re-qualify as management trainers, organized by a local industrial association; and (b) an association for older workers. The association offers moral and material support to workers who lose their job late in their career. Members are unemployed workers aged over 40 who struggle to re-enter the labour market after a period of unemployment. The activity of the association includes lobbying, training and networking initiatives.

Participants in the training course and members of the association were contacted via email, in order to select upper-level managers who lost their job when they were in their 50s and who were still unemployed or had temporary jobs at the time of the research. In short, individuals who never found a stable job after being made redundant or dismissed when they were in their 50s. The focus was on workers in their 50s (at the time of the job loss) because even though this does not constitute a homogeneous group, literature shows that age makes the situation of these workers unique in many ways (Kira and Klehe, 2016; Steel and Tuori, 2019). Most research investigating the experience of unemployment and precarious work among older workers focuses on individuals aged over 50 (see, for example, Riach and Loretto, 2009; Lain et al 2018; Steel and Tuori, 2019). Moreover, the age of 50 corresponds to the age at which labour force participation begins to decline in many countries (OECD, 2006).

Among the 39 potential participants who met the selection criteria, 15 agreed to participate –13 men and two women; there were only four women in the population from which the sample was derived. Even though the sample is small, it nonetheless meets the recommendations on qualitative sampling for phenomenological studies (Morse, 1994; Creswell and Poth, 2016). Further details about the sample are provided in Table 6.1; the numbers after quotes in the 'Findings' section relate to individuals listed in the table.

A common reason for people's refusal to participate was because it would be too painful to recall their dismissal. The self-selection of participants renders the sample biased, in the sense that people who agreed to participate in the research were willing – and some of them even enthusiastic – to narrate their experiences. It is acknowledged that not all unemployed upper-level managers who lose their job in late-career may have experiences and emotions similar to those discussed in this chapter. Moreover, the limited

Table 6.1: Sample overview of unemployed individuals

ID number	Name (pseudonym)	Age at interview	Age at job loss	Gender	Last stable job	Current position
1	Marco	55	50	Male	ICT manager	Business consultant for one company; he works two days a week
2	Andrea	57	49	Male	Marketing executive	Teacher
3	Stefano	58	50	Male	Finance executive	Management consultant; very casual work
4	Alessandro	58	48	Male	Supply chain operations manager	Temporary manager; very casual work
5	Roberto	56	50	Male	General manager	Secretary at a sailing centre
6	Giuseppe	64	57	Male	Sales executive	Retired (recently retired)
7	Flavio	56	49	Male	Pharmaceutical sales manager	Marketing trainer; self-employed
8	Luca	59	50	Male	Production executive	Business consultant (self-employed)
9	Maria	57	51	Female	Administration manager	Care worker
10	Angelo	63	55	Male	Head of internationalization	Part-time business consultant
11	Gianni	65	59	Male	Finance manager	Unemployed
12	Luigi	60	50	Male	Product manager	Unemployed (caring for his mother)
13	Davide	59	52	Male	Sales manager	Unemployed
14	Paolo	52	48	Male	Product development manager	Trainer (self-employed)
15	Rosa	56	50	Female	General manager	Management consultant (self-employed)

number of female participants – a reflection of the low number of women employed in upper-level managerial positions in Italy (Ferri et al 2018) – delimits the possibility for discussing the gendered dimension of critical issues related to late-career job loss and unemployment, as well as the gendered dimension of ageism (Duncan and Loretto, 2004).

The unemployment periods (absence of any kind of paid work) that followed the job loss lasted from a minimum of two to a maximum of seven years. One of the participants, after two years of unemployment decided to dedicate his time to care for his chronically ill mother.

As mentioned earlier, some of the individuals contacted declined to take part in the study as they did not wish to relive the painful experience of being dismissed. In order to address the potential distress deriving from the narration of the dismissal, participants were first invited to briefly give some background information on their professional career. This allowed them to open up and gradually approach the most recent episode of involuntary job loss. They were then invited to comment on the experience of job loss and on how their view of this experience has changed from the moment of the dismissal to the present moment. The interview then focused on the recent years of unemployment/(under)employment. Participants were invited to comment on the experience of job seeking, on the jobs they had had over the last years and on their status at the time of interview. Instead of a specific set of questions, using an interview agenda allowed them to reflect on a broad range of issues related to the domains of enquiry, commenting on previous experiences as well as present feelings and future expectations (Zikic and Richardson, 2007).

Interviews lasted between 30 (one case) and 90 minutes, they were audiotaped, responses were transcribed verbatim and translated into English. A bilingual colleague verified the translations.

Analytic memos on each interview were developed over the data collection period. Coding techniques (Weston et al 2001) were then employed to analyze memos and transcripts in order to identify processes and cultural resources participants use in order to make sense of their experiences (Riach and Loretto, 2009). In a second stage of the analysis, connections and contradictions between participants' accounts were examined through comparison within and between cases.

Findings

The analysis of the interview materials led to the emergence of the processes that were key to participants' meaning-making of the experience of unemployment and the attempts to revive their careers. The obstacles participants encountered in finding a new stable job mainly related to suffered and self-imposed age discrimination (Duncan and Loretto, 2004;

Macnicol, 2006). These experiences forced them to relate, for the first time, to the identity of the older worker (Riach and Loretto, 2009) and with precarious work (Kalleberg and Vallas, 2017). The strategies they adopted to deal with these experiences included constructing the stereotype of the unenthusiastic job seeker, described as the antithesis of the idealized proactive worker (Sennet, 2007; Lane, 2011), and using it to refer to older workers and contrast them with their younger colleagues. By distancing themselves from this stereotypical character, they were able to feel legitimized to re-enter the labour market. Moreover, participants tried to re-affirm their previous professional identity (Riach and Loretto, 2009; Spyridakis, 2016; Daskalaki and Simosi, 2018) through accepting forms of precarious work that allowed them to maintain some sort of continuation. This implied embracing and adapting to a new structuring of work.

The strategies adopted by participants to give a meaning to the world of experienced uncertainty they came to know with the job loss and find a new valuable place within it are now described in detail.

Finding a new job: age discrimination and the unenthusiastic older worker

Nearly all the participants in this study viewed unemployment as a temporary episode immediately after the job loss, rather than the end of their career (Gabriel et al 2013). In fact, they described the immediate aftermath of the lay-off as a period in which they had continued to actively and intensively attempt to find a new job because they were sure that unemployment was a temporary condition. This was based on their previous employment transitions, the 'prestigious' jobs and 'ascending career' they had. In short, they were confident of being able to find a new managerial job quickly, and they considered their experience and expertise as their strongest asset in the search for a new job (Gabriel et al 2013).

Many of them had previous experiences of voluntary or involuntary job loss (before they reached the age of 45), variously described as "normal" and "very easy to cope with". They proactively welcomed the challenge of finding a new job and considered these transitions as an opportunity for their career development. Often, when they were younger, they re-entered the labour market right after the job loss, because they were offered a new opportunity through head-hunters or friends employed in similar positions in other companies.

During the first year of unemployment after losing their job in late career, they engaged in an active and confident job search, for they were confident that their "being proactive and not expecting help from anyone" would have produced the same (positive) ending as in the past. They contacted friends and former colleagues in their professional network who could have potentially helped, and they "sifted through hundreds of job offers" (11) (numbers after direct quotations indicate the interview participant number).

However, as one of the participants described, this active job search often led to few or zero interviews: "I applied for more than 60 or 70 positions, I had three or four job interviews ... but nothing happened" (10). Some participants remarked that despite the intense job search, they had never – "not even once – been offered the possibility of discussing [their] applications at interview" (11).

Soon, they realized that the present situation was very different from the employment transitions experienced in the past. In particular, all of them underlined the progressive prolongation of unemployment periods:

'When you are in your 60s, nobody thinks about the possibility of hiring you. Working as an executive, since when I was 45 finding new jobs has become more and more difficult and unemployment periods have progressively lasted longer ... from one to six months ... to one year and then nothing.' (11)

Consequently, they began thinking of their unemployment condition as a "prelude of retirement, rather than the starting point of a new career stage" (4). Even though they never stopped searching for a new job, they maintained that after some time they "realized that the last episode [lay-off] was the final act of [their] career", an "unexpected end" that had "completely changed [their lives] from one day to another" (4).

What influenced the shift from confidence to disillusionment was their first-hand experience with few opportunities and even fewer job interviews. Moreover, the experience of friends and colleagues of the same age who were facing the same situation, and media reports describing the tendency of Italian companies to dismiss managers and executives during the economic crisis, contributed to a change from a positive attitude to a negative feeling of disillusionment and frustration (Mendenhall et al 2008).

Job search exposed all participants to episodes of age discrimination. As the following quote helps to clarify, they ran into many – directly or indirectly – discriminatory job adverts: "Most job opportunities advertised are blatantly for young workers, for graduates at their first experience ... are jobs that a person over 50 cannot do" (6). In the few cases in which they succeeded in the first stage of selection and gained the opportunity to discuss their application at interview, they maintained that they were openly told that they were too old for that particular job.

Self-imposed age-discrimination is another relevant issue which emerged from their stories. Participants admitted that on more than one occasion they did not apply for a job for which they were qualified, because in their opinion the company "was clearly looking for a young candidate" (6). Even when they were selected for an interview, sometimes they renounced it: "I arrived there and there was a line of guys, aged around 25, probably at their first job interview. ... I looked at them and I decided to leave" (14).

Being discriminated against on account of age pushed the participants to reflect on what it means to be labelled as "older" in the labour market. Their accounts highlighted that the barriers to reviving their career were constructed through judgements of them based on their age and the fact that they were too old, and not on the assessment of their knowledge and competences. Despite expressing frustration at this, their narratives reproduced the same logic when, for example, they maintained that workers over 50 cannot apply for certain kinds of job. They tended to refer to chronological age as a factor capable of determining, in itself, the difference between those who succeed and those who do not (in recovering their career), those who can and those who cannot (discussing their application at interview).

Confronted with the identity of the older worker – which they felt was imposed upon them through being labelled as "too old" during the job search – participants engaged in an argument counterposing younger and older workers. This argument was put forth through two main strategies.

First, participants constructed the stereotype of the unenthusiastic job seeker to refer to older unemployed workers, described through a number of attributes and behavioural claims. Specifically, they referred to them as those who "do not react, continuously complain, are not proactive enough in developing their competences and often do not enough to solve their situation" (15). The stereotype of the unenthusiastic job seeker was built as the antithesis of the idealized worker typical of the neoliberal culture: one who is entrepreneurial and self-directed and can easily cope with frequent transitions in the labour market, embracing them as an opportunity (Sennet, 2007; Lane, 2011).

In participants' accounts, the unenthusiastic job seeker coincided with older unemployed workers, while the characteristics of the idealized proactive worker were attributed to younger workers. For example, they described younger workers as "a natural power ... younger workers have much more energy and many ideas, their minds work better. They have ideas and are eager to get involved, even for free. They have determination and enthusiasm ... they never give up" (10).

It is interesting to note that they viewed working for free as commendable. In line with this, participants stressed, reluctantly, that older workers "cost more [than their younger colleagues] and they have been guaranteed certain rights that may cause inefficiencies for the company" (13). The practice of self-exploitation (working passionately for free) – typical of neoliberal labour markets (Schmiz, 2013; Brienza, 2016) – which participants attributed to younger workers, is described as an opportunity to improve workers' marketability, and is contrasted with the outdated and inefficient work standards of 'payments and dependence' (Finn, 2000, p 393), embodied by the older workers.

Participants used the stereotypes of the unenthusiastic job seeker and the idealized younger worker in two ways. First, on the one hand, by highlighting that they "have never quit searching for a job", or again "have immediately rolled up their sleeves to face the situation" (4), they were able to juxtapose their actions with others who are in the same situation but are not entrepreneurial enough or proactive, thus distancing themselves from the stereotypical older worker. On the other hand, they stressed their admiration for younger workers and their feeling much more comfortable "with them, than with those of [their] age" (1) as a means to affirm their affinity to the character of the idealized proactive worker.

Second, participants positioned themselves within the debate on intergenerational conflict (Hess et al 2017). They stressed the fact that "younger workers are those who deserve to work" (5). By having a conscience that youth employment "must be prioritized" and highlighting that with their participation in the labour market they do not "intend to deprive young people of work opportunities" (15), participants were able to legitimize their desire to re-enter the labour market. Moreover, by stressing the fact that they "take young people's side" in this imagined battle between younger and older workers, they were able to reject, once again, the identity of the older worker. Their accounts reflected the common (wrong) belief that older workers' employment and the prolongation of work careers is to blame for younger workers' unemployment (Marcaletti, 2013). This idea has been reinforced in Italy by recent pension system reforms which have reintroduced early retirement options, justifying them based on the young-in, old-out logic.[1]

New employment conditions: chasing activity, embracing precarity

Participants did not succeed in finding a new stable job. Nevertheless, nearly none of them had ever considered giving up paid work and, once they had abandoned the idea of recovering their careers as upper-level employees, they started searching for whatever job, "just to work". This magnified the possibility of facing discrimination on account of their age, because their long career and their previous qualified experience made them unsuitable for jobs requiring no qualifications or experience. The main reason behind their desire to find a stable job, even a low-level job, was not financial. Many participants did not express concern over possible financial distress. On the contrary, they maintained that their past earnings and the "golden parachute" that accompanied the lay-off could have allowed them "to sit and wait for retirement" (2).

However, they could hardly entertain the idea of giving up paid work because it "is fundamental to feel active and … one must continue doing something in order to keep a useful role in the couple and in the family" (6). Again, as the following quote explains, they considered it key to personal well-being: "When you stop working you can easily go insane. If you stay still and you don't try to do something, you are going to go insane very soon" (3).

When talking about "being active" and "doing something" they were referring to productive activity. From their accounts it was clear that feeling well and useful to their family and to society was inextricably linked to having a paid job. Activity was thus interpreted only with reference to the traditional notion of labour. They did not engage in a personal renegotiation of the meaning of work (Riach and Loretto, 2009). As one of them affirmed: "Nothing has changed in the way in which I look at the meaning and value of work in my life and in the way in which I define myself as a worker. … I am an upper manager … simply as it is. … I am just doing my job in a different way" (4). Only in one case, a participant, after two years of trying to find a job, decided to give up and spend his time and energy caring for his chronically ill mother. The other interviewees, including the two women in the group, never mentioned caring or volunteering as possible alternative ways of utilizing their time in their years of unemployment.

As the aforementioned quote shows, participating in paid employment, even if it implied a downgrade in terms of position and salary, allowed them to continue defining themselves as upper-level professionals.

As a result of an active and intense job search and the desire to do "whatever job", all interviewees had some sort of work experience after the lay-off. They had never been able to re-enter the labour market on a stable and qualified contract, even if they declared they would have preferred it. Nevertheless, nearly all of them had temporary, underpaid and underqualified jobs that "not even remotely could compare with [their] previous job" (15), as one of the participants stated. Specifically, they reported working self-employed and part-time jobs that included: short-term consulting contracts, tutoring and teaching and commission-based sales jobs. All jobs were found through personal contacts.

In financial terms, these jobs were described as "very similar to unemployment" (15). Moreover, participants stressed the fact that these new jobs were always temporary and very discontinuous: "I am happy to change job every six months … however, the problem is that between one job and the other I often wait up to one year" (14).

Despite the poor working conditions they experienced, their accounts around these forms of employment never included terms such as 'instability' or 'insecurity'. Even if, as mentioned previously, nearly all of them were currently working – or had experienced working – with short-term, unstable and underpaid contracts, none maintained that they were in bad jobs. Instead, they variously referred to these jobs as "flexible", "interesting" and "satisfactory". Overall, they described the new (and worst) (under) employment conditions positively (Gandini, 2016). In other words, despite these working conditions, which were not through choice but the only available option, they never described it as bad. The interpretation around the experiences they were living excluded any form of contestation of precarious low-paid work, as well as any attempt to construct alternative selves outside the structural spaces of paid work and traditional work organizations (Daskalaki and Simosi, 2018).

Only a few interviewees developed a narrative of liberation and said that this new life allowed them "to find a new balance between work, family and personal interests" (2); thus, an opportunity to escape an undesirable job. For the majority of participants the new conditions that characterized their work experience did not correspond to what they actually wished for but, at the same time, it was not something they felt they were able to complain about.

Specifically, they used terms such as "normal" and "nothing to complain about" when describing employment conditions that are typical of the risk economy (Mendenhall et al 2008), with its emphasis on flexibility and contingent workforce. Moreover, they declared to "understand" and "justify" companies that had dismissed many managers and executives, due to economic and financial reasons.

Participants' accounts seemed to reflect an interpretation of their personal experience around job termination as the natural consequence of changes that have affected work, labour markets and, more generally, the economy. They interpreted their condition as the average condition of contemporary workers. They did not consider themselves particularly unlucky or unsuccessful: on the contrary, they maintained that their situation "mirrors the condition that most workers are currently forced to cope with" [13]. In addition, this condition was not something one could complain about, because it "is one's own responsibility to be able to cope with a flexible and competitive market ... it is not companies' fault" (13): "If you are not able to find a new job, to recover your career, it means that you have not been able to adequate your skills and competences to the new needs of the market ... that you have not invested enough in your development and in creating a network of helpful people" (8). As shown, participants blamed workers who are not able to "adapt to these new [employment] conditions" and maintained that, regardless of their age, these people are not enough "self-entrepreneur" (15). Immersed in the neoliberal culture of meritocratic individualism, which permeates the managerial world (Lane, 2011) they inhabited for a long time, participants tended to interpret the failure in finding a new job as the consequence of personal flaws and, in particular, the absence of an enterprising attitude.

It is worth mentioning that being one among many others workers did not imply the development of a sense of solidarity, nor the idea that a collective action could sustain the improvement of the situation for all. Since what participants are facing is interpreted as natural in the contemporary economic system, and companies are justified in their choices and their personnel policies and practices, the responsibility for succeeding in finding a new job rests on the shoulders of every worker.

Discussion

Participants' stories clearly show the huge obstacles that older workers – even those who previously had prestigious and highly paid jobs – are faced with when trying to recover their career after job loss, in the Italian context. As data on late-career unemployment show, finding a new job is difficult and finding a job similar to that lost seems to be almost impossible. Participants' experiences reflect a context characterized by few concrete opportunities to getting back into paid employment and in which age discrimination – either suffered or self-imposed – is evident.

The experience of late-career job loss and unemployment leads older workers to engage in a process of meaning-making and (re)construction of a coherent sense of self (Riach and Loretto, 2009; Gabriel et al 2013). Findings suggest that this process seems to imply an individual transformation oriented towards the production of a self that is fit for work in contemporary labour markets (Bandinelli, 2019): a self-directed entrepreneurial individual that bears all the responsibility of managing work transitions (Lane, 2011) and surviving job instability. The logics of efficiency and productivity (Bröckling, 2016; Daskalaki and Simosi, 2018) dominate the time of unemployment and do not leave room to imagine alternative selves outside the domain of paid labour. In fact, in contrast with what emerges from other studies (Riach and Loretto, 2009), respondents do not negotiate the meaning of work and seek to affirm a continuation of prior professional identity in order to demonstrate their capacity to successfully adapt to an uncertain situation. There is no room to contest precarious, low-paid work and the structural causes of a growing insecurity that dominates the world of work.

Being discriminated against on account of age is lived by participants as a frustrating experience that leads them to construct a negative stereotyped character they use to describe older workers and to distance themselves from this identity. This negative stereotype is described as the antithesis of the idealized proactive worker: the older worker is one who does not successfully manage work transitions, due to their limited flexibility and entrepreneurial attitude. The contrast between the older worker and the proactive worker is reinforced through stereotyping younger workers as adaptable to company needs and deserving of work. Thus, the common discourse of autonomy and self-responsibility (Lane, 2011), espoused by participants, nurtures an ageist attitude that manifests through stereotyping younger and older workers as respectively deserving or not of work. At the same time, respondents try to make their age invisible by juxtaposing their attitudes and actions with those of the older workers, stressing their admiration for younger workers and expressing their solidarity with them. The lack of reaction towards the poor working conditions brought about by the progressive process of employment de-regulation drives respondents to the point where older workers are also the ones to blame for the difficulties that younger Italian workers face in finding a job.

Overall, work-related problems that may occur when one experiences late-career job loss are attributed to a supposed decreasing usefulness of workers as they age, and the responsibility for finding a solution to these problems is entirely put on individuals' shoulders. This idea delimitates the spectrum of possible and acceptable work-related attitudes and behaviours in late career because it is based on an interpretation of vulnerability as a personal responsibility, rather than as the consequence of structural conditions. If people find themselves out of the labour market and experiencing precarious work, the only acceptable way out of this condition is to adopt an entrepreneurial attitude and a free-agent mentality in the search for a new job. According to this logic, unsuccessful experiences are the result of not being as active and proactive as needed.

This interpretation of unsuccessful late-career transitions out of unemployment undercuts importantly the possibility of individual and collective resistance to age discrimination because it is sustained by ageist attitudes which seem to be internalized (and thus invisible) by those who suffer from discriminatory practices, as well as because it diverts attention away from any possible political solution.

Conclusion

The research discussed in this chapter has explored the lived experience of attempted transitions out of unemployment among older workers who had high-level managerial jobs, in Italy. Findings show how participants' interpretation of the experiences that follow the job loss are shaped by concrete obstacles – in particular, related to episodes of age discrimination – that limit the possibilities of successfully reviving the career, as well as common discourses about ageing and work in contemporary labour markets (Thomas et al 2014).

Inevitably, any conclusion based on this study must be explorative. No generalizations can be drawn from these data, but this was not the aim of a research based on qualitative interviews. Yet, they allow for a reading of individual accounts of personal events in light of specific contextual conditions and socio-cultural processes (Murgia, 2011). Further research is needed in order to explore the gendered dimension of late-career employment transitions, especially in a context where women still face major disadvantages in their working lives.

Notes

[1] It is worth mentioning that at the beginning of 2019 the Lega-Five Stars Movement government approved a new early-retirement scheme: Quota 100. Quota 100 introduced the possibility for workers aged 62 years with 38 qualifying years to retire, thus allowing them to retire five years earlier with a limited reduction of the pension amount. The new scheme was approved as an experiment to run for three years, and it was due to be replaced with a new early-retirement scheme (but the Lega-Five Stars Movement's government fell in August 2019). The first data regarding beneficiaries show that Quota 100 was applicable to workers with a long contributory history, from the private sector (50 per cent) or self-employed (20 per cent), thus mostly men living in the North (Perri, 2019).

[2] According to the OECD (2019), less than 10 per cent of older workers in Italy have access to training.

References

Bandinelli, C. (2019) 'The production of subjectivity in neoliberal culture industries: the case of coworking spaces', *International Journal of Cultural Studies*, 23(1): 3–19.

Brienza, C. (2016) 'Degrees of (self-) exploitation: learning to labour in the neoliberal university', *Journal of Historical Sociology*, 29(1): 92–111.

Bröckling, U. (2016) *The Entrepreneurial Self: Fabricating a New Type of Subject*, London: Sage.

Checcucci, P., Principi, A., Quattrociocchi, L., Tibaldi, M. and Zurlo, D. (2020) 'Employment of older people across Italian regions: an exploration of drivers and barriers based on the active ageing index', *Journal of Population Ageing* [online first], 1–13.

Creswell, J.W. and Poth, C.N. (2016) *Qualitative Inquiry and Research Design: Choosing Among Five Approaches*, Thousand Oaks, CA: Sage.

Daskalaki, M. and Simosi, M. (2018) 'Unemployment as a liminoid phenomenon: identity trajectories in times of crisis', *Human Relations*, 71(9): 1153–78.

Duncan, C. and Loretto, W. (2004) 'Never the right age? Gender and age-based discrimination in employment', *Gender, Work & Organization*, 11(1): 95–115.

Eurostat (2019) *Ageing in Europe. Looking at the Lives of Older People in the EU* [online], Luxembourg: Publications Office of the European Union, available at: https://ec.europa.eu/eurostat/documents/3217494/10166 544/KS-02-19%E2%80%91681-EN-N.pdf/c701972f-6b4e-b432-57d2-91898ca94893 [accessed 27 September 2021].

Eurostat (2020a) *Population (Demography, Migration and Projections)* [online], available at: https://ec.europa.eu/eurostat/web/population-demography-migration-projections/data/database [accessed 27 September 2021].

Eurostat (2020b) *Employment and Unemployment (Labour Force Survey)* [online], available at: https://ec.europa.eu/eurostat/web/lfs/data/database [accessed 27 September 2021].

Ferri, V., Ricci, A. and Sacchi, S. (2018) *Demografia Imprenditoriale e Tessuto Produttivo in Italia*, INAPP Policy Brief N. 5 [online], available at: http://oa.inapp.org/bitstream/handle/123456789/140/Inapp_Ferri_Ricci_Sacchi_Demografia%20imprenditoriale_2018.pdf?sequence=3 [accessed 27 September 2021].

Finn, D. (2000) 'From full employment to employability: a new deal for Britain's unemployed?', *International Journal of Manpower*, 21(5): 384–99.

Floridi, G. (2020) 'Social policies and intergenerational support in Italy and South Korea', *Contemporary Social Science*, 15(3): 330–45.

Franco, D. and Tommasino, P. (2020) 'Lessons from Italy: a good pension system needs an effective broader social policy framework, *Intereconomics*, 55(2): 73–81.

Frosch, K. (2006) *Reemployment Rates Over the Life Course: Is There Still Hope After Late Career Job Loss?*, Thünen-Series of Applied Economic Theory Working Paper, No. 64, Rostock: University of Rostock.

Gabriel, Y., Gray, D. E. and Goregaokar, H. (2013) 'Job loss and its aftermath among managers and professionals: wounded, fragmented and flexible', *Work, Employment and Society*, 27(1): 56–72.

Gandini, A. (2016) *The Reputation Economy: Understanding Knowledge Work in Digital Society*, London: Palgrave.

Garrett-Peters, R. (2009) '"If I don't have to work anymore, who am I?": job loss and collaborative self-concept repair', *Journal of Contemporary Ethnography*, 38(5): 547–83.

Giuliani, G.A. (2020) 'The distributive implications of welfare reform packages. The Italian case during and after the great crisis', *European Politics and Society* [online first], 1–15.

Gray, D.E., Gabriel, Y. and Goregaokar, H. (2015) 'Coaching unemployed managers and professionals through the trauma of unemployment: derailed or undaunted?', *Management Learning*, 46(3): 299–316.

Hess, M., Nauman, E. and Steinkopf, L. (2017) 'Population ageing, the intergenerational conflict, and active ageing policies: a multilevel study of 27 European countries', *Population Ageing*, 10(1): 11–23.

Hood, J.C. (2007) 'Orthodoxy vs. power: the defining traits of grounded theory', in Bryant, A. and Charmaz, K. (eds) *The Sage Handbook of Grounded Theory*, London: Sage, pp 151–64.

Istat (2018) *Annuario Statistico Italiano* [online], available at: www.istat.it/it/files//2018/12/Asi-2018.pdf [accessed 27 September 2021].

Jessoula, M., Graziano, P.R. and Madama, I. (2010) ' "Selective flexicurity" in segmented labour markets: the case of Italian "mid-siders" ', *Journal of Social Policy*, 39(4): 561–83.

Jin, Y., Fukahori, R. and Morgavi, H. (2016) *Labour Market Transitions in Italy: Job Separation, Re-employment and Policy Implications*, OECD Economics Department Working Papers, No. 1291 [online], Paris: OECD Publishing, available at: www.oecd-ilibrary.org/economics/labour-market-transitions-in-italy_5jm0s95j78s1-en [accessed 27 September 2021].

Kalleberg, A.L. and Vallas, S.P. (2017) 'Probing precarious work: theory, research, and politics', in Kalleberg, A.L. and Vallas, S.P. (eds) *Precarious Work*, Bingley: Emerald Publishing Limited, pp 1–30.

Kira, M. and Klehe, U.C. (2016) 'Self-definition threats and potential for growth among mature-aged job-loss victims', *Human Resource Management Review*, 26(3): 242–59.

Lain, D., Airey, L., Loretto, W. and Vickerstaff, S. (2018) 'Understanding older worker precarity: the intersecting domains of jobs, households and the welfare state', *Ageing and Society*, 39(10): 2219–41.

Lane, C.M. (2011) *A Company of One: Insecurity, Independence, and the New World of White-Collar Unemployment*, Ithaca: Cornell University Press.

Legard, R., Keegan, J. and Ward, K. (2003) 'In-depth interviews', *Qualitative Research Practice: A Guide for Social Science Students and Researchers*, 6(1): 138–69.

López-Andreu, M. (2019) 'Neoliberal trends in collective bargaining and employment regulation in Spain, Italy and the UK: from institutional forms to institutional outcomes', *European Journal of Industrial Relations*, 25(4): 309–25.

Macnicol, J. (2006) *Age Discrimination: An Historical and Contemporary Analysis*, Cambridge: Cambridge University Press.

Marcaletti, F. (2013) 'La dinamica intergenerazionale nei mercati del lavoro: tra conflitto, mutua esclusione e misure per l'inclusività', *Studi di Sociologia*, 51(3–4): 307–16.

Mazzola, P., Rimoldi, S.M.L., Rossi, P., Noale, M., Rea, F., Facchini, C. et al (2016) 'Aging in Italy: the need for new welfare strategies in an old country', *The Gerontologist*, 56(3): 383–90.

Mendenhall, R., Kalil, A., Spindel, L.J. and Hart, C.M. (2008) 'Job loss at mid-life: managers and executives face the "new risk economy" ', *Social Forces*, 87(1): 185–209.

Morse, J.M. (1994) 'Designing funded qualitative research', in Denzin, N.K. and Lincoln, Y.S. (eds) *Handbook of Qualitative Research*, Thousand Oaks, CA: Sage, pp 220–35.

Murgia, A. (2011) ' "Flexible narratives": discursive positionings of gender and identity in precarious times', *Qualitative Sociology Review*, 7(11): 55–68.

OECD (Organisation for Economic Co-operation and Development) (2006) *Live Longer, Work Longer* [online], Paris: OECD Publishing, available at: www.oecd.org/employment/livelongerworklonger.htm [accessed 27 September 2021].

OECD (2015) *Pensions at a Glance 2015: OECD and G20 Indicators* [online], Paris: OECD Publishing, available at: www.oecd-ilibrary.org/social-iss ues-migration-health/pensions-at-a-glance-2015_pension_glance-2015-en [accessed 27 September 2021].

OECD (2017) *Pensions at a Glance 2017: OECD and G20 Indicators* [online], Paris: OECD Publishing, available at: www.oecd-ilibrary.org/social-iss ues-migration-health/pensions-at-a-glance-2017_pension_glance-2017-en [accessed 27 September 2021].

OECD (2019) *Pensions at a Glance 2019: OECD and G20 Indicators* [online], Paris: OECD Publishing, available at: www.oecd.org/publications/oecd-pensions-at-a-glance-19991363.htm [accessed 27 September 2021].

Perri, S. (2019) 'Italy on the way to Trumpism', *International Journal of Political Economy*, 48(3): 238–52.

Raito, P. and Lahelma, E. (2015) 'Coping with unemployment among journalists and managers', *Work, Employment and Society*, 29(5): 720–37.

Riach, K. and Loretto, W. (2009) 'Identity work and the unemployed worker: age, disability and the lived experience of the older unemployed', *Work, Employment and Society*, 23(1): 102–19.

Schmiz, A. (2013) 'Migrant self-employment between precariousness and self-exploitation', *Ephemera: Theory & Politics in Organization*, 13(1): 53–74.

Sennet, R. (2007) *The Culture of the New Capitalism*, New Haven, CT: Yale University Press.

Spyridakis, M. (2016) *The Liminal Worker: An Ethnography of Work, Unemployment and Precariousness in Contemporary Greece*, London: Routledge.

Steel, T. and Tuori, A. (2019) 'Older jobseekers' temporal identity work: relating to past, present, and future', *Nordic Journal of Working Life Studies*, 9(3): 25–43.

Stier, H. and Endeweld, M. (2015) 'Employment transitions and labor market exits: age and gender in the Israeli labor market', *Research in Social Stratification and Mobility*, 41: 92–102.

Thomas, R., Hardy, C., Cutcher, L. and Ainsworth, S. (2014) 'What's age got to do with it? On the critical analysis of age and organizations', *Organization Studies*, 35(11): 1569–84.

Unioncamere (nd) *Dirigenti: 50 Anni e Licenziati* [online], available at: www. filo.unioncamere.it/P42A4538C4529S0/Dirigenti--50-anni-e-licenziati. htm [accessed 27 September 2021].

Walker, A. (2006) 'Active ageing in employment: its meaning and potential', *Asia-Pacific Review*, 13(1): 78–93.

Weston, C., Gandell, T., Beauchamp, J., McAlpine, L., Wiseman, C. and Beauchamp, C. (2001) 'Analyzing interview data: the development and evolution of a coding system', *Qualitative Sociology*, 24(3): 381–400.

Zikic, J. and Richardson, J. (2007) 'Unlocking the careers of business professionals following job loss: sensemaking and career exploration of older workers', *Canadian Journal of Administrative Sciences/Revue Canadienne des Sciences de l'Administration*, 24(1): 58–73.

7

Divorced Women Working Past Pension Age in Germany and the UK: The Long Shadow of the Female Homemaker Model

Anna Hokema

Introduction

Demographic ageing, pluralization of life courses as well as major welfare state reforms across Europe have already, and will continue to, change the life phase of and transition into retirement in the years to come. It is well documented that divorced women in particular face difficult living conditions in old age, including their financial situation (see, for example, Jenkins, 2003; Price, 2006; Fasang et al 2013; Klammer, 2017). Daly writes in her comparative study on the impact of the German and British welfare states on gender relations that 'the well-being of existing lone mothers and divorced and separated women is a litmus test of the range of choices that states and societies make available for women' (Daly, 2000, p 216). But at the same time, women are particpating in greater numbers in the labour market, have longer work careers as well as their own pension entitlements. This societal context informs the analysis of divorced women working past state pension age (SPA) and living on their own in Germany and the UK. In line with the findings mentioned earlier, the influence of their income on their motivation to work past pension age will be explored. However, the analysis will go further by investigating more broadly the subjective reasons these women give for their continued employment, so that the significance of non-financial reasons can be assessed and a more holistic understanding of working in this life phase can be developed. Furthermore, the analysis will incorporate their family and work history as well as their subjective experiences and views on family models. This information will be related to their motivation and their overall experience of working past pension age. With this comparative approach, the influence of welfare state institutions such as the pension or employment system but also the gender regime can be tentatively considered.

This chapter aims to contribute to life course research on retirement as well as knowledge on work, gender and ageing (Ní Léime et al 2017). In particular, the distinct and often different experiences of women retiring from paid work and their subsequent life in retirement is only slowly being incorporated into mainstream research on ageing and retirement (see, for example, Price, 2003; Duberley et al 2014; Loretto and Vickerstaff, 2015; Duberley and Carmichael, 2016; Denninger and Schütze, 2017; Calvo et al 2018). Furthermore, employment past SPA is increasing throughout Europe and research is only gradually catching up with this development (see, for example, Alcover et al 2014; Scherger 2015). Nevertheless, many open questions remain with respect to this particular group of workers. Again, the gender perspective has only received limited attention (Pleau, 2010; Finch, 2014; Wildman, 2020). This holds especially true for the subjective experience from a comparative perspective of post-retirement employment (Hokema and Scherger, 2016).

The chapter proceeds in the following way: in the first main section, theoretical perspectives on post-retirement employment will be presented; the data collection and interpretation methods as well as the sample for this study will be described in the second section; the results will be presented in the third section and discussed in the final conclusion.

Theory and research on the life course, gender, welfare and post-retirement employment

Life course concepts

In this chapter, the lives of divorced women who have not re-partnered and work beyond pension age will be analyzed from a life course perspective, because this approach allows events and processes to be considered that have occurred in the past but still influence the current situation (see, for example, Elder et al 2003), and it facilitates the study of the influences of welfare state institutions on individual lives (Kohli, 1986; Leisering, 2003). The institutionalized life course is understood to be organized around the employment system and foresees a tripartite life course particularly for men, namely one life phase of education, one of work and one in retirement, where people live from the benefits accrued in midlife. Accordingly, the retirement life phase is understood to be free of the obligation to pursue paid work. Moreover, it is assumed that the institutionalized life course provides orientation for individuals. Moen and Flood use Krüger's concept of the life course regime (2003) when they write that individuals encounter 'age-graded institutionalized guidelines that open up or close down opportunities' (Moen and Flood, 2013, p 210) as they move through their lives. However, the institutionalized life course for women was not precisely explicated in the founding texts on this approach, but must implicitly be understood to consist of: education in childhood and youth, a short period of employment and then unpaid care work after marriage and birth of children – retirement is experienced via the husband (see, for example, Kohli, 1986: footnote 5). Moen calls this the 'gendered life course' (Moen, 2010, p 9), because the male breadwinner model is ingrained in state and business policies and practices as well as into expectations and assumptions about paid and unpaid work, which lead to the institutionalization of two different life courses for men and women. In a similar fashion, Krüger and Levy argue that institutions do gender as well (Krüger and Levy, 2001, p 163) and in this way offer men and women different and often complimentary roles (2001, p 158) in different spheres, such as in family and work life. Hence, they suggest that simultaneous and not just sequential participation in different life spheres should be analyzed in life course research (2001, p 160).

Life phases are connected by status passages involving changes in roles and statuses (Elder et al 2003). Heinz describes the function of status passages in the following way: 'status passages link institutions and actors by defining time-tables as well as exit markers for transitions between social status configurations' (Heinz, 1996, p 58). Obviously, retirement is the relevant status passage for this study, however, it remains to be seen whether individuals also experience it as a biographical interpretation point, which implies that an individual reinterprets his or her past, present and future after navigating the transition (Rosenthal, 1995, p 141). A further important biographical interpretation point for this study is divorce, which is explicitly named by Rosenthal in her works.

Agency is also an important concept in life course research and for this study, but it is also an elusive one and difficult to define. Without going into too much detail concerning the problems, I will use the following understanding offered by Elder et al who describe agency as an '[i]ndividual['s] construct[ion of] their own life course through the choices and actions they take within the opportunities and constraints of history and social circumstance' (2003, p 11). In this study, the welfare state and gendered cultural norms will be considered as opportunities and constraints of social circumstances.

The concept of gender regimes helps to conceptualize hierarchal gender arrangements in a society. It includes and distinguishes the normative and cultural level, institutional rules and regulations as well as lived practice (see, for example, MacRae, 2006). This means that it can also capture differences and irritations between these levels, such as a structural lag between the guidelines inherent in institutional rules and regulations and actual behaviour (Moen, 2003). As seen earlier, the historical embeddedness of life courses is also an important theme in life course research. Of particular interest for this study is the change in the normative model for family life during the lifetimes of the group observed here from the male breadwinner to the modified male breadwinner model (for more details see later).

Older divorced women

In line with the analysis of different male and female life courses, previous research on old-age incomes has consistently shown that – like the gender pay gap – a marked gender pension gap still exists in Europe. Data from across the European Union can show that in 2018 the gender pension gap was 37.4 per cent in Germany and 34.2 per cent in the UK (Eurostat, 2021). These lower pension incomes of women are related to more intermittent work careers, including longer phases of atypical employment, breaks from paid work to care for others, but also gender-segregated labour markets and gender discrimination more generally that lead to wage differences and overall fewer years spent in work (see, for example, Möhring, 2014; Tinios et al 2015; Ní Léime et al 2017). In the past, female employment careers ended earlier than male ones, on the one hand because of lower pension ages but also because of looser labour market attachment and alternative responsibilities resulting from other social roles, such as looking after grandchildren or older relatives in need of long-term care (see, for example, Moen, 2001; Duberley et al 2014).

When looking at old-age incomes it is important to consider the household context (Loretto and Vickerstaff, 2013). Married women feature the lowest in terms of individual pension income compared to divorced women in West Germany and the UK, but they have a spouse with whom to pool their income (see, for example, Evandrou et al 2009; Fasang et al 2013). Women who never married have the highest pension income but cannot – like divorced women – share their resources with someone else, unless they are cohabiting with a partner (Evandrou et al 2009; Fasang et al 2013). Price et al can show that in 2006, in the UK 43 per cent of divorced or separated women over 65 were living in poverty (defined as having an income below 60 per cent of the median population income and adjusted for household size), for men the poorest groups were widowed (31 per cent) and never-married men (29 per cent) (Price et al 2016, pp 1808–09). Finding equivalent numbers for Germany is more difficult because officially published poverty rates (such as in the Federal Reports on Poverty and Wealth) are not differentiated by marital status and sometimes not even by gender (see, for a critical discussion, Bundesministerium für Familie, Senioren, Frauen und Jugend, 2011, p 207), but a general tendency can be discerned. The latest old-age income report of the Ministry of Work and Social Affairs names the average monthly income of divorced women over 65 as 1,393 Euro and that of divorced men as 1,710 Euro in 2019 (Bundesministerium für Arbeit und Soziales, 2021, p 102). Divorced women have the lowest incomes compared to all single women. Married men have an average net income of 1,945 Euro and it is the second-highest income of all compared groups. To put these incomes into context, the at-risk-of-poverty threshold was calculated at 1,175 Euro a month in 2019, which represents 60 per cent of the median of the net equalized income (Bundesamt für Statistik, 2021).

The question is, how large is the group of divorced women that did not re-partner? Research has shown that divorced women are less likely than men to re-partner or remarry in old age and subsequently spend old age alone, and that this group is growing (Moen, 2001, p 179). In Germany, in 2014, 14.8 per cent of the 55–69-year-olds were divorced or separated, which was a steep increase from 6.2 per cent in 1996 (Engstler and Klaus, 2016, p 205). Of these, 13.3 per cent were men and 16.2 per cent were women (GeroStat – Deutsches Zentrum für Altersfragen, 2018). In the UK, 12.2 per cent of men and 16.0 per cent of women aged 50 and older are divorced or separated and in the age group 65–69, 12.9 per cent of men and 19.3 per cent of women are divorced or separated (Matthews and Nazroo, 2016, p 228).

Working beyond state pension age

Both changes in pension and employment policies as well as older people's changing self-perceptions have shifted social perceptions of older people in society away from the disengaged, inactive, family-centred, often poor old person to the active, engaged, self-sufficient senior citizen who wants and is expected to contribute to society (see, for example, Walker, 2007). The active ageing concept has surfaced in international policy debates and corresponds with gerontological concepts such as active and successful ageing (see, for a critical discussion, van Dyk, 2014). However, this generally positive development of understanding older people as a more diverse group that participates in various ways in society (volunteering, working, caring) also has negative side effects, because it raises expectations about what older people have to do and contribute once they are past pension age (Moulaert and Biggs, 2013; van Dyk, 2014).

Increasing numbers of people go on working past pension age. Developments across Europe are heterogeneous and result in different employment rates in this age group. The employment ratios of people aged

Table 7.1: Population/employment ratio of the age group 65–69 in per cent in Germany and the UK

		2000	2005	2010	2015	2020
Germany	Men	7.4	8.4	10.8	18.3	20.6
	Women	3.1	4.7	6.5	11.0	13.4
United Kingdom	Men	14.4	18.5	23.9	25.9	27.6
	Women	8.4	10.6	15.9	16.6	20.5
European Union 27	Men	11.2	11.9	13.2	15.1	16.5
	Women	6.1	6.2	7.7	8.6	10.0

Source: OECD, 2021 – own compilation

between 65 and 69 years in the two countries under investigation in this chapter increased steadily over the past 15 years (see Table 7.1). Additionally, the table shows that more people in this age group work in the UK than in Germany and that in both countries more men than women work past SPA. However, both countries have a higher employment ratio than the EU average.

Research on working beyond pension age in Germany and the UK has shown that good health and higher education have a positive effect on the probability of working past pension age (Scherger et al 2012). As we saw earlier, being female has a negative influence on the probability. With respect to the role of income, studies arrive at differing and mixed results. For the UK, the need for individual income seems to be a more consistent finding because Lain (2015) and Lux (2016) can both show that household income (without the income from employment) is lower for people working past pension age compared to non-workers in the same age group. Slightly older German studies are not that conclusive in their findings. Brenke (2013), for example, shows that it is not financial hardship that drives people to work past pension age. However, working pensioners' household incomes are lower without the income from work compared to non-working households, but then with the income added they are higher than the non-worker household incomes (Brenke, 2013, p 10).

Quantitative and qualitative studies looking both at Germany and the UK find that, when looking at individual reasons for working past pension age, financial reasons are mentioned less often than non-financial reasons (Engstler and Romeu Gordo, 2014; Hagemann et al 2015; Hokema 2016; Hokema and Scherger, 2016). Non-financial reasons include fun and enjoyment of the work activity, to be physically and mentally active, to structure the day, to create biographical continuity, social contacts, and respect (Hagemann et al 2015). However, when gender, marital status and social class are included in the analysis, financial reasons become more important in the overall motivation for divorced women or working men and women in the lower classes (Hokema and Lux, 2015; Hokema and Scherger, 2016). Country differences become only tentatively visible in the subjective accounts, even though the institutional set-ups are very different, as will be seen in the next section.

When looking at retirement intentions and actual behaviour, Damman et al (2015) can show for their Dutch sample of older female workers that divorced women who did not re-partner intend to and actually do retire later than married and re-partnered divorced women. But the effect of partnership status on actual retirement behaviour seems to be mediated by having a challenging job, good health and a perceived pension shortfall, because after adding those aspects to their statistical model, being single, divorced and retiring later was no longer statistically significant (Damman et al 2015, pp 357–8).

Institutional context: pension system, male breadwinner model, female employment

With paid employment beyond pension age being shaped by earlier work careers and pensions, the following institutions frame individual employment decisions and behaviour. The West German welfare state was for a long time considered to be the archetypical conservative welfare state (see, for example, Esping-Andersen, 1990), aiming at status preservation with its social insurances to cover unemployment, old age, sickness and long-term care of the male breadwinner and through him also a wife and children. Furthermore, the welfare state was, and to a certain extent still is, marked by explicit familialism (Leitner, 2003, p 371), because the family was and is seen as the major provider of unpaid care work for children and the elderly, and this role is encouraged by leave options and compensatory benefits (Daly, 2000). Until the early 1980s, the male breadwinner model was the normative family model inherent in the welfare state and was also the widely lived family practice in West Germany. It subsequently changed into a modified male breadwinner model, which encompassed full-time employment for men across the life course until (early) retirement and the homemaker role and major responsibility for childcare for wives, supplemented with only an additional earner role in part-time employment. The German welfare state to this day supports and favours this living arrangement of married couples through the taxation system and derived welfare rights for wives such as pension payments.

For a long time the German pension system was defined as a 'social insurance pension system' (Bonoli, 2003), which implied the primacy of the public pension and only an additional and rather marginal role for occupational and private pensions. This has changed since the major pension reforms at the beginning of this century (Schulze and Jochem, 2006), but has not affected the generation of pensioners considered in this study. Since the German pension system is organized in such a way that lifelong full-time employment yields the highest pensions, women and especially mothers (except for the current generation of older women from East Germany) have lower pensions. However, married women are covered through their husbands' pensions and receive survivor's benefits consisting of 55 per cent of the deceased's pension. Pension entitlements are shared in the event of divorce (Meyer and Pfau-Effinger, 2006). Meyer and Pfau-Effinger (2006) show that the German pension system moderately supports the male breadwinner model, because it always gave wives the chance to gain individual pension rights, either through paid employment or care-related pension rights for unpaid family care. But in other parts of the welfare state, the gender culture and actual lived family practice was more traditional.

Even though the British welfare state belongs to a different regime type, namely that of the liberal welfare state (Esping-Andersen, 1990), the normative family model, including the division of labour between men and women, and the associated labour force participation patterns of women, did not and still do not look so different to Germany. One marked difference is that British women started to participate earlier in greater numbers in the labour market than German women and that in contrast to Germany, part-time employment remained constant over the years. Part-time employment of mothers was and still is high, because the market, which is the main provider, only offers a moderate amount of affordable childcare. Except for healthcare, the British welfare state can be framed as a residual welfare state that leaves caring to the family or the market and only provides support when all other options are exhausted and then often only after a means test as a low flat-rate payment (Daly, 2000).

The British pension system is characterized as a multi-pillar system (Bonoli, 2003), which means that the basic state pension only provides a low flat-rate pension that needs to be complemented by occupational and/or private pensions. The opportunities to pay into occupational or private pensions are unequally distributed across the British labour market: women and low qualified workers have less access to them and are less able to pay into them continuously because of their intermittent work careers (Ginn and Arber, 1999; Ginn, 2003). Meyer and Pfau-Effinger describe the British pension system up to the 1970s as based on a strong male breadwinner model, because married women could choose to be exempt from paying National Insurance contributions when in paid work, but would thereby forgo the possibility of receiving their own state pension. This so-called Married Women's Option was difficult to avoid until it was abolished in 1975. Also in the same year, the Home Responsibilities Protection was introduced, which made caring periods count as credit for the basic state pension. From this period on (married) women could build up their own pension rights and were slightly less dependent on their husbands' old-age incomes, hence Meyer and Pfau-Effinger describe the British pension system from then on – like the German one – only moderately enforcing a male breadwinner model (Meyer and Pfau-Effinger, 2006). In the event of divorce, pension rights are shared as well. Both pension systems allow people over the SPA to work and earn as much money as they want without reducing pension payments.

Preliminary conclusion

Even though data for the two countries on the different topics mentioned earlier are very different, it becomes clear that women, especially mothers and even more so divorced women, are a vulnerable group in old age, as Orloff quotes feminist researchers 'women are often only a husband away from poverty' (Orloff, 1993, p 319). Even though the pension systems of the two countries under investigation have tried to tackle this problem by splitting pension entitlements in half for the time of the marriage at divorce, research has shown that this is not sufficient, because divorced women often reduced their working hours or even stopped working while married and raising children and they have difficulty making up for this after the divorce (see, for example, Ginn and Price, 2002; Price et al 2016; Klammer, 2017).

Pulling together these research findings and theoretical perspectives, the intention in this analysis is to examine the subjective self-reported reasons for working beyond pension age of divorced women who have not re-partnered, as well as their decisions and actions concerning pension saving and retirement. The influences of the normative family model and the welfare state that come to light in the individual accounts of life choices will be explored. The question will be discussed of whether the institutionalized (female) life course served as an orientation during the respondents' lives and whether it is mentioned as a reference point in the interviews, especially since interviewees in this study deviate from it in several ways: first, because they are working during a life phase that is understood to be free of the obligation to work; second, they lived their adult lives during a time period that foresaw the worker role for them at best only as an additional activity to the main responsibility of unpaid care work; third, they experienced a divorce which includes the termination of the implicit contract of being safeguarded by the spouse or his derived welfare rights; fourth, they lived their subsequent life as a single person – marriage, especially in Germany, enjoys supremacy over other forms of family life in law as it is mentioned specifically in the Basic Law of Germany. Additionally, they are unable to pool their financial resources.

Methods

The empirical basis for the findings presented later is a subsample of a larger qualitative study on post-retirement employment in Germany and the UK (Hokema, 2016). The sample for this study consists of ten interviewees, who, at the time of the interview, lived by themselves, but who had been married until midlife and had children (see Table 7.2 for more detail). The ten women are between the age of 68 and 79 years (all names are pseudonyms). Three women live in the UK and seven in Germany. Education and jobs

Table 7.2: Sample overview of female divorced interviewees

Name (pseudonym)	Country	Age	Children	Education	Job before SPA	Job after SPA
Edith Fichte	Germany (GDR till 1990)	76	2	Degree in teaching	Teacher	Private tutor
Marianne Lorenz	Germany	71	1	Vocational training as assistant tax accountant	Assistant tax accountant	Assistant tax accountant
Erika Hoffmann	Germany	74	1	Vocational training as a travel agent	Travel agent	Supervisor in museum
Olivia MacDonald	UK	73	4	None	Office clerk	Canteen assistant
Margrit Peters	Germany	79	4	Vocational training as office clerk	Accountant	Proofreader for local newspaper
Elke Schwab	Germany	75	3	None	Office clerk	Courier
Christa Stark	Germany	71	1	Vocational training in accounting	Office clerk in bank	Canteen assistant
Monika Weber	Germany	68	1	Vocational training as multilingual secretary	Secretary	Secretary and proofreader
Linda Wilson	UK	68	2	Degree in teaching	Teacher, adult teacher	Supply teacher
Judy Wood	UK	68	1	Degree in teaching	Teacher	Language teacher and language teacher trainer

before and after SPA vary enormously and will be discussed in more detail in the next section. All women have children, and the number of children varies between one and four.

The data was collected in the form of problem-centred interviews (Witzel and Reiter, 2012), which varied between 50 and 120 minutes in length and touched on the topics of work before and after pension age, leisure time activities, the experience of ageing and health, pension saving and views on the pension system. Each section generated a lengthy narrative by the interviewees on the topic, which guaranteed that individuals could mention the topics that were relevant to them and could set their own emphasis. The interviews were transcribed verbatim and were analyzed in several thematic coding cycles (Saldaña, 2013), the cycles moved from open coding to more analytic coding and the development of theoretically influenced categories. Additionally, biographical case reconstructions were written to help identify patterns across the life course and to counteract the rather dissecting method of coding. The institutional influences in particular came to light in the case reconstructions and could be traced across the cases.

Results

The analysis of the group of British and German female divorcees working past pension age shows a distinct life course pattern that can in parts be traced back to them following the normative family ideal – as depicted earlier – and then deviating from it through the divorce and reaping the consequences of this into old age, which has implications for post-retirement employment and the subjective reasoning behind it. Their life courses look as follows: first, the period before the divorce entails education, family formation and an intermittent work career; second, the divorce happens in midlife, consequently they re-enter the labour market or switch to full-time employment as well as start individual pension planning; and third, they continue employment past SPA in various ways and for several subjective reasons. Since a qualitative approach is followed, not only the similarities but also the differences between the women can be explored in the following section.

Post-retirement employment as a deliberate retirement activity to increase one's finances and independence

The divorced women in this study present their continued or newly found employment as a consciously chosen activity. One reason for this is that the divorced women living by themselves continue working because they rely on this income. This is how Judy Wood describes it:

'because in a way I always feel as I didn't really have a choice about not working, stopping working. Because I would have managed but it would've been a struggle and I would have had to not [do] a lot of the things I like doing which is travelling and going on holidays and so on. And, so, in a way it was never when I was approaching 60 ... it never entered my head not to work over the age of 60 because I always knew that I would have to and when I got the state pension, financially it was a little bit easier and I was able to save because what I feel I'm doing now is all of those years when I opted out of paying into a pension scheme I now manage to save ... and I kind of get it paying into my pension now although I'm not in a pension scheme I'm saving and making up for the years when I didn't.' (Judy Wood, 68, English language teacher, UK)

Similarly, Elke Schwab and Linda Wilson present retirement and not working as not possible.

All except two interviewees present financial reasons as equally important or more important than non-financial reasons. This is not surprising when the literature on older divorced women is considered (Ginn and Price, 2002; Price, 2006). Divorced and single women have the lowest financial incomes compared to their married peers (Evandrou et al 2009). The interviewees directly connect their financial situation in old age to their life course and divorce. Erika Hoffmann opens the interview with the following statement: "Yes, well, how I came to work is, well, [it] comes from my life, worked for 14 years only part-time and got divorced after a 25-year-long marriage and then the pension is of course not so great, right" (Erika Hoffmann, 74, supervisor in museum, Germany). However, it is well worth looking in detail at the financial reasons presented. As the earlier quote from Judy shows, she describes that not working would mainly prevent her from being able to travel and to save money. Others use it to finance a car or extras that they could not afford otherwise. What becomes clear in these examples is that they mostly use their additional income to maintain their standard of living from before retirement age.

When comparing the accounts, something else becomes apparent when they talk about their income from work: working also makes it possible for them to live an independent and self-sufficient life. In light of their life course as a homemaker and additional earner before their divorce, this aspect gives the interviewees a great deal of satisfaction. Edith Fichte, for example, talks in great detail about how she likes working because it gives her something interesting to do and structures her day, and then she says the following: "and these are all things that are let's say three quarters, and apart from all of these positive things enough money comes in that I won't get rich but I have the feeling I can make it alone" (Edith Fichte, 78, self-employed tutor, Germany). Pensions, saving and money in general are important themes in the interviews. Two women want to save a concrete sum of money and then they will stop working. Others speak with great pride about what they have saved already. Being responsible for one's own finances and handling them well brings satisfaction.

Non-financial reasons as an important driving force: enjoyment of the activity and meeting other people

Looking at the accounts where they talk about the reasons for their employment past pension age, it becomes evident that the women also present a wide array of non-pecuniary reasons for why they work. The most important ones are enjoyment of the activity, the possibility of meeting and being with people and the structuring of the day through work. The former seems to act as a prerequisite, they would not do it if they did not enjoy the activity or feel positively challenged. The interviewees describe in great detail what they like about their work. Erika Hoffmann says: "yes, and that [the work] is fun and you know it is then as well the mind will dry up slowly, right, a lot is getting lost and eh, when you're only at home, no, I can't imagine that" (Erika Hoffmann, 74, supervisor in museum, Germany). In this quote something else becomes apparent: the interviewees believe that through their work they can counteract mental decline.

A high level of agency can be observed to fit the work to their needs. They talk about how they got rid of less satisfying work tasks or only work the hours they like. Nearly all interviewees work part-time, sometimes only a couple of hours per week, often on a self-employed basis, which gives them the freedom to set their own times. Being with people is also very important to those women who have not re-partnered. Even though most women mention extensive social networks in the interviews, including family and friends, meeting other people through work seems to fulfil a special need. They especially emphasize being with younger people through work. All women mention how being by themselves in old age can be difficult sometimes, especially with respect to finances but also with respect to social integration, because they observe that friends who do have a spouse spend a lot of time with them and family. Interestingly, volunteering – a typical activity in retirement – is not pursued by the women in this sample, because it directly competes with time for work and family and friends.

In sum, there is never just one reason why the women work; it is mostly an even balance of non-financial and financial reasons. This contrasts with other studies on the topic, where non-financial reasons dominate the accounts of partnered female and male working pensioners (Hagemann et al 2015; Hokema, 2016). In general, all interviewees portray a positive experience of working past pension age. Only few in this group feel that they need to work, for most it is by choice to improve their situation. Even though some interviewees believe that they had no choice but to work past pension age, they all feel that they could stop working anytime they want. This might seem contradictory, but it sets post-retirement employment apart from work before SPA and is in line with the normative perception of being past pension age or being of retirement age, because even for those women retirement is the life phase without a work obligation, even though they are working. The orientation function of the tripartite life course is still meaningful to them. This might also explain the positive experience of working, even though some of the jobs have poor working conditions, such as the canteen assistant jobs of Olivia MacDonald and Christa Stark or the courier job of Elke Schwab. These jobs are physically demanding and especially for Elke Schwab, the courier driver, involve long hours, but the positive aspects such as meeting people and having a structure to the day outweigh this to some extent.

Divorce as a biographical turning point: taking (work) life into their own hands

The divorce is portrayed as a significant turning point, which spurs narratives on agentic action in the interviews. Most of the interviewees divorced in their late 40s or early 50s and it proves to be a biographical interpretation point (Rosenthal, 1995) in their lives. Correspondingly, all of these women started to take a stronger interest in their work careers, increasing to full-time work and changing employers secure better career prospects. Their narratives about work become more important in the interviews, their descriptions of the work tasks take up more room and a lot of agency can be observed, but in addition the difficulty these women faced returning to the labour market after years of staying home also become apparent. A number of women report difficulties in finding the right job during that time and that they had to move from job to job until they found a suitable arrangement for themselves, as the quote from Monika Weber demonstrates:

'I had a part-time job and my employer was practically a one-man-show and my boss was already older and I thought about this very clearly, he will maybe close shop in a couple of years, then you are 50 or a bit over 50 and you will perhaps not get a proper job again and what will happen to your pension then? You'd better start looking for something else' (Monika Weber, 68, secretary, Germany)

She finds a full-time job as a public employee, which also enables her to pay into an occupational pension scheme, and she stays in this position until she reaches SPA. This quote is exemplary for the increased agency the freshly divorced women show to improve their situation. In contrast to their accounts from before the divorce, they exhibit a work orientation and an interest in individual pension planning. Most interviewees report in the interview that they received part of their ex-husband's pension entitlements after the divorce or National Insurance contributions in the UK. However, the process of sharing occupational pension entitlements is more complicated and often they did not bother. The interviewees in this study present very different reasons for not doing so: most just did not want to prolong the painful period of splitting up and did not want any further contact with their former spouses, others say that they did not know that they also had a right to private and occupational pension pots, and some receive other compensation such as property. Edith Fichte constitutes a very special case in the study, as she divorced in the GDR which means she has no right to receive half of her ex-husband's public or occupational pension entitlements.

Accordingly, the divorced women spent the period after the divorce making up for the time they lived in accordance with the normative family model as a homemaker or additional earner. Before pension age, they all work in full-time positions to save as much as possible for their retirement. The female life course as an orientation frame loses its meaning.

Various ways of becoming a working pensioner

In this study, three different patterns of becoming a working pensioner become visible: Marianne Lorenz, Linda Wilson and Judy Wood just keep on working in their jobs past pension age and until the point of the interview. Marianne Lorenz says, when asked how it came about that she kept on working:

> 'That topic never arose, that I should stop working. I only thought at some point I need to claim my pension and at that time as a woman you could retire earlier and you had no [pension] deductions, because deductions I couldn't afford at all ... I went into retirement at 64 [she means that she started to draw her state pension at 64] my pension comes in anyway and I never considered stopping work' (Marianne Lorenz, 71, tax accountant, Germany)

As can be seen, for these women, reaching retirement age is not a biographical turning point in which they reinterpret their life – they go on as before and they postpone the status passage indefinitely. The literature on post-retirement employment calls these workers 'stayers' (Smeaton and McKay, 2003, p 34). 'Stayers' in this and in other studies work in higher-skilled jobs and take home higher wages than so-called 'movers'. Their employers did not encourage their retirement, and everything stayed the same.

A similar attitude towards retirement age can be observed in the accounts of Edith Fichte, Olivia MacDonald and Elke Schwab, but they present a different employment pattern: they are in and out of jobs before and after SPA, but none of the exits are presented as retirement. Edith Fichte and Olivia MacDonald are unemployed around SPA and find a new job and Elke Schwab changes jobs voluntarily from being employed to working on a self-employed basis. Moen et al observe that female work careers of this generation have been very intermittent, and this also influences women's retirement experiences. They write that '[m]oving in and out of the workforce meant that women often viewed their exits as simply another "leaving" rather than an official retirement' (2005, p 238). This description is suitable for this group of women, and consequently their return or re-entry into the labour market past pension age is experienced as simply one more re-entry. The jobs pursued by these women are either on a self-employed basis or low skilled.

In contrast, four German interviewees indicate that they formally retired from their career job. Erika Hoffmann and Christa Stark both take early retirement because they feel tired and exhausted. Monika Weber and Margrit Peters retire at SPA because their employer indicates that they cannot stay. These four do not work for a few years until they find a new job. However, all of these jobs are low skilled, low paid and with flexible work arrangements.

In all narratives on working beyond pension age the influence of the employer becomes visible, either as an encouraging or discouraging factor (see also Vickerstaff, 2006). In Germany, SPA is perceived as quite a strong age limit to end working careers (Kohli, 2000). However, it becomes clear that all women found individual ways to break through this barrier, either by staying on or finding a new and different work arrangement.

Institutional influences in the life stories: the long shadow of the female homemaker model

Throughout the interviews, institutional influences become visible: the pension systems, the normative family model that is inherent in the welfare states and society at large, how it changes as well as the gendered educational and employment systems.

All women chose female-dominated occupational training or university subjects, for example vocational training for office work or university courses for teaching. The British women in the sample either did not enter formal occupational training or went to university, which is typical for the British education system, because it does not feature a formalized vocational training system for intermediately qualified jobs as is typical for Germany. One German and two British women studied to become teachers.

Having children implied for all (except two) interviewees taking a break from paid work for a couple of years and concentrating on non-paid caring. The accounts of leaving the labour market differ. Some just state it as a matter of fact and the division of labour between mother, father and state is not called into question, such as in the case of Margrit Peters: "I have four children and while the children needed care I didn't work" (Margrit Peters, 79, proofreader for the local paper, Germany). But others portray it retrospectively as not exactly according to their own wishes. Marianne Lorenz says:

> 'Because, you know, back then when you were married and a mother – today, fortunately, a woman can go on working, I am all for that, I support my daughter-in-law, I say to her "you'd better go on working so that you get on with your career", it wasn't like that for my generation, you stayed at home and I was never the type, I thought no, I don't want to only stay at home and when my son started nursery school, he was born in 1966, I thought, that was 1969, right, now you start again' (Marianne Lorenz, 71, assistant tax accountant, Germany)

It does not become clear in this quote who made her stay at home, the absence of adequate child care facilities, the social role available to her or – such as in the case of Olivia MacDonald – her husband, as the following quote shows: "[W]hen I had my family I didn't work [because] my man didn't believe in me working, he didn't want me working, he said 'I'm the breadwinner' so it kind of kept me down a wee bit" (Olivia MacDonald, 73, canteen assistant, UK). Three women return to work after about six months or a year, one because of a looming early divorce, one lived and worked in the GDR where the state strongly encouraged a speedy return to work, and one interviewee refers to the influence of the women's liberation movement as the reason. This is the only interview in which the women's liberation movement is mentioned directly. Indirectly, all women were affected by it, because it helped to transform the family model from a male breadwinner to a modified breadwinner model, which implied the part-time worker role for married mothers. None of the interviewees mentioned that fathers were so actively involved in the care of the young children that they reduced their paid work.

In sum, very different influences become evident in the accounts of taking over the unpaid family caring tasks: the women's own wishes and beliefs about family care, the influence of the state as the facilitator of care outside the home (in Germany) only after a certain age, the influence of social roles, of spouses but also cultural influences such as the women's liberation movement. Retrospectively, it is not possible to distinguish which was strongest. What does become clear is that taking on the caring responsibilities at home often went hand in hand with not engaging in individual financial and pension planning, which is not surprising since the male breadwinner and female homemaker model implied the family wage was provided by the husband or welfare state rights accrued through the husband. This becomes obvious in the quote from Monika Weber: "No, that [pension planning] didn't worry me at all and I didn't even realize it, I didn't think about it at all, because it was still this old-fashioned attitude back then, after all I had this well-earning husband and basically nothing could go wrong any more" (Monika Weber, 68, secretary, Germany). Also, when asked about pension planning the interviewees who returned to the labour market when their children started school or nursery school, do not recount pension planning before the divorce. Similarly, no active career planning or job changes are reported. All of these women returned to work part-time and into jobs that did not foresee career advancement. Only Judy Wood and Christa Stark, the two early divorcees in the sample, report job changes and promotions during their employment career very similar to male life courses.

The two quotes in this sub-section also show that the women in this study all acknowledge that the family model, including the assigned role for women, has changed. Hardly surprisingly, most women comment favourably on this change. Their life courses changed accordingly and more so because they worked full-time before SPA and even go on working past SPA. This deviation is justified by their divorce.

Conclusion

The detailed exploration of the life courses of divorced women working past pension age who have not re-partnered makes clear that these women were affected by the cultural norms and institutional incentives of the time that encouraged them to follow the (modified) male breadwinner model and to trust the promise that their husbands and/or their acquired welfare state rights would look after them in old age. However, at the same time the analysis shows how meaningful the biographical interpretation point of divorce in late midlife was for these women to reinterpret their plans and actions to live independent and self-determined lives into old age. Even the quite strong age boundary of retirement age becomes blurry for the majority of the women. This might also be connected to the fact that retirement age in general is less influential for female than for male life courses (Moen et al 2005). Employment past pension age is pursued with the explicit goal of enhancing their old-age incomes, but also a great variety of non-pecuniary reasons are described in detail. They act as a kind of prerequisite: if the women did not like the activity, they would not pursue it. Agency is observed with respect to pension saving, finding appropriate jobs and adjusting working times and the work content to their needs before and past pension age.

Although the work careers and educational backgrounds are quite heterogeneous in this study, it becomes evident that unlike in other studies (for example, Hokema and Lux, 2015; Repetti and Calasanti, 2018), the women's perspective on working is not so different after all. The divorce and the resultant financial burden were so influential that possible class differences become less important or invisible in the subjective accounts. Country differences are also not pronounced in this study. This might be due to the small sample or to the fact that the gender regimes of the two countries are not that different compared to the pension and labour market systems. With respect to the orientation function of the (female) life course, the results are mixed: the women started their adult lives in accordance with the then dominant family model, but most interviewees only see that as a problem retrospectively. Most work full-time in the second half of their work biography until SPA, which is more in accordance with the male than the female life course, and this is justified by their divorce. Pension age is not that decisive and definitely not a strong turning point for most, which can be explained either as typical for females or because the normative life course has lost its orientation function. The tripartite structure is, however, not generally called into question, because they feel working past pension age is a voluntary activity to better their situation but also for fun. Working before SPA is definitely seen as a different activity.

It has been agued elsewhere that working pensioners in general are a selective and privileged group that have the health and skill resources as well as individual interest to work into old age (Scherger et al 2012; Brenke, 2013), something that cannot be observed for all members of this age group and should not be expected of all retirees. This holds especially true for the group that has been investigated here. It can be understood as a remarkable achievement on the part of these women that they were able to return to reasonably good and pensionable jobs after being quite distant from the labour market or having worked in part-time jobs with few prospects for career development. Many other divorced older women were unable to do so and hence are classified as one of the most vulnerable groups in old age (Klammer, 2017).

Lastly, the overall positive experience of working past pension age, despite a financial incentive to do so, can be traced back to the normative assumption that retirement is a life phase free of the obligation to work that is also shared by the women in this study. They present their continued employment past pension age as an option to increase their income in old age but also as an activity that brings them joy, social integration and a mechanism to structure the day or week. Other activities such as being with friends and family, travelling and pursuing hobbies are also important pastimes that these women mention, which are typical for that life phase. Initiatives such as making productive activities obligatory or the excepted behaviour in retirement must be seen as problematic in this context as well as pension reforms that reduce pension levels further. This is especially the case when considering that unpaid caring activities are still expected from and predominantly carried out by women.

References

Alcover, C.-M., Topa, G., Parry, E., Fraccaroli, F. and Depolo, M. (eds) (2014) *Bridge Employment: A Research Handbook*, Oxford: Routledge.

Bonoli, G. (2003) 'Two worlds of pension reform in Western Europe', *Comparative Politics*, 35(4): 399–416.

Brenke, K. (2013) 'Immer mehr Menschen im Rentenalter sind berufstätig', *DIW Wochenbericht*, 80(6): 3–12.

Bundesamt für Statistik (2021) *Armutsgefährdungsschwelle und Armutsgefährdung (monetäre Armut) in Deutschland* [online], available at: www.destatis.de/DE/Themen/Gesellschaft-Umwelt/Einkommen-Konsum-Lebensbedingun gen/Lebensbedingungen-Armutsgefaehrdung/Tabellen/armutsschwelle-gefaehrdung-silc.html [accessed 14 September 2021].

Bundesministerium für Arbeit und Soziales (2021) *Ergänzender Bericht der Bundesregierung zum Rentenversicherungsbericht 2020 gemäß § 154 Abs. 2 SGB VI (Alterssicherungsbericht 2020)*, Berlin: BMAS.

Bundesministerium für Familie, Senioren, Frauen und Jugend (2011) *Neue Wege – Gleiche Chancen. Gleichstellung von Frauen und Männern im Lebensverlauf. Erster Gleichstellungsbericht der Bunderegierung*, Berlin: Bundesministerium für Familie, Senioren, Frauen und Jugend.

Calvo, E., Madero-Cabib, I. and Staudinger, U.M. (2018) 'Retirement sequences of older Americans: moderately destandardized and highly stratified across gender, class, and race', *The Gerontologist*, 58(6): 1166–76.

Daly, M. (2000) *The Gender Division of Welfare. The Impact of the British and the German Welfare States*, Cambridge: Cambridge University Press.

Damman, M., Henkens, K. and Kalmijn, M. (2015) 'Women's retirement intentions and behavior: the role of childbearing and marital histories', *European Journal of Population*, 31(4): 339–63.

Denninger, T. and Schütze, L. (eds) (2017) *Alter(n) und Geschlecht: Neuverhandlungen eines sozialen Zusammenhangs*, Münster: Westfälisches Dampfboot.

Duberley, J. and Carmichael, F. (2016) 'Career pathways into retirement in the UK: linking older women's pasts to the present', *Gender, Work and Organization*, 23(6): 582–99.

Duberley, J., Carmichael, F. and Szmigin, I. (2014) 'Exploring women's retirement: continuity, context and career transition', *Gender, Work and Organization*, 21(1): 71–90.

Elder, G.H., Johnson, M.K. and Crosnoe, R. (2003) 'The emergence and development of life course theory', in Mortimer, J.T. and Shanahan, M.J. (eds) *Handbook of the Life Course*, Boston: Springer, pp 3–19.

Engstler, H. and Romeu Gordo, L. (2014) 'Arbeiten im Ruhestand – Entwicklung, Faktoren und Motive der Erwerbstätigkeit von Altersrentenbeziehern', in Kirstler, E. and Tischler, F. (eds) *Reformen auf dem Arbeitsmarkt und in der Alterssicherung – Folgen für die Einkunftslage im Alter*, Düsseldorf: Hans-Böckler-Stiftung, pp 115–48.

Engstler, H. and Klaus, D. (2016) 'Auslaufmodell „traditionelle Ehe"? Wandel der Lebensformen und der Arbeitsteilung von Paaren in der zweiten Lebenshälfte der Lebensformen und der Arbeitsteilung von Paaren in der zweiten Lebenshälfe', in Mahne, K., Wolff, J.K., Simonson, J. and Tesch-Römer, C. (eds) *Altern im Wandel: Zwei Jahrzehnte Deutscher Alterssurvey*, Wiesbaden: Springer VS, pp 201–13.

Esping-Andersen, G. (1990) *The Three Worlds of Welfare Capitalism*, Cambridge: Polity Press.

Eurostat (2021) *Gender Pension Gap by Age Group – EU-SILC Survey* [online], available at: https://ec.europa.eu/eurostat/de/web/products-eurostat-news/-/ddn-20200207-1 [accessed 12 September 2021].

Evandrou, M., Falkingham, J. and Sefton, T. (2009) *Women's Family Histories and Incomes in Later Life in the UK, US and West Germany*, CASE Discussion Paper 138, London: London School of Economics.

Fasang, A.E., Aisenbrey, S. and Schömann, K. (2013) 'Women's retirement income in Germany and Britain', *European Sociological Review*, 29(5): 968–80.

Finch, N. (2014) 'Why are women more likely than men to extend paid work? The impact of work–family life history', *European Journal of Ageing*, 11(1): 31–9.

GeroStat – Deutsches Zentrum für Altersfragen (2018) *Deutscher Alterssurvey (DEAS) – 1996, 2002, 2008, 2014*. DOI 10.5156/GEROSTAT.

Ginn, J. (2003) *Gender, Pensions and the Lifecourse*, Bristol: Policy Press.

Ginn, J. and Arber, S. (1999) 'Changing patterns of pension inequality: the shift from state to private sources', *Ageing and Society*, 19(3): 319–42.

Ginn, J. and Price, D. (2002) 'Do divorced women catch up in pension building?', *Child and Family Law Quarterly*, 14(2): 157–74.

Hagemann, S., Hokema, A. and Scherger, S. (2015) 'Erwerbstätigkeit jenseits der Rentengrenze. Erfahrung und Deutung erwerbsbezogener Handlungsspielräume im Alter', *BIOS – Zeitschrift für Biographieforschung, Oral History und Lebensverlaufsanalysen*, 28(1–2): 119–47.

Heinz, W.R. (1996) 'Status passages as micro-macro linkages in life course research', in Weymann, A. and Heinz, W.R. (eds) *Society and Biography: Interrelationships between Social Structure, Institutions and the Life Course*, Weinheim: Deutscher Studien Verlag, pp 51–66.

Hokema, A. (2016) *Deferred, Reversed or 'Normal' Retirement? The Subjective Experience of Working Beyond Pension Age in Germany and the UK*, PhD thesis, Bremen: University of Bremen.

Hokema, A. and Lux, T. (2015) 'The social stratification of work beyond pension age in Germany and the UK: quantitative and qualitative evidence', in Scherger, S. (ed) *Paid Work Beyond Pension Age. Comparative Perspectives*, Basingstoke: Palgrave Macmillan, pp 57–80.

Hokema, A. and Scherger, S. (2016) 'Working pensioners in Germany and the UK: quantitative and qualitative evidence on gender, marital status, and the reasons for working', *Journal of Population Ageing*, 9(1–2): 91–111.

Jenkins, C.L. (2003) 'Introduction: widows and divorcees in later life', *Journal of Women and Aging*, 15(2–3): 1–6.

Klammer, U. (2017) 'Alterssicherung von Frauen revisited – aktuelle Entwicklungen und zukünftige Perspektiven', *Sozialer Fortschritt*, 66(5): 359–75.

Kohli, M. (1986) 'The world we forgot: a historical review of life course', in Marshall, V.W. (ed) *Later Life: The Social Psychology of Aging*, Beverly Hills, CA: Sage, pp 271–303.

Kohli, M. (2000) 'Altersgrenzen als gesellschaftliches Regulativ individueller Lebenslaufgestaltung: ein Anachronismus', *Zeitschrift für Gerontologie und Geriatrie*, 33(1)(Supplement): S057–70.

Krüger, H. (2003) 'The life-course regime: ambiguities between interrelatedness and individualization', in Heinz, W. and Marshall, V. (eds) *Social Dynamics of the Life Course: Transitions, Institutions, and Interrelations*, Hawthrone: Aldine De Gruyter, pp 33–56.

Krüger, H. and Levy, R. (2001) 'Linking life courses, work, and the family: theorizing a not so visible nexus between women and men', *Canadian Journal of Sociology*, 26(2): 145–66.

Lain, D. (2015) 'Work beyond age 65 in England and the USA', in Scherger, S. (ed) *Paid Work Beyond Pension Age. Comparative Perspectives*, Basingstoke: Palgrave Macmillan, pp 31–56.

Leisering, L. (2003) 'Government and the life course', in Shanahan, M.J. and Mortimer, J.T. (eds) *Handbook of the Life Course*, Boston: Springer, pp 205–25.

Leitner, S. (2003) 'Varieties of familialism: the caring function of the family in comparative perspective', *European Societies*, 5(4): 353–75.

Loretto, W. and Vickerstaff, S. (2013) 'The domestic and gendered context for retirement', *Human Relations*, 66(1): 65–86.

Loretto, W. and Vickerstaff, S. (2015) 'Gender, age and flexible working in later life', *Work, Employment and Society*, 29(2): 233–49.

Lux, T. (2016) *Dissecting Later-life Employment: The Social Structure of Work after Pension Age in Germany and the United Kingdom*, PhD thesis, Bremen: University of Bremen.

MacRae, H. (2006) 'Rescaling gender relations: the influence of European directives on the German gender regime', *Social Politics*, 13(4): 522–50.

Matthews, K. and Nazroo, J. (2016) *Social Domain Tables*, in Banks, J., Batty, G.D., Nazroo, J. and Steptoe, A. (eds) *The Dynamics of Ageing. Evidence from the English Longitudinal Study of Ageing 2002–2015 (Wave 7)*, London: Institute for Fiscal Studies, pp 218–48.

Meyer, T. and Pfau-Effinger, B. (2006) 'Gender arrangements and pension systems in Britain and Germany: tracing change over five decades', *International Journal of Ageing and Later Life*, 1(2): 67–100.

Moen, P. (2001) 'The gendered life course', in Binstock, R.H. and George, L.K. (eds) *Handbook of Aging and the Social Sciences*, San Diego, CA: Academic Press, pp 179–96.

Moen, P. (2003) 'Linked lives: dual careers, gender, and the contingent life course', in Heinz, W.R. and Marshall, V.W. (eds) *Social Dynamics of the Life Course*, Hawthrone: Aldine De Gruyter, pp 237–58.

Moen, P. (2010) *From 'Work–Family' to the 'Gendered Life Course' and 'Fit': Five Challenges to the Field*, Discussion Paper SP I 2010-501, Berlin: Social Science Research Center Berlin.

Moen, P. and Flood, S. (2013) 'Limited engagements? Women's and men's work/volunteer time in the encore life course stage', *Social Problems*, 60(2): 206–33.

Moen, P., Sweet, S. and Swisher, R. (2005) 'Embedded career clocks: the case of retirement planning', *Advances in Life Course Research*, 9: 237–65.

Möhring, K. (2014) 'Der Einfluss von Kindererziehungszeiten und Mütterrenten auf das Alterseinkommen von Müttern in Europa', *Vierteljahrshefte zur Wirtschaftsforschung*, 83(2): 139–55.

Moulaert, T. and Biggs, S. (2013) 'International and European policy on work and retirement: reinventing critical perspectives on active ageing and mature subjectivity', *Human Relations*, 66(1): 23–43.

Ní Léime, Á., Street, D., Vickerstaff, S., Krekula, C. and Loretto, W. (eds) (2017) *Gender, Ageing and Extended Working Life: Cross-national Perspectives*, Bristol: Policy Press.

OECD (Organisation for Economic Co-operation and Development) (2021) *Labour Force Participation Rate by Gender and Age (65–69) in Per Cent in Germany, UK and the European Union* [online], available at: https://stats.oecd.org/Index.aspx?DataSetCode=lfs_sexage_i_r# [accessed 12 September 2021].

Orloff, A.S. (1993) 'Gender and the social right of citizenship: the comparative analysis of gender relations and welfare states', *American Sociological Review*, 58(3): 303–28.

Pleau, R.L. (2010) 'Gender differences in postretirement employment', *Research on Aging*, 32(3): 267–303.

Price, C.A. (2003) 'Professional women's retirement adjustment: the experience of reestablishing order', *Journal of Aging Studies*, 17(3): 341–55.

Price, D. (2006) 'Why are older women in the UK poor?', *Quality in Ageing*, 7(2): 23–32.

Price, D., Glaser, K., Ginn, J. and Nicholls, M. (2016) 'How important are state transfers for reducing poverty rates in later life?', *Ageing and Society*, 36(9): 1794–825.

Repetti, M. and Calasanti, T. (2018) '"Since I retired, I can take things as they come. For example, the laundry": gender, class and freedom in retirement in Switzerland', *Ageing and Society*, 38(8): 1556–80.

Rosenthal, G. (1995) *Erlebte und erzählte Lebensgeschichte: Gestalt und Struktur biographischer Selbstbeschreibungen*, Frankfurt/New York: Campus Verlag.

Saldaña, J. (2013) *The Coding Manual for Qualitative Research*, Los Angeles, CA: Sage.

Scherger, S. (ed) (2015) *Paid Work beyond Pension Age. Comparative Perspectives*, Basingstoke: Palgrave Macmillan.

Scherger, S., Hagemann, S., Hokema, A. and Lux, T. (2012) *Between Privilege and Burden. Work Past Retirement Age in Germany and the UK*, ZeS Working Paper 4/ 2012, Bremen: Centre for Social Policy Research.

Schulze, I. and Jochem, S. (2006) 'Germany: beyond policy gridlock', in Immergut, E.M., Anderson, K.M. and Schulze, I. (eds) *The Handbook of West European Pension Politics*, Oxford: Oxford University Press, pp 660–712.

Smeaton, D. and McKay, S. (2003) *Working after State Pension Age: Quantitative Analysis*, Department for Work and Pensions Research Report, No 182, London: Department of Work and Pensions.

Tinios, P., Bettio, F. and Betti, G. (2015) *Men, Women and Pensions* [online], available at: http://ec.europa.eu/justice/gender-equality/files/documents/vision_report_en.pdf [accessed 16 June 2018].

van Dyk, S. (2014) 'The appraisal of difference: critical gerontology and the active-ageing-paradigm', *Journal of Aging Studies*, 31: 93–103.

Vickerstaff, S. (2006) '"I'd rather keep running to the end and then jump off the cliff". Retirement decisions: who decides?' *Journal of Social Policy*, 35(3): 455–72.

Walker, A. (2007) 'The new politics of old age', in Wahl, H.-W., Tesch-Römer, C. and Hoff, A. (eds) *New Dynamics in Old Age*, Amityville, NY: Baywood Publishing Company, Inc., pp 307–24.

Wildman, J.M. (2020) 'Life-course influences on extended working: experiences of women in a UK baby-boom birth cohort', *Work, Employment and Society*, 3(2): 211–22.

Witzel, A. and Reiter, H. (2012) *The Problem-centred Interview*, Los Angeles, CA: Sage.

8

Expectations of Transitions
to Retirement in Ireland

Áine Ní Léime

Introduction

This chapter explores expectations about the transition to retirement for older women workers in Ireland in the context of policies introduced in recent years to extend working lives (EWL). It focuses on the retirement plans of workers in two very different occupations – teaching and home care work. Teaching is a well-paid and predominantly secure occupation in Ireland, with a generous occupational pension, while home care is physically demanding and often precarious, with relatively low pay and unfavourable conditions.

The chapter first discusses the changing policy context influencing transitions from work into retirement in Ireland. The research methodology, which draws on a life course lifecourse perspective, is outlined next. Qualitative findings from interviews with ten teachers and ten healthcare workers are then presented; these offer valuable insights about these individuals' expected transitions into retirement and their views about extended working life (EWL). The discussion demonstrates the contrasting implications of EWL policies for these two different groups of women, with teachers to a large extent being protected from many of the disadvantages that raising state pension age poses for home care workers. Finally, the implications of the findings for pensions and employment policy in Ireland are considered.

The policy context for transitions into retirement in Ireland

Institutional context for women's retirement in Ireland

Ireland has been commonly designated as a liberal welfare state (Esping-Andersen, 1990), where cash benefits and state pensions have been provided at modest levels by European standards. It has also historically been regarded as a 'male breadwinner' state with gender discriminatory legislation in the past, including a marriage bar until 1973, which meant that women working in the public sector were legally compelled to leave their jobs when they married. Taxation policies historically discouraged married women from paid employment, and employment policies to promote gender equality were not introduced until after Ireland joined the European Union in 1973 (Mahon, 1998). These earlier discriminatory policies affected many of today's older women workers, limiting their employment possibilities. Consequently, as we saw in Chapter 1, female employment in Ireland is lower than in other 'liberal' welfare states, although it has risen significantly since the early 2000s.

Pensions system in Ireland

The Irish pension system is composed of three pillars – state, occupational and private pensions. There are two state pensions – a contributory state pension (SPC) and a lower 'safety net' non-contributory pension (SPNC) for those who do not qualify for the SPC. The amount of the SPC depends on the number and years of contributions, and a full SPC is €12,911.60 per annum as at 2019 (Department of Social Protection, 2021a). A higher proportion of women (61 per cent) than men receive the lower SPNC (€12,324 in 2019), while a lower proportion of women (37 per cent) than men receive a full SPC (Ní Léime et al 2020). Periods spent caring from 1994 onwards can be credited towards the SPC (up to a maximum of 20 years), but many older women (including some in this study) will not benefit from this because they were out of the labour market looking after children before 1994 (Ní Léime et al 2020). Similar proportions of Irish men and women have occupational or private pensions, or both (46 per cent for women and 47 per cent for men). However, there is a lower level of personal (private) pension coverage for women (11 per cent), compared to men (25 per cent) (Central Statistics Office, 2016). Private pension coverage is nevertheless low for men and women, despite tax incentives, partly due to a loss of trust in private pensions in Ireland following the global financial crisis of 2008.

Policies to extend working life

The government (following Organisation for Economic Co-operation and Development [OECD] recommendations) has introduced policies to EWL, although Ireland has a relatively young population with 13.8 per cent of people aged 65 or over (CIA, 2021). These policies have been critiqued as being economistic and overly focused on the narrow neoliberal goal of reducing pension costs without sufficiently assessing the impacts for different groups in society (Mouleart and Biggs, 2013). A series of reforms was announced in 2012 when new pension bands were introduced, the effect of which was to link the pension more closely to participation in the labour market, making it more difficult for women to build up full state contributory pensions (Bassett, 2017). A Total Contributions Approach was subsequently introduced to address some of the disadvantages of the new pension bands; however, this still links pension amounts more closely than previously to participation in the labour market. The number of contributions required for a minimum state contributory pension was doubled from 260 to 520.

Ireland is noteworthy in terms of raising the state pension age to 66 comparatively early, in 2014, and not making a reduced pension available at an earlier age (see Chapter 1). There were also further plans for the state pension age to rise to 67 in 2021 and 68 by 2028. However, prior to the 2020 general election, there were strong objections by trade unions and other organizations to the proposed increase, based on potential hardship for those in physically onerous jobs and because many workers would have worked for between 40 and 50 years by the age of 66. In response, most political parties announced that they would postpone increasing the state pension age (SPA). The current government has suspended the increase in SPA that was due to be introduced in 2021 and set up a Commission on Pensions to reconsider the issue. The Pensions' Commission report has recommended introducing a more gradual change to the SPA – to increase by three months each year, starting in 2028, reaching 67 in 2031 with further increases of three months every second year to reach 68 in 2039. The government is currently considering the recommendation (Department of Social Protection, 2021b) and at the time of writing (May 2022) an announcement is expected later in the year. Nevertheless, the increase in SPA to 66 has already intensified the need to work longer. An anomalous situation in Ireland is that although the SPA is 66, employers can still legally retain a contractual retirement age, typically 65, leaving a gap between retirement and SPA. This was the case for the private healthcare workers in this study at the time of the interviews, although public sector workers have since been granted the right to work to 70. In such instances of people leaving jobs at 65 they are likely to be reliant on Retirement Benefit (formerly Jobseekers' Benefit) for a year, or an occupational pension.

The context for the retirement of teachers and carers in Ireland

Teachers

Teaching is a feminized occupation in Ireland: 85 per cent of primary school teachers and 69 per cent of secondary school teachers were women in 2017–18, while women accounted for only 67 per cent of primary school principals (Department of Education and Skills, 2021). It is a predominantly public sector occupation with most teachers being trade union members who receive information on pensions from the union. Entry to the profession requires specialized third level training typically involving a three-year degree for primary school teachers and usually a primary degree and a master's degree (formerly a Higher Diploma) for secondary school teachers. Teachers' pay in Ireland is relatively generous. The average salary for a primary school teacher with 15 years' experience in Ireland is €62,179 per annum, well above the OECD average of €46,801; pay is €62,781 for equivalent secondary school teachers (Department of Education and Skills, 2020). Teaching has traditionally been a secure job, although it can take time to gain a permanent contract. Pay levels were reduced for new teachers recruited after the 2008 global financial crisis.

Transitions to retirement for teachers

Teachers in second-level schools recruited before 2004 (most teachers participating in this study) may retire voluntarily at any time from age 60 onwards. There is provision for early retirement (from age 55, with 35 years' service) and for retirement on disability grounds subject to minimum service and medical verification. Those recruited after 2004 may retire from age 65 onwards. Those recruited after 2013 are enrolled in the Public Service Single Pension Scheme, where the minimum pension age is linked to the SPA which is currently 66. A minority of study participants were recruited post-2004. In December 2018, the government introduced an Act to allow public sector workers, including teachers, to continue working until age 70; as noted earlier, this was introduced after these interviews were conducted. Teachers (recruited before 2004) have a relatively generous occupational pension calculated at 1/80th of final salary for a maximum of 40 years and they are also entitled to a gratuity calculated as 3/80th of final salary for each year of pensionable service. The amount of pension for teachers with 40 years of contributions is considerably higher than the full state contributory pension. More women than men teachers in Ireland take career breaks or job share (Department of Education and Skills, 2021).

Previous Irish research indicates that teaching can be stressful – especially at second level and that teachers are facing increasing demands related to administration and child welfare (Kerr et al 2011). Teaching is also acknowledged to be psychologically demanding (Grayson and Alvarez, 2008). Even though teaching is not physically demanding in the same way as caring, it is recognized that teaching at all levels requires considerable energy (Viotti et al 2017).

There is evidence that teachers internationally tend to retire earlier than workers in other occupations (Droogenbroeck and Spruyt, 2014). Pension systems, especially defined benefit systems, appear to have a strong influence in creating a relatively early 'normalised retirement age' (Furgeson et al 2006). US research on teachers' retirement shows a strong link between having amassed a full or nearly full pension and the timing of retirement (Friedberg and Turner, 2010). Other factors affecting teachers' decisions to retire early are physical and emotional burnout and bullying (Fahie and Devine, 2014). Physical burnout is more relevant for teachers of young children. The influence of peers – retiring when they retire – is also important (Droogenbroeck and Spruyt, 2014).

Home care workers (carers)

Home care work is a growing sector in Ireland, due to demographic ageing and is also a predominantly female occupation (Timonen et al 2012; Timonen and Lolich, 2019). This chapter focuses on workers involved in personal care for older people in their homes. In Ireland, although government rhetoric states that home care for older people in the community is the preferred option, current funding structures favour care in residential settings. Community care provision is limited and is increasingly being outsourced to private agencies, although the state's Health Service Executive (HSE) do employ some home care workers. Timonen and Lolich (2019) note that there is little regulation of the formal home care sector or recognition of home care workers. The terms 'home care workers' and 'carers' will be used interchangeably in this chapter. Those employed by the HSE have better pay and conditions and are more likely to be unionized than those employed by private agencies. Carers employed by the HSE have the option of contributing to an occupational pension. This is unlikely to be the case for those employed by a private agency, and low pay and inconsistent hours make it difficult for them to contribute to a private pension. Many, therefore, are likely to depend on state pensions (Ní Léime and Street, 2019).

A scoping review of health care aides found that there has been relatively little research on these workers, despite the importance and expansion of the sector (Hewko et al 2015). Carers in Ireland provide personal care to older people in their own homes. They may help their clients to shower, dress, eat, ensure they take medication and may also perform some light housework (Timonen and Lolich, 2019). Such work may be physically demanding as it often involves assisting clients to move around their homes, and such workers are known to be at greater risk than other workers of musculoskeletal injuries (McCaughey et al 2012). Carers, particularly those working for private agencies are usually poorly paid and often do not have regular hours of work from week to week (Ní Léime and Street, 2019). Government cutbacks mean that carers are often only allowed minimal time to perform instrumental tasks for clients and do not have sufficient time to talk to them, a situation which many carers find stressful (Duffy et al 2015). The relatively scarce research on older home care workers in Ireland has primarily focused on specific groups such as migrant care workers (Doyle and Timonen, 2009; Walsh and O'Shea, 2009; Cangiano and Walsh, 2014).

Attitudes to extended working life in Ireland

As we saw in Chapter 1, retirement in Ireland has historically occurred relatively late. In the early 2000s Ireland had the highest effective male and female 'retirement' ages of all the countries examined, at over 65. Research indicates that workers in Ireland today for the most part do not support extending working life further, and in fact most would like to retire well before the current pension age of 66 (Eurofound, 2017). However, there has been little research that analyzes the perspectives of older workers on EWL policies at an occupational level in Ireland (although see Ní Léime and Street, 2019) and none that specifically examines these attitudes in the context of their retirement plans as the current chapter does. Research on the attitude of workers to extending working life in the Netherlands found strong negative reactions to having to work longer, especially where job demands are high and personal. They found that anger and worry were more prevalent among older workers in lower occupational and manual jobs, and among those with longer careers, poorer health, and less favourable finances and social resources (Van Solinge and Henkens, 2017). Recent research shows that retirement norms and health concerns affect health professionals' views on EWL; however, this chapter offers additional insights by exploring how the health concerns of carers are affected by working in low-paid, precarious employment (Roy et al 2018).

Methods

The interview data drawn upon for this chapter are 20 interviews conducted in 2017 with ten female teachers and ten female home care workers in Ireland. This is a subset of a larger study with a purposive sample of teachers, academics, healthcare workers and janitors in Ireland and the United States. Participants were recruited through trade unions and other contacts initially and then through snowball sampling. Interviews were conducted in a variety of locations chosen by participants – their workplace, the interviewer's office, their homes or a location nearby. Interviews were audio-recorded and lasted between 55 minutes and 2 hours. Participants gave an account of their work-life history, their current working conditions, experiences and health. They were asked when they planned to retire, what influences their decision and for their views on the increase in SPA. Data are anonymized and pseudonyms are used.

A life course framework (drawing on Giele and Elder, 1998) was used initially to analyze the interview transcripts. Work-life trajectories were identified with attention paid to timing, location in time and space (including policy and events in the economy), the degree of agency, and linked lives (influence of family and friends). For this chapter, participants' retirement timing plans, the main influences on their retirement decisions and their perspectives on extending working life were analyzed thematically.

Table 8.1 sets out features of the socio-economic profile of the workers. Teachers were younger, because at the time the study took place they were required to retire by age 65, while three of the home care workers were aged over 65. Most women in both occupations were married. Carers had a lower level of education and a lower income; all but one teacher earned more than the highest-paid carer. Teachers had occupational pensions, while most carers were going to be reliant on the state safety net non-contributory pension or a partial contributory pension; some had partial pensions from abroad. A similar number of teachers and carers had chronic health conditions; however, for teachers these were not work-related, while for carers, they were.

Findings

Work-life trajectories for teachers and carers

The work-life trajectories of teachers and carers differed in several respects (see Ní Léime and Street 2019 for a more extended discussion). Many of the teachers interviewed were strongly encouraged by their families to become teachers, to participate in higher education and/or had teachers as role models in their families. Alice's account of her decision was typical:

> 'Well, I'd say my father decided for me. He kept saying it would be a lovely job and a cushy job [laughs]. And he kind of ... he was such a persuasive man that I was nearly doing it to half please him nearly. And sure I didn't have any other major thought anyway at the time, so I thought well ... teaching is in both sides of the family – my granny was a teacher on one side.' (Alice, teacher, age 57)

Their families encouraged higher education and most had the resources to support it. For several teachers, this led to a trajectory of stable employment, with mostly uninterrupted pension-building. Six teachers had worked in their current jobs for an average of 29 years. For others their careers and pension-building were interrupted by job-sharing or taking career breaks or both in order to travel and/or to care for their children; as a result they needed to work longer and/or pay additional voluntary pension contributions

Table 8.1: Profile of teachers and carers

	Teachers	Carers
Age group		
45–54	2	3
55–64	8	4
65–74	0	3
Marital status		
Married	9	8
Single	1	1
Divorced/separated	0	1
Education: highest level	*UGD: 2 *UGD + **H Dip: 5 *UGD + **H Dip+ master's: 2 *UGD + 2 **H Dips: 1	Primary: 1 Lower secondary: 1 Leaving certificate: 7 *UGD: 1
Number of children		
0–3	7	4
4 or more	3	6
Annual income range	€20–40,000 per year: 1 €60–80,000 per year: 7 €80–100,000 per year: 2	Under €20,000 per year: 7 €20–40,000 per year: 3
Pensions	Full/near full occupational pensions: 6 Lower pensions: career breaks, job-shares: 4	***SNCP only: 6 ***SNCP + small private pension: 2 ****SCP part + small UK/US pension: 2
Health	Back, knee or osteoarthritis: 3 Generally healthy: 7	Arthritis, aneurysm or depression: 3 Generally healthy: 7

*UGD: Bachelor of Education or BA or BSc. **H Dip: Higher Diploma in Education.
***SNCP: State Non-Contributory Pension. ****SCP: State Contributory Pension.

in order to have full pensions. One woman who moved to Ireland from abroad expected to have a much lower pension.

The reasons carers gave for leaving school were markedly different to those given by teachers. Two left school in their teens because they came from large families where the money from their wages was needed, or because they wanted to contribute. For example, Ita, from a family of 14, left school at age 13: "I thought I would go to work, I would help my mother and father" (Ita, carer, age 62).

Many healthcare workers left paid work for lengthy periods – 13 years on average – to care for their children and tended to have larger families than the teachers (see Table 8.1). Many moved between low-paid work, unpaid care and paid caring roles across the life course leading to interrupted (state) pension contributions. Several women began work as carers in the community at the request of neighbours, community organizations or families of older people after caring for their own children for many years. While some loved the work, others entered home healthcare because they felt unqualified for other work: "I suppose I was at home a long time and, you know, I suppose hadn't sort of done anything in between except look after children" (Alex, carer, age 68).

For others there were few alternative employment opportunities in rural areas, or the hours fitted in with childcare. These very different work-life trajectories, working conditions, pay levels and access to pensions led to different attitudes to retirement timing.

Retirement timing for teachers
Financial/pension influences for teachers

In general, many of the teachers interviewed wanted to, and were in a position to, retire early with generous pensions. Several were also married to husbands with high earnings (teachers, accountants, other professionals) and/or good pension prospects. For example, three teachers planned to retire in their late 50s – two at age 57 and one at age 59. One of the main reasons these teachers gave for retiring early was that they had sufficient pension contributions to be financially comfortable in retirement: "I have enough years and I've paid back years and all that kind of thing ... there is a maximum amount of years which I won't have done but ... you can buy back years [with additional pension contributions]" (Alice, teacher, age 57). Another who planned to retire at age 57 also cited having full service as a motivation: "I am in the happy position where I have my service and I can go when I want to" (Caitriona, teacher, age 55).

Emer, aged 59, planned to retire in a few months and would have retired earlier had she not been the main breadwinner:

'Well, I suppose really most teachers now once they reach 55 and they have 33 years done they can retire, and a lot of ... my colleagues would have done that so I had the option of doing that ... but having children and my husband doesn't work at the moment so I'm kind of the breadwinner in the family so I decided I would keep going just a little bit longer.' (Emer, teacher, age 59)

This quote illustrates that it is normative for teachers with full service to retire early, demonstrating the influence of the occupational pension scheme.

Other teachers planned to retire at age 60. Two said that they would have retired earlier than this, but they needed to keep working either because they job-shared and/or took a career break and needed to contribute more to their pension. Another said she would stay until age 60 because she enjoyed her work and it was an important part of her identity, but she did not want to stay past the point where she was an effective teacher.

Finally the remaining four planned to stay until between the ages of 60 and 65. One was going to retire at age 62–63 – she still had financial commitments with children in college and a mortgage, but planned to retire as soon as possible because she wanted healthy years in retirement. Two expected to stay until age 65 as they were the family breadwinners and had insufficient years of service. One had returned to Ireland after many years abroad while another had moved to Ireland from abroad and had to retrain as a teacher in Ireland. Only one person stated that she *wanted* to stay to age 65 because she enjoyed working and disliked the prospect of retirement.

Health influences for teachers

While many teachers cited financial reasons as a main factor influencing retirement timing, for several health was also an important consideration. For example, some had existing health conditions. One, though she loved her job, recognized that it adversely affected her health and planned to retire at 57 for that reason:

'But ... there is one reason I'm retiring really, I suppose, and that is I suffer from rheumatoid arthritis for the last 25 years, and the one downside I find is the tiredness nowadays. So I want to try and kind of look after my health in that sense, so, you know, when I come out of school I am tired and I'm fine after a day or two so I realized it's the early getting up in the mornings and all that, you know. You get so busy, when I'm there I get so busy and I love it but ... I feel as I'm getting older I should look after my health a bit.' (Alice, teacher, age 57)

Others cited the fear of developing ill health as part of their motivation for retiring:

'I had a health scare a couple of years ago and that made me think about it more and a lot of, there is another teacher now who is a couple of years older than me and she is very sick at the moment ... but I think, God, if something like that happened, yeah, well, you would have to retire then to get your lump sum for your family.' (Caitriona, teacher, age 55)

Others said that they had worked for long enough and that they wanted some healthy years in retirement to engage in other activities: "At this point, 36 years, I think, really is long enough, you know, I suppose for the family and for my own health and well-being as well and it's enough – it's time to stop now and just concentrate on other things" (Emer, teacher, age 59). While some teachers said they enjoyed their job, for all but one, the prospect of retiring on a good pension while still healthy made retirement more attractive than staying on. Some emphasized the physical demands of teaching. One woman felt that teaching had become increasingly tiring as she aged; she also wanted healthy years in retirement, and believed that staying until 65 would compromise her health. She cited the example of her mother who worked to age 65 and died early as a motivation to retire:

> 'Yeah. I've to travel too far. I suppose if I was teaching next door I might stay on a bit longer. And it is a young person's job. You need a lot of energy for it. And also my mother is one of eight and they were all teachers; primary, secondary or third level. She is the only one that went to 65 and she is the only one that's dead. The rest of them are all, are still alive and kicking.' (Deirdre, teacher, age 57)

For these reasons, she planned to leave at age 60, even without a full pension – she could afford this because her husband was still working and had a good income.

While most said they would discuss retirement with their husbands/partners, most were not coordinating their retirement timing with them. There was little reference to grandparenting as a motivation for retirement, perhaps, partly because most did not yet have grandchildren.

Retirement timing for carers

In contrast to teachers, most home care workers said they were going to be dependent on the SPNC or a partial contributory pension (SPC) in retirement; they did not have generous occupational pension schemes that would enable them to retire early. Several were married to men who did not have occupational pensions. A few had partial HSE occupational pensions, but most could not afford to pay additional contributions to these pensions to compensate for years spent out of paid employment. Those working for private agencies were not offered a pension and most could not afford private pensions. Unlike the teachers, none planned to retire before age 60. Two said they would like to retire at age 60. One of these individuals said this would not be possible, however, because she needed to work to 65 for financial reasons. The other felt that 60 was a good age to retire and spend time with her family, and she was in a financial position to do this. Two women planned to retire at age 66 when they qualified for the state pension, while a third had already retired at age 66 because of health and financial reasons and the feeling that she had worked for long enough. Finally, some wanted to work to age 70, two because they enjoyed the work and were healthy, one, a family breadwinner out of financial necessity; and another to supplement her (partial) state pension (although she felt she would be unable to work past age 70 due to the physical demands of the job). One of these individuals wanted to work to age 70, but already had a work-related back injury and was unsure whether this would be possible.

Financial influences for carers

Those who were working because they liked the job and the extra money it provided expected to work for as long as they were healthy enough. Others who were family breadwinners stated that they needed to work longer. For example, one woman who was separated, believed she may have to work until age 70, although she did not want to: "I do have four children and I have a mortgage on my house so you can well imagine by the time I come to retire ... I'll still probably be paying a mortgage until I'm 70 and even ... as hard as I work, I don't really want to be working until I'm 70" (Jane, carer, age 48). Fiona, whose husband did not have a good pension, said she would have to work longer than she would like to: "Em, I kind of had 60 in my head but I think that's gonna be pushed on more than that ... just financially, I'll have to keep going for another while" (Fiona, carer, age 54). Bridget, whose husband had a good occupational pension, was relieved to have retired when she qualified for her state pension at age 66:

'I just simply retired at 66 on the date of my birthday. I was so glad to leave all the work behind me and spend time at home. And of course then I had my pension and I had a "salary" every week anyway. It made it very easy, because I would probably not have earned maybe the same [from caring] as my pension and a lot less at times. So I felt that I was getting a salary every week and I could be in my own home. It was a good feeling.' (Bridget, former carer, age 69)

Bridget's experience illustrates both the low level and the inconsistency of pay for agency home care workers.

Health influences for carers

Health considerations influenced carers' retirement decisions. Some had already developed chronic musculoskeletal health issues that were worsening with age and likely to prevent them from continuing with this type of work. For example, Evelyn had osteoarthritis:

'I always remember people talking years ago about, you know, as you get older you have less energy and I used to think to myself, "What are they on about?" But now I do realize it that definitely it makes a difference, yeah. Or maybe it's because I have this thing in my feet [osteoarthritis] that slows me down'. (Evelyn, carer, age 66)

Both Evelyn and others said that the desire to retire while relatively healthy influenced their retirement timing expectations: "And you don't know how your health is going to turn out, you know, as you get older you just don't know what's happening from day to day, so I want to have that bit of freedom before anything does happen to me" (Evelyn, carer, age 66). For these workers, there was an awareness that the work was physically demanding and may prompt them to retire: "But, you know, because sometimes it's very physical as well, you know, mentally and physically, you know. So yeah, I suppose if I thought to myself no, I don't want to do this any more, no, I'm not able to do it" (Alex, carer, age 68). Others felt that they had worked long enough, were tired and wanted time to care for themselves: "I felt I was getting a little bit tired, and I felt I had done my bit for society. I just kind of felt it was time to look after myself and to take time out to rest and exercise and, yeah, I was well ready ... really ready to retire at 66" (Bridget, carer, age 69). For some carers, health concerns were exacerbated by onerous working arrangements.

Difficult working conditions for carers

One carer noted the toll that working long, piecemeal hours required by employers took on her energy and her time:

'You need a lot of energy for this caring and driving and like it's not a continuous, you know, if you went and you're back with somebody in the morning you'd have to go back again in the afternoon and then again at night time so it's kind of your whole day would be taken up, I suppose.' (Evelyn, carer, age 66)

She was looking forward to retirement partly to avoid having to work long disrupted days. Another in her mid-50s wanted to leave the job because of the poor pay and conditions, but was unable to due to financial needs – she had four children, and she and her husband had had to spend much of their savings during the recession caused by the global financial crisis.

Enjoying the work

Some health care workers stated that they wanted to stay on at work for a long time, because they loved the work and were very healthy: "I hope I'll be able to keep going 'til around 70 … because I think if – when I see, when I leave the person's house – my client's house and they're happy, well, I'm on cloud nine" (Greta, carer, age 56). Some carers said they hoped to spend time with grandchildren when they retired, although this was not cited as a direct motivation for retiring and they were currently combining helping out with grandchildren with their work.

Teachers' views on extended working life

Many teachers had a negative view of raising SPA. Others felt that it was necessary, but that working until 67 should be a choice and that it should not be imposed on people in physical jobs.

Some felt that working past age 65 would be challenging for teachers, especially teachers of younger children. For example, one teacher said:

> 'In terms of teaching, yeah, well, I think it depends on the class you have, I mean, I think definitely I couldn't see somebody who is very old teaching junior infants. You need a lot of energy and a lot of moving up and down and that kind of thing. … I think by 67 they [teachers] will be well spent and they'll be well wrecked, I think they [the government] should leave it [pension age] at 65 really. (Barbara, teacher, age 60)

Most of those interviewed would not need to continue working because of the increase in SPA as they had occupational pensions. However, most stated that the proposed increase was unfair for a variety of reasons including disrupted expectations, health issues for those in physically demanding work and there was a strong view that retirement after age 65 should be a choice. Caitriona, for example, discussed the difficulties caused by disrupting people's pension expectations:

> 'I think … it is rotten to change it halfway through when you have something set in your head. I mean, if you're very young say and you're starting out working you don't care because you don't even imagine what you will be like at that age, but if you're kind of coming up to retirement I think people shouldn't be forced to work longer than they want to work.' (Caitriona, teacher, age 55)

Other teachers highlighted the health challenges of working to age 67:

'And if they are expecting people to work until they're 67 and 68 should that not be a strand, you know, it's obligatory on the part of the state to ensure that the people are healthy enough to be able to continue and if they're not then – is there another role that they can go into instead.' (Geraldine, teacher, age 56)

These individuals suggested that the government should support people to change jobs if necessary. Others felt that people should be entitled to enjoy a portion of life in retirement:

'I always kind of said, "Isn't it lovely to have that slice of life, to be able to do that because life is so precious it's not all about utilitarian part of it", you know, utilizing the person to work and have, like to have an input but that there should be a slice that when you can say, "Now I can enjoy not having to work", you know.' (Barbara, teacher, age 60)

Other teachers felt it was necessary to increase SPA to ensure pensions are sustainable, but felt it would be difficult for those who suffered stress or burnout:

'I can see why they are doing it because we are an ageing population, and they won't have the money. … The biggest problem in this country is going to be pensions in the future. … I am not surprised. I feel sorry for people who will feel burnt out and won't be able to retire.' (Alice, teacher, age 57)

Even those who felt it was a good idea to increase SPA said that working later should be a choice:

'Well, I think, you know, 67, 68, it's become, you don't even think of being old at that stage any more. People's health, it's a lot better and I think they'd be a lot more able to work and I think a lot of people would be glad to work. But then I think I always liked people to have the choice, where they're not being forced, you know. I don't like the idea of them *having* to [stay on at work].' (Emer, teacher, age 55, emphasis added)

Next, we turn to the views of healthcare workers on extending working lives.

Carers on extended working life

Most healthcare workers had a negative attitude to increasing SPA. They gave a variety of reasons for this including the long period of time many people have already worked, the compromised health of some workers, the heavy physical demands of some jobs including healthcare and the desirability of enjoying some healthy time in retirement.

Bridget, a healthcare worker, cited the long years of work that many have had at current SPA:

'I think that is absolutely the worst decision that has been made in a long, long time, because say a person of ... 66 is pension age, isn't it, now? ... will have worked for 40 odd years. ... Now, let no one tell me that somebody who has worked for 40, or sometimes 50 years – people start at straight out of national [primary] school working, nobody can tell me that they're not ready to retire ... at 66 and I think it's actually very cruel on the part of the government.' (Bridget. former carer, age 69)

Another home help worker who had osteoarthritis and was about to retire shortly at age 66 was relieved that she would not have to work past age 66, because of her health and the difficulty of working due to diminishing energy as she ages:

'Oh God, I'm just glad I escaped it so. ... Like I mean, as I said, as you get older, when you pass 60, some people do like to work into the 70s maybe but definitely my experience is you have less energy. ... Well, I'm 66 this week but I feel tired at this stage. Like I feel I've done enough. And I mean if you wanted to, when that [increase in SPA] comes in, you'll still have to keep going until 68 before you get anything which, you know, an extra two years is a while when you're that bit older, you know.' (Evelyn carer, age 66)

Others believed that workers deserved to have some healthy time in retirement and that the proposed changes would prevent this. Fiona felt that workers in certain types of physically demanding work should not have to work past the age of 65:

'Em, I don't know. I think, certainly [in] construction, I think people can't keep up that pace. ... You know, I see people in their 50s and they've kind of had it with, you know tradespeople can't do what they used to do ... and a worker in their 60s is a whole lot different from a worker in their 30s. (Fiona, carer, age 54)

The most common response from carers was that workers should have the option to retire – that they should be able to continue to work if they wished to, but that they should not be forced to do so because of a higher SPA.

Few said that, personally, they would be happy to continue to work past age 66 – one was still working at age 68 – because they enjoyed their job and had good health, but they felt that not all workers should have to since they may have health difficulties. The following quote, where Jane refers to the plight of her friend who is ill, exemplifies this position:

'I really think it's not just a one-size-fits-all, I think that … you have to take everything into account and while I might be spared my health to work as long as I can and I'm very hopeful I will be, somebody like my friend … wouldn't physically be able to work and I think it would … be very, very unfair to expect her to work.' (Jane, carer, age 48)

Only one healthcare worker was happy with the proposed increase in SPA: "Well, I think it's better to leave it later" (Ita, carer, age 62). She felt that the pension age should be increased to 70, although she planned to retire at 66.

Conclusion

This chapter with its in-depth focus on women workers in two contrasting occupations highlights that extending working life through raising SPA is a blunt policy instrument that has markedly different effects on women depending on their work-life trajectories, the physical demands of their jobs and their occupational pension status. Using a life course perspective reveals that from the start of their working lives, teachers were encouraged by their families who had the resources to ensure that their daughters pursued higher education and teaching while some had a strong tradition of teaching in the family. This set most of them on a stable work-life trajectory to a well-paid job with a relatively generous occupational pension. Even where teachers had periods of career breaks and/or job sharing to travel or care for their children and/or parents, most were able to compensate for lower pension accumulation by making additional voluntary contributions, and/or by having access to their husband's income. A minority who had long career interruptions, had moved country and/or who were family breadwinners needed to work to age 65 out of financial necessity. Most teachers were healthy, or if not, their health issues were not work-induced.

By contrast, most healthcare workers did not receive encouragement to pursue third-level education. Some came from large families and joined the workforce early to help with family finances. Some left school before completing secondary education while most had completed it. This led to lower qualifications for most, and to work in factories, or service jobs, often followed by lengthy periods of unpaid care (13 years on average) for their own children. Carers tended to have larger families than teachers. While some actively enjoyed their jobs, some undertook care work because they were not qualified for other work or because of limited work availability in rural areas.

As a result of their stable trajectories many of the teachers could retire at or before the age of 60 on good pensions; this supports previous research which emphasizes the impact of qualifying for a full pension in allowing teachers to retire early (Furgeson et al 2006; Friedberg and Turner, 2010). Teaching is obviously not physically demanding in quite the same way as care work, and the teachers interviewed did not appear to have work-related ill-health (Maguire and O'Connell, 2007). However, most teachers regarded their job as requiring considerable stamina and energy and this provided a further push towards retirement, which supports previous research (Viotti et al 2017). Most teachers interviewed planned to retire well before age 65, while a few needed to work until age 65, out of financial necessity.

The majority of teachers objected to the proposal to raise SPA to 67 on the basis that teaching requires energy and that it is normal to retire at or before 60. This largely resonates with the results of a 2015 Eurofound survey which found that there was a gap of 5.8 years between the age at which Irish women want to retire and the SPA (then 66) (Eurofound, 2017). They felt it was wrong to 'change the rules' and disrupt expectations and that workers in more physically demanding jobs were at a particular disadvantage. They felt that people were entitled to some healthy time in retirement, which resonates with previous international research (Pond et al 2010). While a few teachers felt that raising SPA was necessary, all expressed the view that working past age 65 should be a choice, not something imposed by pension reforms.

Perhaps not surprisingly, given the physical demands of the job, more home care workers than teachers strongly disagreed with increasing SPA, resonating with the findings of Van Solinge and Henkens (2017). In addition to the reasons given by the teachers, the carers emphasized the long years many workers had already worked by age 66. They stated that the combination of health challenges with lower levels of energy makes working after the age of 65 extremely unattractive, if not impossible for workers in their occupation. Yet, because of their lower pay, the length of time spent out of the labour market in childcare, and unpredictable working hours and (for most) lack of access to an occupational pension, they were far more likely than teachers to *need* to work to at least age 66. This highlights the fact that increasing SPA decreases the options available to carers and puts them in a difficult position.

The findings emphasize the very different options facing teachers and home care workers as they approach retirement age. They indicate that most teachers are protected from the possible health disadvantages of having to delay their retirement by their occupational pension scheme, which allows them to retire on an adequate income by around age 60. In contrast, evidence from the carers demonstrates the likely negative implications of increasing SPA for low-paid workers in physically demanding, precarious work. This provides a strong rationale for the need to enable those engaged in physically demanding work to retire earlier on full pensions. This calls for a modification of the one-size-fits-all policy approach of having the same (increased) pension age for all workers. Because of the reliance of most home care workers on the state pension, it is important that the level of the state pension be maintained, or preferably increased. So too, it seems only fair that those who started work in their teenage years and have worked (paid or unpaid) for 40 to 50 years should be able to retire on a full state pension before age 66. The Homemakers' Scheme needs to be made retrospective pre-1994 so that older home care workers with children may benefit from it. If the government expects workers to provide for their own pensions, as the pension privatization agenda suggests, the wages of private sector home care workers need to be increased. Working conditions need to be regularized so that workers may have a consistent income that would enable them to contribute regularly to occupational or private pensions. Since it is clear that home care work can lead to work-related ill health, private and public sector employers need to introduce flexible policies to enable home care workers to find alternative work in non-physically demanding roles and the government needs to introduce skills retraining for those older workers who cannot be so accommodated.

The introduction of legislation enabling public sector workers to continue working to age 70 in 2018 is a positive measure and provides opportunities for teachers who do not have full pensions and who are the main providers to continue earning. However, there is no similar legislation to cover private sector workers, including some carers in this study. While there is currently a demand for carers and therefore they may continue to work as long as they are healthy, this is not necessarily the case for other workers, who remain at a disadvantage if they need to retire at age 65 and do not receive their state pension until age 66 or 67 if the planned increase in 2021 goes ahead.

This chapter indicates the limitations of using a one-size-fits-all increase in SPA as a primary policy measure to address the pension costs associated with an ageing population. It demonstrates the need for nuanced government and employer policies to avoid exacerbating pension and health disadvantages for carers and other workers in similar occupations.

References

Bassett, M. (2017) *Towards a Fair State Pension for Women Pensioners*, Dublin: Age Action.

Cangiano, A. and Walsh, K. (2014) 'Recruitment processes and immigration regulations: the disjointed pathways to employing migrant carers in ageing societies', *Work, Employment and Society*, 28(3): 372–89.

Central Statistics Office (2016) *Quarterly National Household Survey: Pension Provision Quarter 4 2015 Summary*, Cork/Dublin: Central Statistics Office.

CIA (2021) *CIA World Factbook, Ireland. People and Society* [online], available at: www.cia.gov/the-world-factbook/countries/ireland/#people-and-society [accessed 1 March 2021].

Department of Education and Skills (2020) *National Briefing Note on Education at a Glance 2020 OECD Indicators: A Country Profile for Ireland, September 2020*, Dublin: Department of Education [online], available at: www.asti.ie/document-library/department-of-education-and-skills-education-at-a-glance-2020/ [accessed 19 May 2022].

Department of Education and Skills (2021) *Teacher Statistics*, Dublin: Department of Education [online], available at: www.gov.ie/en/publication/c97fbd-teacher-statistics/ [accessed 19 May 2022].

Department of Social Protection (2021a) *State Pension Non-contributory* [online], available at: www.gov.ie/en/service/e21eee-state-pension-non-contributory/ [accessed 3 March 2021].

Department of Social Protection (2021b) *Report on the Commission of Pensions* [online], available at: www. gov.ie/en/publication/6cb6d-report-of-the-commission-on-pensions/?section=state-pension-age [accessed 18 October 2021].

Doyle, M. and Timonen, V. (2009) 'The different faces of care work: understanding the experiences of the multi-cultural care workforce', *Ageing and Society*, 29(3): 337–50.

Droogenbroeck, F. and Spruyt, B. (2014) 'To stop or not to stop', *Research on Aging*, 36(6): 753–77.

Duffy, M., Armenia, A. and Stacey, C. (2015) *Caring on the Clock. The Complexities and Contradictions of Paid Care Work*, New Brunswick, NJ: Rutgers University Press.

Eurofound (2017) *Extending Working Life. What do Workers Want?*, Dublin: Eurofound.

Fahie, D. and Devine, D. (2014) 'The impact of workplace bullying on primary school teachers and principals', *Scandinavian Journal of Educational Research*, 58(2): 235–52.

Friedberg, L. and Turner, S. (2010) 'Labor market effects of pensions and implications for teachers', *Education Finance and Policy*, 5(4): 463–91.

Furgeson, J., Strauss, R. and Vogt, W. (2006) 'The effects of defined benefit pension incentives and working conditions on teacher retirement decisions', *Education Finance and Policy*, 1(3): 316–48.

Giele, J. and Elder, G. (1998) 'Life course research: development of a field', in Giele, J. and Elder, G. (eds) *Methods of Life Course Research: Qualitative and Quantitative Approaches*, Thousand Oaks, California: Sage, pp 5–27.

Grayson, J.L. and Alvarez, H.K. (2008) 'School climate factors relating to teacher burnout: a mediator model', *Teaching and Teacher Education*, 24(5): 1349–63.

Hewko, S., Cooper, S., Huynh, H., Spiwek, T., Carleton, H., Reid, S. and Cummings, G. (2015) 'Invisible no more: a scoping review of the health care aide workforce literature', *BMC Nursing*, 14(1): 1–17.

Kerr, R.A., Breen, J., Delaney, M., Kelly, C. and Miller, K. (2011) 'A qualitative study of workplace stress and coping in secondary teachers in Ireland', *Irish Journal of Applied Social Studies*, 11(3): 27–38.

Maguire, M. and O'Connell, T. (2007) 'Ill-health retirement of schoolteachers in the Republic of Ireland', *Occupational Medicine*, 57(3): 191–3.

Mahon, E. (1998) 'Class, mothers and equal opportunities to work', in Drew, E.R. and Mahon, E. (eds) *Women, Work and the Family in Europe*, London: Routledge, pp 170–81.

McCaughey, D., McGhan, G., Kim, J., Brannon, D., Leroy, H. and Jablonski, R. (2012) 'Workforce implications of injury among home health workers: evidence from the National Home Health Aide Survey', *Gerontologist*, 52(4): 493–505.

Mouleart, T. and Biggs, S. (2013) 'International and European policy on work and retirement: reinventing critical perspectives on active ageing and mature subjectivity', *Human Relations*, 66(1): 22–43.

Ní Léime, Á. and Street, D. (2019) 'Extended working life in Ireland and the US: gender implications for precarious and secure workers', *Ageing and Society*, 39(10): 2194–218.

Ní Léime, Á., Duvvury, N. and Wijeratne, D. (2020) 'Gender, health and extended working life policy in Ireland', in Ní Léime, Á., Ogg, J., Rašticová, M., Krekula, C., Street, D., Madero Cabib, I. and Bédiová, M. (eds) *Extended Working Life: International Gender and Health Perspectives*, Cham: Springer, pp 297–307.

Pond, R. Stephens, C. and Alpass, F. (2010) 'How health affects retirement decisions: three pathways taken by middle-older aged New Zealanders', *Ageing and Society*, 30(3): 527–45.

Roy, D., Weyman, A., George, A. and Hudson-Sharp, N. (2018) 'A qualitative study into the prospect of working longer for physiotherapists in the United Kingdom's National Health Service', *Ageing and Society*, 38(8): 1693–714.

Timonen, V. and Lolich, L. (2019) '"The poor carer": ambivalent social construction of the home care worker in elder care services', *Journal of Gerontological Social Work*, 62(7): 728–48.

Timonen, V., Doyle, M. and O'Dwyer, C. (2012) 'Expanded, but not regulated: ambiguity in home-care policy in Ireland', *Health and Social Care in the Community*, 20(3): 310–18.

Van Solinge, H. and Henkens, K. (2017) 'Older workers' emotional reactions to rising retirement age: the case of the Netherlands', *Work, Aging and Retirement*, 3(3): 273–83.

Viotti, S., Martini, M. and Converso, D. (2017) 'Are there any job resources capable of moderating the effect of physical demands on work ability? A study among kindergarten teachers', *International Journal of Occupational Safety and Ergonomics*, 23(4): 544–52.

Walsh, K. and O'Shea, E. (2009) *The Role of Migrant Care Workers in Ageing Societies: Context and Experiences in Ireland*, Galway: National University of Ireland.

PART III

Conclusions and Discussion

9

Retirement and Responsibilisation: Current Narratives about the End of Working Life

David Lain, Sarah Vickerstaff and Mariska van der Horst

Introduction

Across many countries we have seen the development of a raft of policies designed to encourage an extension of working lives, and indeed people are working later than in recent decades (see Chapter 1). We have also seen the development of a discourse of active ageing in which living longer brings new obligations on older citizens to keep working, stay fit and age well (Moulaert and Biggs, 2013). This has occurred against a wider backdrop of neoliberalism and welfare state retrenchment, which has led to an increasing individualization of responsibility for welfare that was previously collectively assured. In response to these changes, the bulk of previous research has focused on the factors that encourage or inhibit extended working lives; experiences of later life working are rarely explored.

In this book we have sought to increase our understanding of these experiences by exploring different types of job transitions experienced by older workers in a range of European countries. This included job redeployment/mobility within the organization; temporary employment; attempted transitions from unemployment; and employment beyond pension age. We have attempted to move beyond the increasingly common way of framing job transitions in Europe as 'bridge jobs', a concept that we think obscures more than it reveals about the diverse range of experiences of older individuals in the contemporary world of work and welfare. We do not claim to cover all transitions older workers can make – we do not, for example, cover transitions into self-employment. However, we believe this volume makes an important contribution to the literature, by exploring transitions in a more disaggregated way and looking at the lived experiences of older workers themselves in a changing policy, employment and cultural context.

In this final chapter we first elaborate on why we think the concept of bridge jobs is problematic for the purpose of making sense of job transitions. In the subsequent sections we draw on qualitative evidence from the country chapters to explore the key themes of the book. First, we look at why job transitions in older age must be understood in the context of neoliberal responsibilisation and 'appeals to freedom'. Second, we explore 'psychological reactance' as a means of understanding older workers' job transitions. Third, we look in more depth at the constraints on individuals exercising control over the transitions they make and the inequalities that result. We conclude by reflecting on the contributions of the book to the literature.

Moving beyond 'bridge employment' to explain job transitions

The adoption of the language of 'bridge jobs' in Europe as a way of making sense of older worker job transitions originated in the United States (US). The idea that 'bridge jobs' dominate late career transitions in the US emerged in the 1990s, following the development of longitudinal surveys that tracked interviewees over time. These surveys seemed to suggest that, contrary to expectations, most people did not move from a full-time 'career job' to 'full' retirement at 'pension age', but instead moved into a so-called 'bridge job'. As a result, retirement came to be conceptualized as a 'process', rather than a one-off event. The 'bridge employment' stage was consequently seen as 'working in retirement', or more precisely 'the labour-force participation patterns observed among older workers as they leave their career jobs and move toward complete labor-force withdrawal (i.e., full retirement)' (Wang et al 2014, p 195). The numbers of people making such transitions were said to be very high. For example, Cahill et al (2005, p 2) reported that: 'one-half to two-thirds of the ... respondents with full-time career jobs take on bridge jobs before exiting the labor force completely'.

The terminology of 'bridge jobs' generally gives a positive impression – the reference to 'career' arguably implies some stability over the earlier stages of the working life, and the term 'bridge' implies a functional mechanism by which the individual is able to reach a point at which they can afford to retire. However, this interpretation is open to question and the usefulness of the idea of bridge jobs as a categorization for understanding job transitions in older age is debatable. What constitutes bridge employment and how it is measured in the US varies considerably in the literature. Wang et al illustrate how broad the category is: 'bridge employment can be categorized into five distinct types in the current literature: career bridge employment in the same organization, career bridge employment in a different organization, non-career bridge employment in the same organization, and non-career bridge employment in a different organization, as well as full retirement (i.e., complete labor-force withdrawal)' (Wang et al 2014, p 196). The concept of bridge employment is therefore defined so broadly, often including multiple dimensions in the same piece of research, that it ends up obscuring more than it reveals.

Likewise, the decision to define a career job as having stayed in the same job for ten years in this literature seems to reflect the fact that Americans *in general* often do not have secure 'career jobs' in a meaningful sense, and instead have to move jobs throughout their working lives. Average job tenure for Americans aged 25 plus is only around five years, and is only about eight years at 45–55 (BLS, 2020). This is in the context of a very unregulated labour market in which employers have a lot of discretion over retaining employees. The concept of a career job, upon which bridge employment rests, is therefore questionable in the US, and people typically move jobs regularly before they reach older age. Furthermore, the concept does not neatly capture a range of transitions that do not start from a 'career job'. The diversity and complexity of later life working transitions and arrangements cannot adequately be covered by the concept of 'bridge jobs'.

If bridge employment is a problematic concept in the US context, it has even less relevance in Europe. Europeans with a full-time 'career' job of ten plus years were less likely to move into a new 'bridge job' after age 50 than their American counterparts, according to Brunello and Langella (2013). This is not to say that job moves are unimportant in the European context, however. If we avoid the 'bridge jobs' concept, and simply look at moves into new jobs (including among those not previously having a so-called 'career job'), we see that significant minorities of individuals in Europe do move into new jobs in older age. In 2015 around a quarter of workers aged 55–64 had moved into a new job in the previous five years in the UK, and around a fifth had done so in Sweden, with Germany not far behind this (see Chapter 1).

The literature on bridge jobs also fails to adequately address *why* older people make job transitions, or how they experience them, because it is insufficiently informed by theory and there is a lack of in-depth qualitative enquiry. The literature tends to explain the contemporary importance of bridge employment with reference to broad positive demographic changes (for example, in relation to increased health and education among more recent cohorts) and increased financial 'incentives' to remain in work. The move from defined benefit to defined contribution pensions, for example, is arguably presented as creating opportunities to work longer, because continued employment is rewarded financially. It is questionable how much older people do view job transitions and working longer in these terms, however.

Individualization of risk, neoliberal responsibilisation and 'appeals to freedom'

The experiences of older people making transitions may be better understood in the context of what Krekula and Vickerstaff (2020) call an 'individualization of responsibility and risk'. 'Welfare state retrenchment has progressively led to the framing of policy as enabling individual "choices" and "freedoms" and demanding individual responsibility' (Krekula and Vickerstaff, 2020, p 37). This means older individuals have fewer financial supports if they are not in work, but they have the (theoretical) freedom to 'choose' to work (given the introduction of changes such as age discrimination legislation). Retirement in this guise is not something that happens to individuals but something that they must actively construct (Vickerstaff, 2015, p 297). As we argued in Chapter 1, this represents a wider trend towards 'neoliberal responsibilisation' (Pyysiäinen et al 2017; see also Laliberte Rudman, 2006, 2015).

It should be noted that countries started at different positions in relation to welfare provision and labour market regulation, and are not identical in terms of the extent to which neoliberal responsibilisation has taken hold. Nevertheless, according to Vickerstaff et al (2017, p 226), countries as diverse as Sweden, Germany, Ireland, and the United Kingdom have seen: 'a remarkable convergence towards the neoliberal turn with respect to pensions, disability and unemployment benefits, with measures to individualise or privatise the risk of income sufficiency in retirement. Perhaps the most unexpected patterns ... observed ... is the distance that Sweden and Germany have travelled down the neoliberal path'. The question of why there has been this partial convergence between different welfare states is complex. However, it is important to note that a number of challenges to welfare states have intensified over recent decades, including globalization, enhanced global competition and demographic change. There are a number of ways in which countries can respond to such challenges (see, for example, Macnicol, 2015, in relation to pensions in the UK). However, countries appeared to have gravitated towards ready-made solutions and proposals from international bodies such as the Organisation for Economic Co-operation and Development (OECD).

In the field of pensions and extended working lives the OECD advocates policies that are very much consistent with promoting neoliberalism and individual choice/responsibility. In terms of framing the debate, they argue: 'Giving people better choices and incentives to continue working at an older age is crucial for responding to the challenges of rapid population ageing' (OECD, nd). This includes raising pension ages; promoting private pension provision in partial place of state provision; restricting access to 'early retirement' and unemployment/disability schemes that supposedly 'incentivise early retirement for those still able to work'; introducing age discrimination legislation; and reducing the role of mandatory retirement (Ní Léime and Loretto, 2017; OECD, 2018). This helps to set the consensus for what are reasonable responses to the challenges facing OECD Member States, and countries are publicly monitored and reported on in terms of their success, or otherwise, in meeting OECD goals.

In Europe, such neoliberal narratives have been reflected in the emphasis on 'active ageing' as a means of getting people to take greater responsibility for themselves (Moulaert and Biggs, 2013). In order to get people to assume responsibility for their fate, Pyysiäinen et al (2017) argue that narratives around 'appeals to freedom' are used as part of neoliberal responsibilisation. For example, the OECD (1998, pp 14–15, emphasis added) defined 'active ageing' as: 'The capacity of people, as they grow older, to lead productive lives in the society and economy. Active ageing implies a high degree of flexibility in how individuals and families *choose* to spend their time over life in work, in learning, in leisure and in care-giving.' In combination with the policy changes mentioned earlier, individuals are incentivized to 'choose' to continue working.

We saw some evidence of this 'appeal to freedom' narrative to motivate older workers to take more responsibility in a number of places in this book. In particular, this was evident in statements made by HR managers in the chapter on redeployment in a UK local government authority, as the following quote indicates: "it [the redeployment scheme] hasn't got anything to do with age, it is across the board for anybody who wants to either change a role, needs development, needs moving due to ill health, no longer have a job because the service is restructured. It's for all the scenarios" (Fiona, HR). By emphasizing the theoretical freedom and choice open to people of all ages from redeployment, HR shift the responsibility onto (older) people to manage their transitions successfully.

An apparent acceptance of individual responsibility for one's own predicament was reflected in some of the interviews with unemployed older people seeking work in Italy:

'[It] is one's own responsibility to be able to cope with a flexible and competitive market ... it is not companies' fault.' (Davide, aged 59, unemployed manager)

'If you are not able to find a new job, to recover your career, it means that you have not been able to adequate your skills and competences to the new needs of the market ... that you have not invested enough in your development and in creating a network of helpful people.' (Luca, aged 59, unemployed production executive)

In the Belgian chapter there were examples of people working in precarious temporary contracts due to pride in taking responsibility for themselves; likewise, the need to embrace being flexible was emphasized: "That's what's great and difficult at the same time with temping, because you're doing jobs you would never have done otherwise" (Serge, aged 54).

In many cases older workers had ended up in unfavourable circumstances. This was not perceived or framed as freedom, but instead it was sometimes presented in a 'matter-of-fact' way, with little apparent blame for employers, as a set of situations they simply had to respond to. Serge, mentioned earlier, for example, said:

'at my age I didn't have much chance of finding a stable job ... the only solution that was interesting for him [the employer], it was to hire me as a temporary worker. It was almost a week from time to time. Obviously this formula suited me because it was always better than nothing'.

In this way, with varying degrees of enthusiasm, people came to accept the need to take responsibility for their income and career by being more 'realistic' about their employment options (Laliberte Rudman and Aldrich, 2021).

Job transitions and 'psychological reactance' as a means of understanding of older worker behaviour

Across the book as a whole, one of the themes identified is that the act of needing to make a transition of some sort often placed older people in a less than advantageous position, despite coming from countries that have often been assumed to be very different from one another. Older unemployed individuals struggled to find work in Italy; older Belgians were in temporary work because they were unable to find permanent employment; female carers in Ireland were financially unable to leave their jobs; manual workers in Sweden were unable to move to less physically demanding work; and older local government workers in the UK were unable to progress their careers through redeployment, and in some cases took lower-level work. These experiences, therefore, are in stark contrast to the apparent promises in the 'appeal of freedom' narrative associated with the trend towards neoliberal responsibilisation. As noted earlier, most interviewees did not view their circumstances in relation to choice, but nor did they blame employers for the predicament they were in. Instead, they sometimes accepted their unfavourable treatment on the basis of age as being a fact of life, and responded as best as they could to a context in which there were pressures to work longer. Recent work on internalized ageism suggests that older workers may themselves feel less entitled to work or promotion and defer opportunities to younger generations (Beach et al 2021; Vickerstaff and Van der Horst, 2021).

In making sense of this, and the wider response of older individuals to extended working lives, it is arguably useful to draw on the concept of psychological reactance identified by Pyysiäinen et al (2017, p 216), that is, 'responsibilisation through threats to personal control'. Under conditions of uncertainty, and in this case the need to continue working, individuals strive to restore personal control by taking whatever opportunities *are* available to them. This was illustrated, for example, in the chapter on local government workers in the UK under conditions of austerity. Budget cuts had resulted in a cut in the staffing numbers, the removal/restructuring of roles and the introduction of a redeployment scheme to internally move people to areas where staff were needed. This was presented by HR as a development opportunity open to all, irrespective of age; however, older workers rarely saw it in this way and none of the older workers interviewed appeared to have progressed as a result of redeployment. For example, Mary reported: "So I didn't get that job, which would have been a promotion, and on that restructure there was quite a lot of feeling amongst the people over 50 that it was the people over 50 who didn't get the jobs" (Mary, aged 56).

Crucially, individuals were not instructed by managers to move into less favourable jobs. However, in the context of job positions being disestablished and older people being unable to secure jobs at the same level internally, some individuals sought to resolve an uncertain anxiety-inducing situation by taking lower-level or less desirable jobs through redeployment, a form of psychological reactance. Redeployment in UK local government was motivated by the needs of the organization, rather than the older people concerned. Similarly, in the chapter on a manufacturing firm in Sweden it was reported that opportunities for manual workers to move into less physically strenuous jobs in recent years had decreased, rather than increased, due to financial pressures.

In the other chapters we saw examples of older people being resigned to the fact that they have reduced options because of their age and seeking out whatever opportunities are available to continue working. For example, in Belgium, Sonia (aged 48), who was highly educated, had taken temporary work because she had been unable to obtain secure employment: "they [employers] tell you that anyway the problem is your age. Well, now, I've got used to the idea; there's nothing to be done about it, so, wanting ... it's not that I want to be, that's not what I want to say, but the fact is, well, it's something that I know". As we saw earlier, in a similar vein, Serge took temporary work because 'at his age' permanent work was not realistic.

Structural constraints on freedom over transitions and a continuation of unequal outcomes

As the earlier discussion indicates, there were real structural constraints over individuals being able to exercise a meaningful degree of freedom over their employment transitions. This operated by constraining different types of choices – in UK local government we saw examples of older individuals being unable to progress to more senior positions, and in Ireland we heard accounts of older workers not in a financial position to retire.

So-called freedom to work longer also resulted in unequal constraints on people being able to exercise choice over the transitions they made. For example, social class played a significant role in determining choices available to women in Ireland, with female teachers mostly able to choose to retire before state pension ages and carers having to continue working for financial reasons. At the same time, expectations about working longer could also cut across simple occupational divides, with some carers and teachers having to work longer for financial reasons because of household circumstances, such as divorce.

The influence of gender and marital status on employment also cut across different country contexts. In the comparative social policy/ sociology literature Germany and the UK are usually presented as different types of 'regimes' (see Chapter 1). However, in the chapter on working beyond pension age, the experiences of divorced women in Germany and the UK were not that dissimilar. In both countries these women had continued working in part due to financial reasons caused by divorce and the periods spent as a homemaker. Income from work enabled them to live an independent and self-sufficient life, topping up a very basic retirement income, arguably consistent with a context of wider neoliberal responsibilisation and an individualization of risk. In some cases they had simply continued in jobs they already held, and in others they moved in and out of work, demonstrating considerable initiative to remain in employment; those returning after an absence typically ended up in low-paid, low-skilled jobs. This desire to be independent and to keep busy and do something satisfying went beyond financial survival: "apart from all of these positive things [from working] enough money comes in that I won't get rich but I have the feeling I can make it alone" (Edith Fichte, 78).

It should be remembered that, in a sense, the interviewees in the chapter on working beyond pension age were 'survivors', that is, those who *were* able to navigate working at this age. However, we saw in the introductory chapter that the percentage of people working beyond age 65 was rising among men and women in all the countries covered in this book. Furthermore, across the chapters, we have seen older people looking for opportunities that were available to them, consistent with neoliberal responsibiliation, and making choices within structural constraints, based on combinations of social class, gender, family circumstances, health and so on.

Conclusion

In this book we have sought to bring together the lived experience of older people facing job transitions in a European context. In comparative research on employment in older age the focus has all too often relied solely on the use of survey analysis to explore employment and retirement outcomes. It has uncritically accepted employment in older age as being a positive, or successful, outcome, or it has scientifically distanced itself from such assessments. In this vein, job transitions in older age are often framed around the notion of 'bridge employment', which is said to provide a path from 'career' employment to 'full retirement'. Such transitions are assumed to be influenced by a combination of 'incentives' to work longer and positive demographic changes. The relative absence of qualitative research on this means that we have lacked an in-depth understanding of the experiences and motivations of older people attempting to make employment transitions.

This book therefore makes a major contribution to the literature by bringing together qualitative research on older people's experiences of different types of job transitions across a range of European countries. While comparative research often wants to find differences between countries, the analysis in this book shows remarkable similarities between countries in terms of the experiences of older workers. Despite coming from seemingly different welfare state contexts, for example, interviewees in Italy, Belgium and Ireland were on the margins of employment and sometimes struggled in the face of adversity to continue working into older age. Likewise, despite supposedly being a more benevolent employment context, evidence from 'social democratic' Sweden was consistent with that of 'liberal' UK, in terms of indicating that redeployment and job mobility was unlikely to be used as a tool to support older workers in the context of the financial pressures of neoliberal capitalism. In both Germany and the UK divorced women continued working past pension age in part for financial reasons.

In terms of making a theoretical contribution, this book links the lived experience of older people making employment transitions with neoliberal responsibilisation. This is not the first work to link a neoliberal turn to extended working lives (see, for example, Macnicol, 2015; Vickerstaff et al 2017); however, this volume makes a contribution by setting out how people may respond to such pressures to work longer in such a context. Drawing on the work of Pyysiäinen et al (2017), neoliberal responsibilisation enables us to link policy and employer narratives around freedom and choice to individuals' employment decisions. As a framework, it provides sufficient nuance to understand that while some individuals will identify with such narratives, others will seek to restore control over their lives by making transitions that enable them to continue working in the context of financial pressures. We would argue such transitions are likely to become more common in the future across all the countries covered in this book, as pressures to work longer intensify. As the recent COVID-19 pandemic and the great recession of 2008 also both illustrate, ultimately, we always face uncertainty in terms of our continued employment, and older individuals will increasingly have to take individual responsibility for ensuring they make the transitions required to remain in employment.

References

Beach, B., van der Horst, M. and Vickerstaff, S. (2021) *Enabling Age at Work: How Ageism and Ableism Overlap in the Workplace*, London: International Longevity Centre.

BLS (Bureau of Labor Statistics) (2020) 'Table 1. Median years of tenure with current employer for employed wage and salary workers by age and sex, selected years, 2010–2020', US Bureau of Labor Statistics [online], available at: www.bls.gov/news.release/tenure.t01.htm [accessed 23 August 2021].

Brunello, G. and Langella, M. (2013) 'Bridge jobs in Europe', *IZA Journal of Labor Policy*, 2(1): 1–18.

Cahill, K.E., Giandrea, M.D. and Quinn, J.F. (2005) *Are Traditional Retirements a Thing of the Past? New Evidence on Retirement Patterns and Bridge Jobs*, US Bureau of Labor Statistics, Working Papers in Economics, No 166, Cambridge, MA: US Bureau of Labor Statistics.

Krekula, C. and Vickerstaff, S. (2020) 'The "older worker" and the "ideal worker": a critical examination of concepts and categorisations in the rhetoric of extending working lives', in Ní Léime, Á., Ogg, J., Street, D., Krekula, C., Rašticová, M., Bédiová, M. and Madero-Cabib, I. (eds) (2020) *Extended Working Life Policies: International Gender and Health Perspectives*, Cham: Springer Open, pp 29–54.

Laliberte Rudman, D. (2006) 'Shaping the active, autonomous and responsible modern retiree: an analysis of discursive technologies and their links with neo-liberal political rationality', *Ageing and Society*, 26(2): 181–201.

Laliberte Rudman, D. (2015) 'Embodying positive aging and neoliberal rationality: talking about the aging body within narratives of retirement', *Journal of Aging Studies*, 34: 10–20.

Laliberte Rudman, D. and Aldrich, R. (2021) 'Producing precarity: the individualization of later life unemployment within employment support provision', *Journal of Aging Studies*, 57: 1–9.

Macnicol, J. (2015) *Neoliberalising Old Age*, Cambridge: Cambridge University Press.

Moulaert, T. and Biggs, S. (2013) 'International and European policy on work and retirement: reinventing critical perspectives on active ageing and mature subjectivity', *Human Relations*, 66(1): 23–43.

Ní Léime, Á. and Loretto, W. (2017) 'Gender perspectives on extended working life policies', in Ní Léime, Á., Street, D., Vickerstaff, S., Krekula, C. and Loretto, W. (eds) *Gender, Ageing and Extended Working Life: Cross-national Perspectives*, Bristol: Policy Press, pp 53–75.

OECD (Organisation for Economic Co-operation and Development) (nd) *Ageing and Employment Policies*, Paris: OECD [online], available at: www.oecd.org/employment/ageingandemploymentpolicies.htm [accessed 23 August 2021].

OECD (2018) *Recommendation of the Council on Ageing and Employment Policies*, Paris: OECD [online], available at: www.oecd.org/els/emp/Ageing-Recommendation.pdf [accessed 23 August 2021].

Pyysiäinen, J., Halpin, D. and Guilfoyle, A. (2017) 'Neoliberal governance and "responsibilization" of agents: reassessing the mechanisms of responsibility-shift in neoliberal discursive environments', *Distinktion: Journal of Social Theory*, 18(2): 215–35.

Vickerstaff, S. (2015) 'Retirement. Evolution, revolution or retrenchment', in Twigg, J. and Martin, W. (eds) *The Routledge Cultural Gerontology Handbook*, New York: Routledge, pp 297–304.

Vickerstaff, S. and van der Horst, M. (2021) 'The impact of age stereotypes and age norms on employees' retirement choices: a neglected aspect of research on extended working lives', *Frontiers in Sociology*, available at: https://doi.org/10.3389/fsoc.2021.686645 [accessed 23 August 2021].

Vickerstaff, S., Street, D., Ní Léime, Á. and Krekula, C. (2017) 'Gendered and extended work: research and policy needs for work in later life', in Ní Léime, Á., Street, D., Vickerstaff, S., Krekula, C. and Loretto, W. (eds) *Gender, Ageing and Extended Working Life: Cross-national Perspectives*, Bristol: Policy Press, pp 219–41.

Wang, M., Peenn, L.T., Bertone, A. and Stefanova, S. (2014) 'Bridge employment in the United States', in Alcover, C.M., Topa, G., Parry, E., Fraccaroli, F. and Depolo, M. (eds) *Bridge Employment: A Research Handbook*, London: Routledge.

Index

Printed and bound by CPI Group (UK) Ltd, Croydon, CR0 4YY

23/04/2025

14661024-0002